The Use of Social Science Data
in Supreme Court Decisions

The Use of Social Science Data in Supreme Court Decisions

Rosemary J. Erickson and Rita J. Simon

University of Illinois Press

Urbana and Chicago

© 1998 by the Board of Trustees of the University of Illinois
Manufactured in the United States of America

1   2   3   4   5   C   P   5   4   3   2   1

This book is printed on acid-free paper.

Library of Congress Cataloging-in-Publication Data
Erickson, Rosemary J.
The use of social science data in Supreme Court decisions /
Rosemary J. Erickson and Rita J. Simon.
   p.   cm.
Includes bibliographical references and index.
ISBN 0-252-06661-8 (pbk. : acid-free paper).
ISBN 0-252-2355-2 (cloth : acid-free paper)
1. United States. Supreme Court. 2. Judicial process—
United States. 3. Social sciences—United States.
4. Sex and law—United States. I. Simon, Rita James. II. Title.
KF8742.E75 1998
347.73'26—dc21   97-4657

CIP

Contents

Acknowledgments

Rosemary Erickson acknowledges with thanks the help she received from James P. Lynch, Jurg Siegenthaler, and Ken Kusterer at American University in their review of the manuscript. She wishes to thank her husband, Arnie Stenseth, for his encouragement and editing; her mother, for her unyielding faith in her; and her niece, Tessa Erickson, for her assistance with the legal research.

Rita Simon is very appreciative of the extensive and excellent editing that Gabrielle Loperfido did on earlier versions of the manuscript. Bath Bangert was superb in making all the changes from version to version and in seeing the manuscript through to completion.

Introduction

This study considers the uses of social science data by the Supreme Court in decisions made since the 1970s in thirty-five cases concerning abortion, sex discrimination, and sexual harassment. Supreme Court cases were selected for study because the effects of the Court's decisions are more far-reaching than those of any court. The 1970s was selected as the point of departure because that decade marks an increase in the use of social science data in the courtroom. Women's issues were selected because the number of those issues in the courts has grown since the 1970s, largely as a result of the women's movement. We believe that a thorough examination of the cases in question will contribute to the ongoing discussion of the tenuous relationship between the social sciences and the legal community, to the growing body of research on women's issues, and to the nascent literature treating social science data and how it is used by the Supreme Court.

In *Women's Movements in America*, Rita Simon and Gloria Danzinger concluded that a coherent set of beliefs identifies and unifies the members of the women's movement in their pursuit of workplace equality and abortion rights, issues central to our discussion. The women's movement of the late twentieth century has moved beyond the issues near and dear to the suffragists and the women who fought for the right to inherit property, the right to testify in court, and the right to serve on juries. However, the movement has continued to seek important reforms—identifiable goals—within the judicial system as well as among the state and federal legislatures. Considerations of the use of the social sciences in the deliberation of such legal reforms at the state and federal levels will be put aside here in order to focus instead on the way in which the courts have treated research and statistics derived from the social sciences while applying existing law.

The general use of social science evidence within the courtroom has escalated since the 1970s, as documented by Patrick Driessen in his article "The Wedding of Social Science and the Courts: Is the Marriage Working?" as well as by Faust E. Rossi in his book *Expert Witness,* and by Melvin Kraft in his book *Using Experts in Civil Cases.* Analyses of the way in which data from the social sciences have been used by the Supreme Court have been made by Nancy Adler et al. in "Psychological Factors in Abortion"; by Donald Bersoff in "Social Science Data and the Supreme Court: Lockhart as a Case in Point"; by Lee Epstein and Joseph Kobylka in *The Supreme Court and Legal Change: Abortion and the Death Penalty;* by John Monahan and Laurens Walker in "Social Authority: Obtaining, Evaluating, and Establishing Social Science in Law"; and by Gerald Rosenberg in *The Hollow Hope.* Three principle concerns are at stake in the discussion of the use of social science for all cases, including those related to key women's interests. First is consideration of conflicting epistemologies and methodologies: the inductive scientific method, which seeks unqualified truth, versus deductive reasoning and an adversarial or dialectical approach to the truth of a specific case, and the degree to which these approaches are reconcilable. Second is the degree to which the legal community is capable of assimilating social science data. Third is the degree to which the social sciences can inform judicial proceedings.

An increase in the use of social science research has been accompanied by an increase in the use of expert testimony, one of two principle gateways of social science data into the court, the second being that of *amicus curiae* briefs. Standards and procedures for the admissibility of expert testimony are therefore germane to our discussion of the use of social science research in cases pertaining to women's issues, which rely on both expert testimony and *amicus curiae* briefs. These will be addressed at length in chapter 2.

Cases, Data, Questions

The subsets of Supreme Court cases discussed here are 22 cases treating the issue of abortion and 13 cases treating sex discrimination. Of all the cases treating sex discrimination, we have included only cases of sex discrimination with regard to employment (at the expense of examining those regarding issues of credit, jury duty, and alimony). And we considered only those sex discrimination/employment cases where the discrimination was directed against women.

Before examining these 35 cases that the Supreme Court decided between 1972 and 1992, we must define what we mean by social science data, in order to discuss how it is that the Supreme Court justices use such data. We define social science data as information dealing with social, social-psychological, and psychological issues. We do not consider data that are strictly medical, religious, philosophical, ethical, and/or historical in nature to be social science data. We do include statistics such as census data in so far as they have had to do with social issues and were interpreted beyond the mere presentation of raw numbers. We also include public opinion polls and surveys as social science data.

In examining these thirty-five cases with regard to social science data as defined here, we explore and discuss several fundamental questions:

1. Is the use of social science data by the Supreme Court dependent upon whether such data were introduced into and considered by the lower courts?
2. Does the frequency of the use of data from the social sciences in opinions of Supreme Court justices depend on whether the opinion is a majority or dissenting opinion?
3. Is there a significant difference in the kind or nature of the social science data, depending on how the information entered the courts—whether via expert testimony delivered in the lower courts, briefs submitted to the appellate courts, or *amicus* briefs submitted to the Supreme Court?
4. Do certain kinds of social science data carry more weight than others?
5. Are the data used in the courtroom in a manner consistent with the standards of the social sciences community?

With cases and data defined and questions set forth, it remains now to delineate the form our discussion will take. In chapter 1 we will focus on the history and nature of the intersection of the social sciences and the legal communities in the courtroom. In chapter 2 we will discuss the way in which social science data finds its way into the courtroom via expert testimony and *amicus* briefs. We devote chapters 3, 4, and 5 to discussions of the history, findings, and analysis of cases on abortion, sex discrimination, and sexual harassment, respectively. In the conclusion we will address the research questions laid out above and will present the results and conclusions of our study.

We hope that the questions we ask, the discussion of cases we examine, and the conclusions we present will give social scientists the information they need to make their research more amenable to use by the courts. Likewise, it is our hope that the legal community will benefit from taking a closer look at how and when data from the social sciences have been and can be used appropriately and effectively in the courtroom. Such hopes are, of course, quite optimistic given the uneasy nature of the relationship of the social sciences and the law. The nature of that relationship and its history form the basis of the chapter to follow.

1

Social Science and the Law

The breadth and complexity of issues surrounding the Supreme Court's use of social science data in making its decisions stem from the clash of the cultures of law and social science. Central to this clash are differences in method and epistemology that feed the ongoing debate over the validity, neutrality, and objectivity of social science data and the role of statistics, certainty, and probability.

Scholars from Jurgen Habermas to Richard Posner have predicted that the crisis in modern legal culture will lead courts to give social science a more prominent role in the formation of legal policy; that if precedent and judicial intuition cannot supply a clear answer to a legal problem, perhaps empirical social science can, as Alexander Tanford discussed in "The Limits of Scientific Jurisprudence: The Supreme Court and Psychology" (1990). Some members of the legal community agree. James B. McMillan, judge of the United States District Court, Western District of North Carolina, said about the role of social science in the law: "Social science . . . is entitled to a respected place in the halls of justice. The study of people and their problems is a natural prerequisite of the legal decision of problems among people" (1975:163). The extent to which that view is shared within the halls of justice or the social science academy is the focus of this section, beginning with the clash of the methodologies, the nature and ends of the truth-seeking processes, of each community.

The Clash of Cultures

For decades, differences in the law and social science have been argued by social scientists and legal scholars such as Donald Bersoff, Patrick Driessen, David Faigman, Valerie Hans, Edward Imwinkelried, Constance Lindman, Frank MacHovec, John Monahan and Laurens Walker, Alexander Tanford, and John Wisdom. As Tanford points out (1990:156), lawyers and social scientists, like individuals from different national or linguistic cultures, may have such different professional customs and values that they cannot effectively communicate with each other. Among the significant differences are the following binary oppositions: Science is rational, but the law is irrational. Law is specific while science is abstract. Law produces idiographic knowledge while science produces nomothetic knowledge. Legal findings are based on certainties and the absence of reasonable doubt but social science findings are based on probabilities and generalizations. The law is normative and prescriptive, describing how people should behave, and what ought to be. Social science attempts to be value-free, positive, and descriptive, describing how people *do* behave (Driessen 1983; Lindman 1989; Monahan and Walker 1986; Tanford 1990).

As Lewis Coser discusses in *Masters of Sociological Thought* (1977), Max Weber contended that an empirical science can never advise people what they should do, though as Karl Mannheim points out in *Ideology and Utopia* (1936), Louis Wirth said that in studying what is, we cannot totally rule out what ought to be. There is no reason why, as Patrick Driessen maintains, "descriptive social science cannot form the rationale for normative judicial decisions" (1983). Beyond these basic differences lie other fundamental disparities between the two cultures, particularly in terms of their methods of acquiring knowledge or, more broadly, pursuing the truth. As Tanford puts it, law is adversarial, while science is largely cooperative (1990). The adversary method of the courtroom differs from the search for truth in scientific endeavor, although, as Valerie Hans has observed, science has its adversarial moments. Hans wrote, "The ethical tension between the scientific tradition of full disclosure and the more limited role of the adversary expert appears inevitable" (1989:312). In other words, there is tension created between the pursuit of a true picture of the world from a social science perspective, which admits all relevant data, and the pursuit of the merits of a particular claim made in the courtroom, in which data may be admissible only under certain circumstances. It follows, then, as Constance Lindman points out, that there has arisen among social science researchers a belief tinged with fear that the "evidentiary value of social science evidence can be distorted by the adversary process" (1989:755).

Frank MacHovec puts the difference between the communities in still another light: "Law is a limited, closed system, seeking a decision one way or the other while science is a continuous process . . . and therefore more of an open system" (1987:52). Both science and the law seek the truth, but they do it by different means and for different ends. MacHovec recalls William James's take on the difference: James held that the adversary system of law was like science, where "competing theories are tested by biased proponents" (MacHovec 1987:53). In the courtroom, the legal process allows for a judge (or judges) or jury to determine the truth of the merits of a particular case. The search for an accurate picture of the object of social science research is not a qualified one. The trial system values legally accurate verdicts as opposed to the truth in and of itself, suggesting, as Tanford points out, that "legal accuracy" is their "truth" (1990). Legal truth may be explained in this way: "The venerated Anglo-Saxon-American system is deliberately dialectical. . . . Justice comes not from the wisdom and good will of dedicated and sincere people; it comes from a system intended to work with or without wisdom, good will, and sincerity. Truth comes from a system that balances competing views of truth, not from well-intentioned seekers of truth. This is typical of our system of 'laws, not men'—structures are to be trusted, not people" (Chesler, Sanders, and Kalmuss 1988).[1]

Beyond the differences in the kinds of truth the social science and legal communities pursue, another dichotomy arises, between the method of reasoning used by the law and that of social science. Law, departing from a closed set of given information, is deductive, while the social sciences, grounded firmly in scientific method, as Imwinkelried (1986), Lindman (1989), and Tanford (1990) all remind us, is largely inductive: the body of knowledge upon which conclusions are based is continually growing, and conclusions are always subject to revision. Where the law presents its findings as certainties, science attaches a permanent contingency to its results.

At the same time, as Russell Jones notes about Gordon Allport's analysis of knowledge, legal proceedings cultivate idiographic knowledge, that which derives from the individual case and idiosyncratic facts, while social science produces nomothetic information, in which experiences are ordered in such a way as to extract general principles (1985). Lindman points out, however, that the law does make nomothetic pronouncements of general or universal statements (1989). A difficulty arises from relying on nomothetic information following or based upon idiographic inquiry. Idiographic knowledge about the behavior of individuals cannot be reliably inferred from nomothetic knowledge about the behavior of whole classes of people. There is, then, concern about allowing nomothetic evidence before a jury, who must make decisions about particular parties, not society as a whole (Lindman 1989). For example, research conducted within the realm of the social sciences may show a class of people to have been victimized through racism, but such a finding does not necessarily inform a decision about whether a particular individual is guilty of or a victim of such behavior, whether such behavior is in accord with or in violation of existing law, or whether the existing law has been properly applied to the case at hand.

In a complex society in which laws are not written to account by name for each possible infringement, idiographic or otherwise anecdotal analysis may not be sufficient for the court's purposes—either in determining the merits of a particular case in the lower courts, or in determining the justness of the application of the law at the level of the Supreme Court. Under such circumstances, the Court may need to allow nomothetic information supplied by social science data (Lindman 1989). Data from the social sciences may also provide a counterbalance or a hedge against the risk that the jury or individuals may attach disproportionate weight to anecdotal evidence. People are likely to overvalue vivid anecdotes when making important decisions (Tanford 1990). Data from the social sciences may counter that inclination by supplying an accurate picture of the larger social context.

Both the law and science are general, producing principles beyond particular instances, though the law is far more specific to individual cases than is science (Monahan and Walker 1986). For all that science may confidently predict statistical probability, scientific data cannot predict behavior in individual cases. Parole is a good example. When psychiatrists are asked to evaluate whether a particular individual is likely to rape again if released, the scientist knows the odds are great that he will but is averse to predicting individual behavior. Or, as David Faigman points out, broad theories from social science research provide very little certainty in predicting what will happen in a particular case (1989). Here we see the clash of interests. Science is interested in discovering probabilities, where the court is concerned with the particular case put before it. The court has a responsibility to provide for finding the guilt or innocence of an individual, or the merits of a particular claim of one party against another, not the statistical probabilities of guilt or the justness of a claim. Further, the evaluation of the decisions made in the courtroom revolve around the legal accuracy of the decision without questioning the merits of the procedures used. The social sciences permit and often insist upon a critique of the method used to arrive at conclusions, so that a discussion of good-versus-bad results accompanies the presentation of results found.

The legal community traditionally draws at will on all of the available arts and sciences in understanding human behavior: philosophy, history, literature, psychiatry, psychology, economics, political science, sociology, and religion (Faigman 1989). The relevance of the social sciences to legal decision making rests on the validity of a claim to objective knowledge arrived at via the scientific method, but the role of social science data remains undefined and without a standard from the legal community by which to assess their introduction into the court.

Before we look at a few examples of the unsystematic history of the use of social science data, we might conjecture what the effects of the court's systematic reliance upon such data might be. The substantial use of findings in social science could destabilize the law, rendering it subject to the vagaries of the latest scientific discovery and leaving people uncertain at the time of their actions as to how their behavior stands with regard to the law. A reliance upon scientists for knowledge of social facts might result in the fluctuation of the law with every new data set; alternatively, the law might change too slowly while waiting for new data to be collected and evaluated, or while waiting for a new case to provide opportunity for revision, thus producing a certain inflexibility.

An example of the court's inflexibility exists in the change that occurred over nearly six decades, from the time of *Plessy v. Ferguson* in 1896 to that of *Brown v. Board of Education* in 1954. If *Plessy* was a reflection of the Spencerian notion of racial immutability and the doctrine of the "survival of the fittest," then the Court was indeed acknowledging nineteenth-century social science at the time of its decision (Driessen 1983). By the mid-1920s, these "social facts" were no longer considered true, but it was not until 1954 that the Court reversed itself on the basis of new social data and in light of the effects of segregation, in *Brown v. Board of Education* (Driessen 1983). The use of social science data in the courtroom in the *Plessy* and *Brown* cases points to other difficulties with the standards by which social science data are evaluated, and by whom. These are issues that will be discussed at greater length below. Science is by nature innovative, but the law resists innovation, so the law tends toward the status quo. The jurisprudential model assumes that the law is constant from one case to another, while the sociological model assumes it to be variable, changing from case to case as society changes (Black 1989).

Beyond the differences that exist naturally between the social science and legal communities, and apart from the lack of a systematized route for the introduction of any and all extralegal evidence in the court, including that which comes from the social science community, there is an explicit tension within the legal community concerning data from the social sciences. As was alluded to above in the discussion of the data admitted in the *Plessy* and *Brown* cases, not all social science data are equally valid or equally weighted. The legal community must make judgments about them that may or may not adhere to existing standards upheld by social scientists (Faigman 1989). The following statements provide insight into the disparate views on the subject held within the legal community.

Taking a strict constitutionalist view, Justice Frankfurter said in the *Brown* case, "If a proposition is true, I don't need sociologists to tell me that it is true. . . . I do not care what any associate or full professor in sociology tells me. If it is in the Constitution, I do not care about what they say" (Michelson, Rosen, and

Wasby 1980:13). Judges may believe it unnecessary or even inappropriate to consult anything but the law for answers to legal questions (Tanford 1990). The whole issue of whether the Supreme Court justices use social science may, in fact, turn on the question of the appropriateness of its use, rather than the veracity of the science (Tanford 1990).

Judge John Minor Wisdom (1975:143) took a broader view when he was on the United States Court of Appeals for the Fifth Circuit:

> What seemed at first to be antagonism between social science and law has now developed into a love match. What began in the field of education spread to many other fields. In case after case the Fifth Circuit, among other courts, has relied on studies developed by social scientists and other scientists to show pollution, unlawful exclusion of blacks from the jury system, employment discrimination, arbitrary or discriminatory use of the death penalty, discrimination against women, the need for reapportionment, and the cure for malapportionment of various public bodies.

Donald Bersoff, a law professor, gets at the heart of the difference between the attitudes embraced by Justice Frankfurter and Judge Wisdom. In the article "Social Science Data and the Supreme Court," Bersoff remarked that "courts will cite psychological research when they believe it will enhance the elegance of their opinions but data are readily discarded when more traditional and legally acceptable bases for decision making are available" (1987:52). Bersoff's observation confirms Justice Frankfurter's position that precedent is preferred to data. In a 1986 case, *Bowers v. Hardwick,* the Supreme Court clearly rejected scientific evidence and upheld sodomy statutes. Research was ignored in favor of history and morality.

Patrick Driessen lays out twelve "indictments" against the social science–courtroom match, but he then argues that many of the criticisms contained in the indictments can be deflected when the true nature of those criticisms is considered and when practical remedies to counter them are considered; he also points out that the criticisms are equally true of other policymaking methods (Driessen 1983:476).[2] Our investigation attempts to determine whether such arbitrary treatment of data from the social sciences occurs also in cases relating to women's issues.

Given David Faigman's observation that what relevance the social sciences can claim to current legal proceedings rests on the claim of the social sciences to objectivity, we should direct closer attention to the arbitrariness with which social science data are introduced into the courts. While the admission of social science data will be discussed below, the nature and significance of the social sciences claims to objectivity deserve a closer look now.

Objectivity and Validity

The basic organizing principle of the court is the adversarial structure. Given such a structure, lawyers on either side are charged—not with determining truth—but with advancing their clients' interests, often without regard to objectivity, validity, or neutrality. Information known to exist may be withheld if it does not meet basic criteria, a standard at odds with information-gathering within the realm of the social sciences. Alexander Tanford takes a harsh view of the trial system: "Trials . . . rely on incomplete data gathered by biased investigators, operate according to the procedural rules that exclude entire categories of information and permit juries to disregard what little evidence is introduced." He laments that "erroneous conclusions by scientists probably will be exposed by subsequent research. Erroneous decisions by juries cannot be detected because no further investigation or research is permitted" (1990:164).

In the social sciences we have a structure that allows for the pursuit of truth, the presentation of findings, and the indefinite contingency that those findings may be discarded upon the advent of better data at some later time. The adversarial structure of the court, procedures, time limits, prohibitions against double jeopardy, and safeguards against procedural abuses prevent full disclosure of all relevant data and preclude or otherwise restrict the revision of decisions.

Science does not pretend to claim 100 percent accuracy or success with regard to the goal of seeking the truth, but it does attempt to be objective and to remain open to revision. The distinctive character of social science discourse is that every assertion, no matter how objective, has a divergent interpretation of the "factual" situation (Wirth, in Mannheim 1936:xv). In science, this is known as "objectivity," which means to be impartial, have no preferences, predilections, prejudices, biases, or preconceived values (Mannheim 1936).

The question of truly objective social knowledge has been addressed variously over time by Locke, Hume, Bentham, Mill, Spencer, and others (Mannheim 1936). Weber cautioned of the need to be value-neutral and was aware that even the selection of a problem to investigate carried with it a value-relevance (Coser 1977). Scientists do not, in the main, believe that there is one true reality, as a positivist would assert. Twentieth-century social scientists know that it is not possible to succeed in conducting an absolutely value-free investigation, but there is great value in a scientist's awareness of biases in both the selection of a problem and its ensuing investigation.

Keeping in mind the tenuous relationship between the social sciences and the law, based on divergent natures, methods, and ends, let us turn to the history of the interaction of the two cultures. The general history of social science data in the courtroom will then serve as a foundation upon which to build our discussion of the treatment of social science data in the thirty-five cases on abortion and sex discrimination reviewed by the Supreme Court from 1972 to 1992.

History of Social Science in the Courtroom

The use of social science in the courtroom began with *Muller v. Oregon* in 1908 and moved to *Brown* in 1954 (Chesler, Sanders, and Kalmuss 1988; Craven 1975; Driessen 1983; Faigman 1989; Monahan and Walker 1986; Rosen 1972; and Tanford 1990). The court's receptiveness to social science is outlined by Paul Rosen in *The Supreme Court and Social Science* (1972) and is discussed below.[3] History's role in the Court began to wane in the twentieth century as the Court became more deeply enmeshed in the adjudication of contemporary social problems. The Court started to rely upon "extralegal" data, culled from outside the legal community. The Court began recognizing social science and using its findings in place of the less-convincing assumptions that had long influenced its interpretation of the Constitution. At the same time, there was a tremendously successful growth of science in the United States, especially natural science, with a strong emphasis on empiricism.

An emphasis on science in society began in the nineteenth century. Comte outlines three stages of society, beginning with the theological (prior to 1300), which had God as the center; the second was the metaphysical stage (between 1300 and 1800), where nature was the explanation; and then came the positivistic stage (after 1800), characterized by a belief in science (Ritzer 1992). In 1848, Marx and Engels's *Communist Manifesto* appeared, and Darwin's *The Origin of Species* followed in 1859. Together, they inaugurated two of the most influential ideologies of the nineteenth century—communism and social Darwinism. Spencer popularized social Darwinism, including the notions of universal competition, survival of the fittest, and the adaptability of the species. These beliefs affected all forms of social thought and became nearly synonymous with social science itself. Science became part of the culture, which in turn became part of the law, albeit—for the time being—indirectly.

The influence of this nineteenth-century social science on constitutional law was clearly evident in the case of *Plessy v. Ferguson,* decided in 1896. The *Plessy* case served as the constitutional foundation of racial segregation for fifty-eight years. Homer Plessy, who was one-eighth black, had been convicted by a Louisiana court of violating a state statute enacted in 1890 that required the two races to use separate railway facilities. The case was brought to the Supreme Court, charging that the statute violated Plessy's right as guaranteed by the Thirteenth and

Fourteenth Amendments. But Justice Brown on behalf of the Court reasoned that the Louisiana statute did not deprive Plessy of his rights, arguing that a statute that merely established a legal distinction between the two races did not undermine their equality; Brown further denied that the law could create feelings of racial inferiority. Paul Rosen (1972) maintains that, contrary to Brown's statement, the justice not only believed that blacks were different but he accepted as a matter of fact that they were biologically inferior, the underlying rationale of racial segregation based on social Darwinism.

There is little doubt that sociological and psychological theories controlled the Court's decision, even though they were not formally presented or recognized (Bernstein, in Rosen 1972). The Court ruled first that the statute was enacted in good faith, not as an annoyance; second, that racial segregation was a custom or tradition in the South; third, that law which followed custom was reasonable (while law that conflicted was unreasonable); and finally, that the law was incapable of restructuring racial instincts. The majority of the justices were not inclined to see the statute as oppressive, because they believed that racial segregation simply implemented and confirmed the natural inequality of the two races and that laissez-faire policies, given social Darwinism, complemented natural processes that worked toward the improvement of the human species. "Conversely," Rosen observed, "legislation that artificially interfered with the natural order, as Herbert Spencer had argued, posed a real threat to society and was to be regarded as oppressive and arbitrary" (1972:32).

Later, social science was used to support the legal efforts of blacks, but before that was possible, social science would have to abandon its attachment to a nineteenth-century interpretation of Darwinian laws of nature, which regarded nature as a deterministic force that encouraged human inequality. In addition, environmental factors would also come to be considered as a factor in human behavior. Reactions against Darwinism came from several sociologists, including Charles Cooley and George Herbert Mead and the Chicago school of sociology in the 1920s. Thus, while nineteenth-century social science contributed to the slowness with which the courts responded to changes in American culture, the new social science came to exert a more dynamic influence on constitutional law, as we will discuss in the case of *Muller v. Oregon* in 1908.

Muller v. Oregon has become famous because of Louis Brandeis and the "Brandeis brief." In 1905, Curt Muller, the proprietor of the Grand Laundry in Portland, Oregon, was convicted of violating a state statute specifying "that no female be employed in a mechanical establishment, or factory, or laundry more than ten hours during any one day" (Rosen 1972). Muller eventually brought his case to the Supreme Court, but his formidable opponent, representing the state of Oregon, was Louis D. Brandeis, who was later appointed to the Supreme

Court. Brandeis filed a 113-page brief supporting Oregon's maximum-hour law for women, drawing upon foreign, federal, and state studies concerning women's reactions to contemporary working conditions and using the views of American, French, and German doctors as evidence that women could not tolerate the same working hours as men (Craven 1975). His brief was immediately recognized as an innovation in American advocacy (Rosen 1972). The now famous "Brandeis brief" demonstrated the inherent differences between the two sexes, and in apparent reliance on these studies, the Court upheld an Oregon statute prohibiting women from working in factories for more than ten hours per day (Faigman 1989). Brandeis gleaned information from over one hundred sources to establish the legal relevance of extralegal data in support of five hypotheses:

> 1) Women are physiologically different from men and are more susceptible to injury resulting from unregulated industrial conditions. 2) Excessive hours of labor generally endanger the health, safety and morals of women. In particular, the effects on childbirth are disastrous and consequently affect the welfare of the nation. 3) Short workdays foster individual health and improve homelife. The nation in general prospers. 4) Short workdays produce economic benefits. . . . 5) The aforementioned benefits result only from uniform restrictions on the workday. (Rosen 1972:81)

Brandeis formally argued that the existence, not the validity, of facts was conclusive, but the presumption was that the facts were valid. The data Brandeis relied on would not measure up to current social science standards because the data were not systematically gathered, variables were not controlled, and hypotheses were not formally tested; but at the turn of the century, social science was in an embryonic and therefore much less standardized stage of development (Rosen 1972).

It was later observed that when the Court wished to uphold social welfare measures, it accepted the validity of facts of the "Brandeis briefs," but when it chose to reject legislation, the Court found extralegal data spurious and unconvincing (Norman J. Small, in Rosen 1972). The current research will test this assertion. As Judge Craven (1975:151) noted, "The Brandeis brief was an innovation in *Muller v. Oregon,* but is now standard operating procedure in equal employment, ecology, and major school desegregation cases."

The movement for the introduction of social science was slow and tedious after *Muller,* however, and the next major encounter between the Supreme Court and social science was not to occur until over forty years later with *Brown v. Board of Education* in 1954 (Monahan and Walker 1986). The U.S. Supreme Court decided the landmark case in 1954, ruling that racial segregation in public schools violated the equal-protection clause of the Fourteenth Amendment and was therefore unconstitutional (Rosen 1972). The military and private industry were already using social science data, but the Court was slow to come to rely upon it. The Supreme Court was apparently not anxious to use social science findings, even though it repeatedly made judgments that were political, economic, sociological, or psychological in nature. As Justice Oliver Wendell Holmes observed: "Judges commonly are elderly, and more likely to hate at sight any analysis to which they are not accustomed, and which disturbs repose of mind, than to fall in love with novelties" (Rosen 1972:114). Chief Justice Earl Warren pointed out that "The law is slow to move. In the past, seldom has it anticipated conditions and evolved methods to remedy them" (Rosen 1972:159).

One observer stated that the lawyer fears the loss of his age-old function as intellectual broker and his ultimate replacement in terms of power and prestige by the specialist and expert (Rosen 1972). The "threat theory" argues that judges view science as a threat to their power and prestige, and that people with legal training have traditionally occupied high-status positions (Tanford 1990). If the law was to become dependent on science for answers to legal questions, the role of those with legal training would be diminished and scientific techniques, alien to lawyers, might then replace the familiar dialectic of law as the basis for decisions (Tanford 1990). Conversely, of course, social science data could simply become yet another tool in the adversarial armories used in the courtroom.

Rosen (1972) argues that the *Brown* decision was second in importance only to the Emancipation Proclamation. If customs and mores were to change in accord with the Court's decision, then the consequences would be staggering. The tension between social science and the law continued into *Brown*, and it was not at all clear whether the Supreme Court would accept social science findings as a binding definition of the facts. Justice Frankfurter had noted that social science was strictly related to the finding of fact, and as to the finding of law, social science would have no bearing on the matter of whether the Constitution permitted statutory classifications based on race. The factual evidence in *Brown* was presented in an NAACP brief as a social science appendix entitled "The Effects of Segregation and the Consequences of Desegregation: A Social Science Statement." It was relatively short but extensively documented, and it summarized social science findings on the effects of segregation, specifically school segregation, and concluded that enforced segregation is psychologically detrimental to the members of the segregated group (Rosen 1972).

The statement was signed by thirty-five social scientists, including such luminaries as Paul Lazarsfeld, Robert Merton, and Gordon Allport, and testimony at the trial level was delivered by Dr. Kenneth Clark. The modern social science data contradicted the psychological and sociological assumption underlying *Plessy*. The Court acknowledged its implicit use of nineteenth-century social science in the *Plessy* case and stated that the factual finding of psychological harm caused by school segregation—and documented by modern social science—constituted an empirical rejection of the "separate-but-equal" formula (Rosen 1972). Footnote eleven of the *Brown* case referred to and cited seven social science studies. In its decision, the Court had advanced a social science definition of equality that was at the same time one of law (Rosen 1972). Aware of the profound impact the decision would have on the structure of American society, the Court refrained from issuing an immediate decree ordering the termination of public-school segregation (Rosen 1972).

Though it had taken time to reach that point, the Court's use of social science in the *Brown* case confirmed the success of efforts in the *Muller* case to have constitutional law propounded in light of reliable extralegal data, rather than seemingly arbitrary judicial biases. The use of social science in the two cases differed. In *Muller,* empirical data were used to support the rationality of a state statute. In *Brown,* social science data were used to overrule a prior Supreme Court decision (Monahan and Walker 1986). The Court's formal use of modern social science in *Brown* brought hostile reactions, and footnote eleven became the most disputed footnote in American constitutional law (Rosen 1972). Mason, Brandeis's biographer, claimed that the Court had invoked two of the flimsiest of disciplines—sociology and psychology—as the basis for its decision (Rosen 1972). He believed, however, that Brandeis would not have objected to the Court's use of modern social science for the purpose of ascertaining the relevant facts of racial segregation. In fact, the Court's use of social science sounded suspiciously like socialism to some, and the social scientists' loyalty to the United States was even questioned (Rosen 1972).

Social science data were criticized and generally considered weak in certain respects in *Brown* (Rosen 1972): (1) school segregation was not identified as the sole environmental factor that caused injury; (2) the studies did not define the precise psychological effects of school segregation; (3) the studies indicated that the available empirical data were limited; and (4) hypotheses on personality development were tentative. Overall, however, the literature confirmed that disparities in achievement between the races could be explained in environmental, rather than biological, terms, and segregated schools were a critical environmental factor that inflicted psychological harm on black children. The studies were balanced and did not exaggerate, and more than five hundred social scientists had agreed that school segregation was harmful (Rosen 1972). The lesson of *Brown* was that social science can provide factual illumination to a willing court (Rosen 1972). By using social science, the Supreme Court suggested that the longstanding inequality of the two races was not due to any biological traits of blacks.

In other types of cases, especially those having to do with the judicial process itself, the courts have been more reluctant to use social science data. A case in point is *Lockhart v. McCree*, decided by the United States Supreme Court in 1986. The Supreme Court held that in cases in which the prosecution was requesting capital punishment, it is not unconstitutional to exclude those jurists who have moral or religious scruples against imposing the death penalty (Bersoff 1987).

At issue was the scientific soundness of three decades of social science research indicating that the absence of jurors with such scruples created a jury that was pro-prosecution and therefore conviction-prone (Bersoff 1987). The American Psychological Association filed an *amicus curiae* brief that discussed at length the large body of data demonstrating that death-qualified juries are indeed conviction-prone (Tanford 1990). In other words, only individuals who believe in the death penalty can serve as jurors, so the bias is toward execution. Despite assurances that the research was methodologically sound, Justice Rehnquist attacked the empirical studies. He devoted five pages of his majority opinion to assailing the methods used in the cited research (Tanford 1990). "Yet, not a single Supreme Court majority opinion has relied even partly on the psychology of jury behavior to justify a decision about the proper way to conduct a trial" (Tanford 1990:139). The Court in fact decided such cases as if no relevant psychological research existed (Tanford 1990).

Concerning *Lockhart*, Tanford (1990) concluded that (1) most justices are hostile toward social psychology; (2) they do not understand the data; (3) they believe that empirical research on juror behavior is no more reliable than intuition and anecdotal evidence; and (4) they ultimately believe that psychology has little or no place in the jurisprudence of trial procedure (Tanford 1990). Justice Powell stated that he had strong reservations about basing Supreme Court decisions on empirical research even when it supported his position, because of reliance on statistical language, which he disparagingly referred to as "numerology" (quoted in Tanford 1990). Justice Powell doubted the scientific process precisely because it is not adversarial (Tanford 1990). Justices appeared to conclude that if precedent and psychology conflict about jury behavior, they will choose precedent as the basis for a decision (Tanford 1990). Tanford's and Bersoff's analyses of the use of social science by the courts were limited to the judicial process itself. But the court may be less reluctant to use social science in considering issues of broader social scope, such as school desegregation and women's issues, which the current research addresses.

Since appellate courts are not bound by lower courts' conclusions of law, Monahan and Walker (1986) assert that they should not be bound by the lower courts' conclusions regarding empirical research; a reviewing court is completely free to evaluate *de novo* any precedent used in a lower court decision. Therefore, Monahan and Walker conclude that the Court should be unconstrained in its ability to reevaluate any social science research upon which a lower court relied, such as finding that the study cited is insufficiently valid or generalizable, or, conversely, to use research that was dismissed by the court below. The present study will attempt to examine this possibility more thoroughly. Social science research can plausibly be seen as a form of authority in much the same way as prior cases are regarded by the common law (Monahan and Walker 1986). Brandeis argued that realism in law can only be achieved if the court pays closer attention to the facts of life (Rosen 1972). In the years since *Brown*, there has been a change in the scientific issues, data bases, and methods used in the courts and a change as well in the use of expert witnesses, briefs, and other methods of introducing social science into court.

Having addressed the problematic relationship between social science and the law, we will next look at the ways in which social science enters the courts via expert testimony and *amicus curiae* briefs.

Notes

1. Taken from M. J. Saks and R. Hastie, *Social Psychology in Court* (New York: Van Nostrand Reinhold, 1978), 206.

2. The twelve indictments that Driessen (1983) lists are: (1) judges are generalists; (2) legal reasoning is nonprobabilistic and associated with a large tolerance for low-accuracy results; (3) the judiciary is preoccupied with unique cases, attempting to promulgate a general policy from peculiar circumstances; (4) reversibility runs against common judicial practice; (5) expert witnesses, who are not always so expert, may overwhelm judges and juries; (6) hearsay rules hinder the introduction of social science testimony; (7) social scientists brought into the courtroom do not use their best tools; (8) courts emphasize theoretical knowledge over practical or clinical knowledge; (9) a philosophy of school desegregation should not be based solely, or even primarily, on social science evidence; (10) social science results may be presented as less tentative than they really are; (11) the adversarial system in the courtroom sometimes fails to challenge social science evidence; and (12) judges make normative/prescriptive decisions, while scientists attempt to be value-free.

3. Unless otherwise noted, the information on the history of social science in the courtroom is drawn from Rosen (1972).

2

Expert Witness Testimony and *Amicus Curiae*

Expert testimony and *amicus curiae* briefs constitute two of the most important means by which extralegal data enter the courtroom. These gateways of information have great significance for our consideration of the ways social science data are introduced to the court. Relevant to our discussion is the history of expert testimony; the evolution of opinions as to who can be expert witnesses and what constitutes expert evidence; the effect of the Federal Rules of Evidence (FRE), enacted in 1975, on the admissibility of expert testimony; and the brief history of the content and submission of *amicus curiae* briefs to the Supreme Court.

Expert Witnesses

The contribution of expert knowledge to court proceedings predates the advent of the jury system in England in the fourteenth century. Patrick Anderson, in his book *Expert Witnesses: Criminologists in the Courtroom,* and Lawrence Rosen, in his article "The Anthropologist as Expert Witness," both point out that expert knowledge was originally introduced to the court via neighbors acquainted with the facts of a case or through specialists such as scholars, physicians, engineers, and merchants. As Rosen also discusses, the sixteenth century saw neighbors transformed from contributors of their own knowledge of the case to arbiters brought in to bear witness and pass judgment on the evidence presented in court.

The first expert testimony delivered from the witness stand was provided by a civil engineer, John Smeaton, who testified in *Folkes v. Chadd* in 1782. Prior to the *Folkes* case, the first instance of forensic evidence was recorded in England in 1760 when testimony was introduced to the court in the case of Earl Ferrers, on trial for murder, by Dr. John Munro. As Rita Simon and David Aaronson discuss in their book *The Insanity Defense: A Critical Assessment of Law and Policy in the Post-Hinckley Era,* Dr. Munro's testimony was introduced because of the doctor's familiarity with the insane, which the court believed enabled him to distinguish the true features of madness.

At present, expert testimony comes from a wide range of fields, including psychology, psychiatry, economics, statistics, medicine, anthropology, criminal justice, and sociology. The use of evidence from each field in the courtroom has, of course, its own history. Dr. Munro's testimony marks the beginning of the history of psychiatric expert testimony in the courts. Aside from the apparent pattern of redundancy of the professional's affirmation of what the defendant's peers had already concluded or were already disposed to conclude, the history and evolution of the role of psychiatric evidence delivered by experts provides a relevant framework through which to examine the uses and complications of extralegal expert testimony in the court.

The 1987 trial of John Hinckley, who shot President Ronald Reagan, occasioned the examination of medical testimony in the form of psychiatric diagnosis from a historical perspective. The challenge for the psychiatric expert is to determine not what the person's mental condition is at the present time, but what it was at a time in the past. Hinckley's lawyers produced experts for the defense who, while recognized within their professions, had little or no trial experience, whereas the government produced experts for the prosecution who had trial experience and forensic medicine knowledge. The jury concluded, on the basis of testimony provided, that there was a reasonable doubt as to the defendant's mental condition and his criminal responsibility for the attempted assassination and so returned a verdict of not guilty by reason of insanity.

The role played by expert psychiatric witnesses in cases such as Hinckley's should be understood in two contexts: that of the extralegal community from which the evidence originates and that of the legal realm. Within the realm of psychiatry, the expert's judgment differs from that of the lay witness because the expert bases his or her opinion on specialized training and/or theoretical information. The very qualities that confer expertise on the expert—training, methodology, and attempts at objective research—are then subordinated to the procedural concerns and adversarial structure of the court itself. The psychiatric community is concerned that procedural constraints and the adversarial structure of the court may distort scientific findings, but the legal community is concerned that unproven concepts, or those subjected to perpetual revision, may wield undue influence on the law.

As Simon and Aaronson go on to discuss, the court is aware of the potential need for psychiatric testimony. In the case of *Ake v. Oklahoma* in 1985, Justice Marshall, writing for the majority, said that where the defendant's mental condition is critical to the issue of criminal responsibility, the assistance of a psychiatrist may well be crucial to the defendant's ability to marshal his defense. Additionally, as Dr. Alan Stone of Harvard Law School argues (Simon and Aaronson 1988), every defendant in an adversarial legal system is entitled to an ardent advocate, and if there is the possibility of articulating an insanity defense, the system itself demands that the legal advocate obtain psychiatric testimony that will help the client.

An additional complication in the use of psychiatric evidence, alluded to earlier, derives from the issue of consistency of standards within the psychiatric community. Reliable classification, the cornerstone of expert testimony, often eludes the expert because the official diagnostic manual, *The Diagnostic and Statistical Manual of Mental Disorders,* is frequently revised. Further, studies show that the judgments of professional clinicians may not be more accurate than those of laypersons and so there is no body of evidence that a select group of professionals makes consistently better judgments than professionals in general, as Steve Chan discusses in his article "Expert Judgments Under Uncertainty: Some Evidence and Suggestions." Chan states that even when clinicians base their opinions on statistical methods—as opposed to clinical or case-study approaches—their assessments may fall somewhat short of what the court would prefer. Ironically, as the experts remain true to the ideal of expertise in their own fields, they often render themselves unsuitable as expert witnesses in the court.

In addition to the use of psychiatric experts, authorities in fields such as economics, anthropology, sociology, and criminal justice are all called upon to testify in various kinds of cases. For example, as Patrick Anderson (1987) discusses, economists often are brought in to testify in wrongful-death litigation, being called upon to provide data regarding what would have been a victim's future earnings as well as to evaluate special damages.

Anderson, Lawrence Rosen (1977), and Kim Hopper (1990), the latter in her article "Research Findings as Testimony: A Note on the Ethnographer as Expert Witness," discuss the role of anthropologists who have testified in cases dealing with Native Americans and issues of treaties, artifacts, and the use of peyote, as well as racial segregation, miscegenation, child custody, and religious customs. In the Supreme Court case *Wisconsin v. Yoder* in 1972, as Rosen discusses, it was the testimony of John A. Hostetler, an anthropologist and expert witness who was himself raised in the Amish community, to which the Court frequently referred in its opinion. The Court found that the Amish religion and mode of life were inseparable and interdependent, and that the social repercussions of compulsory high school attendance for the Amish would necessarily infringe on the well-being of the community as a religious entity.

As Patrick Anderson and Thomas Winfree (1987), Valerie Hans (1989), and

Lawrence Rosen (1977) discuss in their respective publications, sociologists have been called in to testify in cases concerning the custody of children of mixed racial parentage, race and the death penalty, parental fitness, eyewitness identification, job discrimination, jury selection, sentencing, and, most prominently, school desegregation, in *Brown v. Board of Education*. Mark Chesler, Joseph Sanders, and Debra Kalmuss, in their book *Social Science in Court: Mobilizing Experts in the School Desegregation Cases,* have traced the use of social scientists in seventeen cases of school desegregation since the time of *Brown*.

Criminal justice scholars are brought in as expert witnesses to address institutional issues such as prison overcrowding and excessive use of force by police. The increase in the use of expert witnesses from the field of criminal justice can be attributed to three important shifts in judicial practice that occurred in the 1970s. First, the federal courts abandoned a long-standing hands-off policy with respect to the nation's state-administered prison system (Anderson and Winfree 1987). Second, after 1977, capital punishment was again admitted for sentencing. Third, in 1978, with the resolution of *Monell v. the Department of Social Services,* it became possible to sue units of local government as persons.

Statisticians increasingly appear in the courtroom to explain and demythologize statistics in order to render them intelligible to the jury, as Anne Barton (1983) and David Kaye (1990) discuss. Kaye reports that statistical evidence became to the 1980s what demonstrative evidence such as fingerprints and blood tests were to the 1960s and early 1970s. Considerable use of statistics has been made in cases having to do with employment discrimination, in which the courts have admitted hypothesis-testing to determine, as Edward Imwinkelried (1986) discusses, whether there is a cause-and-effect relationship between the variables. Such a determination would allow them to decide whether patterns in hiring or school enrollment reflect intentional discrimination or are simply the result of chance. The statistician may estimate the number of minority workers one could expect to find at a given company if the employer's hiring pattern was nondiscriminatory. The greater the difference between the statistical expectation and the actual numbers, the stronger the implication of discrimination.

As mentioned earlier, there has been a significant alteration in the source and role of expertise in the court. Expertise was first introduced via neighbors considered to be knowledgeable because of their familiarity with the case in question; it then evolved to the domain of the jury, and subsequently to that of expert witnesses. We will now turn to a discussion of the admission of expert evidence, the effects on admissibility brought about by the Federal Rules of Evidence of 1975, and the ramifications of *Daubert v. Merrell Dow Pharmaceuticals, Inc.* on the application of the FRE. We will then discuss briefs, the second major gateway of expert evidence and social science data into the courtroom.

The Evidence

The kinds of evidence relied upon by the Supreme Court is an important issue in our analysis of the thirty-five cases dealing with abortion and with sex discrimination in the workplace. It dictates that we discuss here the admission of expert testimony to the lower courts. This will allow us to understand how data from the social sciences come to be considered by the higher courts.

As noted above, there is a growing trend in the United States toward the use of more scientifically based evidence in litigation, a phenomenon that Michael Ciresi and Martha Wivell as well as David Faigman, Edward Imwinkelried, Barton Ingraham, Melvin Kraft, Lanelle Montgomery, Faust Rossi, Rita Simon and David Aaronson, and Alexander Tanford each discuss. One survey found that half of the responding lawyers and trial judges encounter scientific evidence in about a third of the cases they try. In addition, virtually every major civil trial involves some kind of expert testimony (Imwinkelried 1986). The principle reason for the increased presence of expert evidence in the courtroom is the liberalization of the rules governing the admission of evidence enacted in 1975 through the Federal Rules of Evidence (rules 702 through 705) (Rossi 1991). Few of the kinds of evidence newly admissible according to the FRE are new or particularly revolutionary in and of themselves. However, they are being admitted and applied in the courtroom with significantly more freedom than under the precedent for the admission of scientific evidence established in 1923 by the *Frye* decision.

Prior to the congressional enactment of the FRE, the rule of *Frye v. United States* (1923)[1] required that expert testimony be based on a method enjoying "general acceptance" in its particular field[2] (Ciresi and Wivell 1991). The Court stated in *Frye* that the "thing from which the deduction is made must be generally accepted by the relevant scientific community" (Block 1990:312). In essence, this meant that a form of peer review must underlie an expert's opinion, thus blocking testimony based on data that might not yet be published in the literature or generally known or accepted by the scientific community. Even though data of questionable validity was effectively filtered out, the courts lagged years behind the laboratories with regard to the quality of the admissible data. The standard set by the *Frye* decision was used in courts for more than fifty years (Ciresi and Wivell 1991; Imwinkelried 1986). Under the old "general acceptance" test of *Frye*, the question about a scientific theory was whether, as a matter of historical fact, it had been embraced by an overwhelming majority of experts in the particular discipline (Imwinkelried 1986).

When Congress passed the FRE in 1975, it intentionally adopted more-receptive standards for admitting expert testimony. The testimony of any knowledgeable expert with special information that might assist the jury was now admissible, thus replacing the more restrictive common-law approach to expert testimony developed over the decades by the federal judiciary (Ciresi and Wivell 1991). The policies set forth by the FRE at the federal level are also used by many states as a model for updating their own rules of evidence (Ingraham 1987).

Thus, if scientific evidence passes the *Frye* test, it will pass the traditional relevancy and expert testimony tests, as outlined in several pertinent rules, among them, "Rule 702. Testimony by Experts. If scientific, technical, or other specialized knowledge will assist the trier-of-fact to understand the evidence or to determine a fact in issue, a witness qualified as an expert by knowledge, skill, experience, training, or education, may testify thereto in the form of an opinion or otherwise" (Block 1990).

The test for Rule 702 admissibility is "whether the untrained layman would be qualified to determine intelligently and to the best possible degree the particular issue without enlightenment from those having a specialized understanding of the subject involved in the dispute" (Ciresi and Wivell 1991:37). In evaluating the weight to be given an expert's opinion, the jury should consider the qualifications of the witness, the theoretical and factual basis for the expert's opinion, and the reasoning process. Further, the jury is not to be bound by the opinions of expert witnesses (Simon and Aaronson 1988). According to the FRE, Rule 702 requires that the testimony be helpful to the trier of fact. The evidence must assist the fact finder in making a more intelligent assessment of the subject matter at issue. It must be presented by a qualified expert and there must be adequate foundation (Block 1990). Modern evidence rules have eroded the scope of expert testimony on what is "beyond the ken" of the ordinary juror and on "general acceptance." Rule 702 says that expert testimony must merely assist the trier of fact, not that it be beyond the ken of lay persons (Rossi 1991). As a result, trial judges allow expert assistance that heretofore would have been considered an invasion of the jury function (Rossi 1991).

Rule 703 permits an expert to base his or her opinion on facts or data not admissible in evidence (Kraft 1982): "Rule 703. Bases of Opinion Testimony by Experts. The facts or data in the particular case upon which an expert bases an opinion or inferences may be those perceived or made known to him at or before the hearing. If of a type reasonably relied upon by experts in the particular field in forming opinions or inference upon the subject, the facts or data need not be admissible in evidence."

Opinions can be based upon facts within personal knowledge or facts supplied in the court by evidence, data that are inadmissible hearsay, or data that violate other exclusionary rules as long as the reliance is reasonable (Rossi

1991). Unlike *Frye,* Rule 703 does not require that the expert's methodology and opinion even be generally accepted (Ciresi and Wivell 1991). Instead, Rule 703 requires that the opinion be based on the kind of scientific evidence usually relied on by experts in that discipline and not be bound by what the court deems reliable (Ciresi and Wivell 1991).

Rule 703 dispenses with the requirement that an expert's testimony be based on reasoning that has been subjected to peer review or on research published in a professional journal (Ciresi and Wivell 1991). Even if a court distrusts testimony that has not been subjected to such scrutiny, the absence of peer review is not grounds for excluding the testimony (Ciresi and Wivell 1991). In addition to dispensing with a standard of peer review, the Federal Rules of Evidence allow an expert to express an opinion based on hearsay (Belli 1982). Opinions offered by experts based on hearsay may be acquired by the expert from sources outside the courtroom and not subject to cross-examination, provided the source is of the type reasonably relied upon within the field (Ingraham 1987). This broadening of admissible testimony has particular relevance to social science evidence in which there is no ruling paradigm and in which the results can have varied interpretations (Ingraham 1987). The purpose of Rule 703 was to expand the base of expert opinion, not to allow the court to abdicate its responsibility to examine the facts upon which the expressed opinions were made (Rossi 1991). The very issue of the duty and role of the court in evaluating evidence will be discussed below in the context of the *Daubert v. Merrell Dow* case.

One of the issues clearly delineated in the FRE is that of the admission of opinion on the ultimate issue to be decided by the jury: "Rule 704. Opinion on Ultimate Issue. Testimony in the form of an opinion or inference otherwise admissible is not objectionable because it embraces an ultimate issue to be decided by the trier-of-fact."[3] Under Rule 704, opinions on ultimate facts are permissible but opinions on questions of law are not. The witness, therefore, still cannot testify about whether particular legal standards have been met (Rossi 1991). Historically, an expert was prevented from giving an opinion on the ultimate issue, reasoning that to allow this would be an impermissible invasion of the jury's province of determining facts (Belli 1982). This restriction was known as the "ultimate fact" prohibition, which barred experts from trying to answer the questions that a trial was being held to resolve. For example, if one of the ultimate facts to be determined was whether a person had died as a result of homicide or accident, a forensic pathologist could not testify directly on that issue (Imwinkelried 1986).

Experts must still stop short of expressing opinions on questions of law. In general, questions of law are answered by the judge and questions of fact are answered by the jury or trier of fact (Monahan and Walker 1986). Today, many courts do allow an expert to express opinions on the ultimate issue. The Supreme Court of Utah explains that to leave an expert's ultimate conclusion undisclosed is to require the jury to speculate as to what conclusion it should draw from the technical facts. The opinion rule should facilitate, not frustrate, jury understanding (Belli 1982).

The typical social science testimony is usually offered at three levels (Ingraham 1987): (1) observations about tests and experiments; (2) discussion of cause-and-effect relationships between behavior and events; (3) consideration of the ultimate issue, that is, negligence, discrimination, guilt. It is at the third level that the expert can, and sometimes does, move into an advocacy position (Ingraham 1987). In general the roles of advocate and expert should not be conflated. In allowing a much broader base of testimony to be admitted, the new rules do not require that an expert lay the basis for that testimony. Rule 705 addresses this specifically: "Rule 705. Disclosure of Facts or Data Underlying Expert Opinion. The expert may testify in terms of opinions or inference and give his reasons therefore without prior disclosure of the underlying facts or data, unless the court requires otherwise. The expert may in any event be required to disclose the underlying facts or data on cross-examination." Rule 705 does not require the witness to lay a foundation for the opinion evidenced by prior disclosure of the underlying facts or data, unless required by the court. This then raises the question of whether the jury can properly evaluate the soundness of the opinion and its factual basis (Ingraham 1987). Rule 706 also has implications for expert witnesses because it authorizes the court, on its own motion, to appoint an expert (Kraft 1982). Some have argued that the adversary system, with its partisan selection of expert witnesses, has been responsible for many of the better scholars' refusal to participate as experts. The partisan selection results in a "battle of experts," which can contribute to confusion and misunderstanding on the part of the jury (Simon and Aaronson 1988). Some suggest that dubious testimony could be countered by a court-appointed expert who would explain what mainstream practitioners of that particular branch of science might think of the witness's theories (Olson 1989). Yet, it may not be assumed that even court-appointed experts would be impartial.

While Rule 705 does not require the expert to lay the foundation for the evidence presented, Rule 401 provides that admissible evidence must be logically relevant; that is, it makes the existence of any fact that is of consequence to the determination of the action more probable or less probable than it would be without the evidence (Block 1990). Rule 403 excludes relevant evidence if there is a danger of unfair prejudice or confusion of the issues, if such evidence is misleading to the jury, or if it is a waste of time (Block 1990). The ultimate question for the judge is whether both sides have a fair opportunity to test the validity of scientific results; if the judge finds this is not the case, he or she must render those results inadmissible. In deciding the ultimate questions, judges must consider the degree to which the accuracy of scientific information has been established (*Federal Rules of Evidence Manual* 1988). The Federal Rules of Evidence, considered the major source in the development of court procedures and the admissibility of scientific evidence, favor the spoken word of expert testimony over the introduction into evidence of the written word, including the study or studies upon which testimony is based (Lindman 1989). The reasoning behind the preference for oral as opposed to written testimony is to avoid having the jury attach undue significance to social science evidence simply because it, unlike some other evidence, is presented in a document that looks reliable and official (Lindman 1989). In sum, the Court's assumption is "that the jury can screen out unreliable evidence and remain unmoved by the aura of expertise. Whether such an optimistic view of the adversary system is justified or not, it reflects the trend of modern evidence doctrine" (Rossi 1991:151).

The Federal Rules of Evidence were put to the test in the case of *Daubert v. Merrell Dow Pharmaceuticals, Inc.,* in which the Supreme Court ruled on how strict judges can be in refusing to allow testimony from expert witnesses and in keeping out testimony derived from various scientific techniques of investigation, especially newer methods. In a decision handed down in June 1993, on *Daubert,* the Court decided that "general acceptance" of underlying scientific evidence is not a necessary precondition to the admissibility of such evidence under the Federal Rules of Evidence. The decision was rendered in a particular case, but the significance of the ruling goes far beyond the case of product liability in which it was raised.

The *Daubert* case has great illustrative value. The Court's opinion (125 L. Ed. 2d 469–89) states that the plaintiffs alleged that two children's birth defects had been caused by the mothers' ingestion of Bendectin (produced by Merrell Dow Pharmaceuticals) during pregnancy. An epidemiologist for the defendant had rendered that no published epidemiological study had demonstrated a statistically significant association between Bendectin and birth defects. In response, the plaintiffs offered expert opinion testimony based on test-tube and live-animal studies that found a link between Bendectin and birth defects. The district court, granting summary judgment in favor of the company, expressed the view that (1) scientific evidence is admissible under the Federal Rules of Evidence only if the principle on which such evidence is based is sufficiently established to have general acceptance in the field to which it belongs; (2) epidemiological studies were the most reliable evidence of causation of birth defects; (3) the testimony based on test-tube, live-animal, and pharmacological studies was inadmissible because such testimony was not based on epidemiological evidence; and (4) the testimony based on reanalyses was inadmissible because the reanalyses had (a) never been published or subjected to peer review and (b) failed to show a statistically significant association between Bendectin and birth defects (727 F.Supp. 570). The United States Court of Appeals for the Ninth Circuit affirmed on appeal. It expressed the view that expert opinion based on a scientific technique is inadmissible if the technique is not generally accepted as reliable in the relevant scientific community. Under the general acceptance standard, the plaintiffs' evidence provided an insufficient foundation to allow admission of expert testimony that Bendectin caused birth defects (951 F.2d 1131).

On certiorari (a process discussed below, in our section on briefs), the Supreme Court vacated the judgment of the Court of Appeals and remanded the case for further proceedings. The opinion was written by Blackmun, who was joined by White, O'Connor, Scalia, Kennedy, Souter, and Thomas. Rehnquist, joined by Stevens, concurred in part and dissented in part. The opinion held that the general acceptance test of *Frye v. United States* (1923) was superseded by the Federal Rules of Evidence. Thus "general acceptance" is not a necessary precondition to the admissibility of scientific evidence under the FRE, given that (1) nothing in the text of Rule 702 of the FRE, governing expert testimony, establishes "general acceptance" as an absolute prerequisite to admissibility; (2) there is no indication that Rule 702 or the FRE as a whole were intended to incorporate a general acceptance standard; (3) under the FRE, a federal trial judge must insure that any and all scientific testimony or evidence is not only relevant but reliable; (4) in a federal case involving scientific evidence, evidentiary reliability is based on scientific validity. The dissent agreed that the Frye general acceptance rule did not survive the enactment of the FRE, and Rule 702 of the FRE confides to the trial judge some gatekeeping responsibility in deciding questions of the admissibility of proffered expert testimony; but the dissent also expressed the view that the Supreme Court should have left the further development of the area of law in question to future cases.

The Court held that the Federal Rules of Evidence, not *Frye*, provide the standard for admitting expert scientific testimony in a federal trial. *Frye*'s general acceptance test was superseded by the FRE's adoption. The FRE, especially Rule 702, place appropriate limits on the admissibility of scientific evidence by assigning to the trial judge the task of ensuring that an expert's testimony rests on a reliable foundation and is relevant to the task at hand. The trial judge, pursuant to Rule 104(a), must make a preliminary assessment of whether the testimony's underlying reasoning or method is scientifically valid and properly can be applied to the facts at issue. Cross-examination, rather than wholesale exclusion under an uncompromising general acceptance standard, is the appropriate means by which evidence may be challenged. Blackmun's opinion states that the debates over *Frye* are such a well-established part of the academic landscape that a distinct term—"Frye-ologist"—has been advanced to describe a person who takes part.[4] Blackmun says (479) that the court agrees with petitioners that the *Frye* test was superseded by the adoption of the Federal Rules of Evidence.

The opinion, in *Daubert v. Merrell Dow Pharmaceuticals,* contains numerous references to scientific articles drawn from the briefs presented to the Court. Blackmun writes (481), "Of course, it would be unreasonable to conclude that the subject of scientific testimony must be 'known' to a certainty; arguably, there are no certainties in science." From *Amici Curiae* 9, he quotes, "Indeed, scientists do not assert that they know what is immutably 'true'—they are committed to searching for new, temporary theories to explain, as best they can, phenomena." From *Amici Curiae* 7–8, Brief for American Association for the Advancement of Science and the National Academy of Sciences, Blackmun quotes, "Science is not an encyclopedic body of knowledge about the universe. Instead, it represents a process for proposing and refining theoretical explanations about the world that are subject to further testing and refinement." Blackmun writes, "In order to qualify as scientific knowledge, an inference or assertion must be derived by the scientific method. Proposed testimony must be supported by appropriate validation . . . based on what is known. In short, the requirement that an expert's testimony pertain to 'scientific knowledge' establishes a standard of evidentiary reliability" (1993:481).

Blackmun maintains (482) that Rule 702's "'helpfulness' standard requires a valid scientific connection to the pertinent inquiry as a precondition to admissibility." A key question, Blackmun determines, is whether a theory is scientific knowledge that will assist the trier of fact. Blackmun quotes Karl Popper: "The criterion of the scientific status of a theory is its falsifiability, or refutability, or testability" (Blackmun, 483).[5] Another pertinent consideration, Blackmun asserts (483), is whether the theory or technique has been subjected to peer review and to publication, which is but one element of peer review and is not the *sine qua non* of admissibility because it does not necessarily correlate with reliability.[6] The fact of, or lack of, publication in a peer-reviewed journal will be a relevant, though not dispositive, consideration in assessing the scientific validity of a particular technique or methodology that is the premise for an opinion (Blackmun, 483).[7] Blackmun asserts (484) that the focus must be on principles and methodology, not on conclusions.

Blackmun notes (484) the importance of a judge's being mindful of the other applicable rules that Rule 703 provides, namely, that expert opinions based on otherwise inadmissible hearsay are to be admitted only if the facts or data are "of a type reasonably relied upon by experts in the particular field in forming opinions or inferences upon the subject." As noted earlier, Rule 706 allows the court at its discretion to procure the assistance of an expert of its own choosing. Finally, Rule 403 permits the exclusion of relevant evidence, Blackmun writes (484), "if its probative value is substantially outweighed by the danger of unfair prejudice, confusion of the issues, or misleading the jury." In conclusion, Blackmun believes that the respondent is being overly pessimistic about the capabilities of the jury and the adversary system generally when stating that abandonment of "general acceptance" will result in a "free-for-all," befuddling juries (484). Blackmun asserts that "vigorous cross-examination, presentation of contrary evidence, and careful instruction on the burden of proof are the traditional and appropriate means of attacking shaky but admissible evidence" (484). Petitioners, Blackmun states, "exhibit a different concern. . . . They suggest that recognition of a screening role for the judge that allows for the exclusion of 'invalid' evidence will sanction a stifling and repressive scientific orthodoxy and will be inimical to the search for truth" (485). To this point, the opinion states: "Scientific conclusions are subject to perpetual revision. Law, on the other hand, must resolve disputes finally and quickly. The scientific project is advanced by broad and wide-ranging consideration of a multitude of hypotheses, for those that are incorrect will eventually be shown to be so, and in itself is an advance" (Blackmun, 485). That, Blackmun says (485), is the balance struck by Federal Rules of Evidence, "designed not for the exhaustive search for cosmic understanding but for the particularized resolution of legal disputes."

Rehnquist says in his dissent that the various briefs filed in this case are markedly different from typical briefs, in that large parts of them deal with scientific knowledge, method, validity, and peer review—in short, matters he considers to be far afield from the expertise of judges. So on the very matter about which the Court was making its decision, Rehnquist opines that he felt overwhelmed by the material on the place of social science in the courts. He agrees that Rule 702 confines to judges some gatekeeping responsibility in deciding questions of the admissibility of expert testimony, but he fears that this latest decision calls upon them to become amateur scientists in order to perform that role, something that he does not believe Rule 702 intends. The majority opinion states that those justices believe the better course is to simply note the nature and source of that duty for the judges.

The Supreme Court's 1993 decision in *Daubert v. Merrell Dow* is likely to blunt efforts to reform the Federal Rules of Evidence and the use of expert witnesses and their testimony. The *Daubert* decision will probably facilitate the trend for using social science data in litigation. It carries, therefore, great import for our study, providing a judicial ruling on the FRE, rules that were in effect throughout almost the entire period in which the thirty-five Supreme Court cases here examined were heard and decided.

Now that we have outlined the history and evolution of expert testimony and discussed the import and relevance of the Federal Rules of Evidence in effect throughout the period that is the focus of our study, we turn our attention to the entrance into the courts of data from the social sciences via briefs.

Briefs

The brief—a written document filed with the Court outlining a party's view of the facts, legal argument, and position—is the primary written presentation that is made to the Supreme Court. The brief filed by the petitioner is usually a more detailed statement of what was contained in the petition for the writ of certiorari, the process by which the Court hears petitions for review (Wagman 1993). The Certiorari Act, passed by Congress in 1925, provided that there would be no right to appeal from a lower court to the Supreme Court of the United States; instead, review of a lower court decision would take place only if the Supreme Court agreed to hear the case. Application for such review is called a petition for certiorari, used for reviewing the decisions of a state supreme court or of a federal court (Rehnquist 1987). If the Supreme Court agrees, it grants the petition for certiorari filed by the party that lost in the court below. Within a few months after certiorari is granted, the Supreme Court hears the case argued orally by lawyers for both sides (Rehnquist 1987).

The process of granting certiorari comprises the first third of the Court's work as outlined by Rehnquist (1987). After that, the court must decide the 150 cases granted certiorari; the decision includes studying of the briefs filed by the petitioner, the respondent, and friends of the court; hearing oral arguments by the lawyers for the parties; and voting on them at conference. Then the Court must prepare the written opinion, supporting the result reached by the majority and separate opinions for the dissenting members of the Court (Rehnquist 1987).

More than 95 percent of all certiorari petitions are denied (Perry 1991). Simply by taking a case, regardless of final outcome, the Court puts the issues raised by the case on the national agenda. When the Court declines to review a case, it lets stand the legal principles established by the lower courts (Conley 1993).

Once certiorari has been granted, briefs must be filed by the petitioner (the party who files the initial statement with the court and who seeks to overturn the lower court judgment) and the respondent (the party who seeks to support the judgment of the lower court) (Rehnquist 1987; Wagman 1993). Briefs may also be submitted by "friends of the court"—parties not directly involved in the litigation, but who believe that the court's decision may affect their interests

(Rehnquist 1987). Several weeks before the oral arguments are to be heard, the briefs are available for the justices to read. The oral arguments for presentation of each side of a case are limited to one half-hour each (Rehnquist 1987).[8]

The primary vehicle through which the Court receives information on social science findings is the *amicus curiae* or Brandeis brief, so called for the precedent established in the *Muller* case discussed above (Rosen 1972). No formal tests are prescribed for the materials that can be included in the brief, thus admitting any kind of extralegal material (Rosen 1972). The Court may receive information through briefs as well as seek information on its own. Witnesses occasionally appear before higher courts to present evidence, but usually the results of research are presented to the appeal judges by attorneys for either side or as a brief of *amicus curiae* by interested third parties. Experts usually participate in the preparation of such briefs (Blau 1984).

Some judges undertake their own search for relevant empirical data, while others obtain data only from trial court records or briefs. Kenneth Culp Davis, a law professor, observed (1986) that when Lord Mansfield was creating English commercial law during the eighteenth century he did not limit himself to what the parties presented. He freely went outside the record for his legislative facts. Needing to know the practices, customs, and attitudes of merchants, he associated with them in local taverns, then returned to his chambers to make law on the basis of what he had learned saying: "I . . . endeavored to get what assistance I could by conversing with some gentlemen of experience" (Davis 1986).[9]

One study reports that 40 percent of the citations to empirical research appearing in the opinions of one state's supreme court had been obtained through the justices' independent investigations; 60 percent came from the record of briefs, including *amicus* briefs[10] (Monahan and Walker 1986). The 40 percent is high, compared to the percentage of citations used by the Supreme Court. In his article "The Limits of a Scientific Jurisprudence: The Supreme Court and Psychology," Tanford notes that neither the Supreme Court justices nor their clerks are trained in the social sciences and would probably be alerted to relevant research only if scientific literature were cited in the briefs or had been presented previously to the Court. Law journals and interdisciplinary journals are easily accessible and contain relevant empirical work, but Tanford's conversations with former Supreme Court clerks indicate that proactive research is almost never undertaken (Tanford 1990). It seems unreasonable to assume that the justices or their clerks should engage in independent fact finding or meta-analysis when judges, lawyers, scientists, and interested parties for both sides have been studying the problem for months or years. The work of these individuals gives greater weight to the data contained within the briefs submitted for inclusion in the Court's review of the cases to which it grants certiorari.

In the following chapters, we shall examine in detail the significance of social science data contained within briefs submitted to the court for the thirty-five cases dealing with abortion and sex discrimination that were heard and decided by the Supreme Court from 1972 to 1992.

Notes

1. *Frye v. United States,* 193 Fed. 1013 (D.C. Cir. 1923), held that certain scientific tests, particularly the polygraph method of determining truthtelling, must gain general acceptance in the particular field to which it belongs before it is admissible in judicial proceedings (Chesler, Sanders, and Kalmuss 1988).

2. The issue in *Frye v. United States* was whether the systolic–blood pressure deception test (which preceded the polygraph) could be used by the defense to show that a defendant was being truthful in asserting his or her innocence. The question was whether the test was demonstrable or experimental. Associate Justice Josiah van Orsdel reasoned that a theory must be "sufficiently established to have gained general acceptance in the particular field in which it belongs" (Imwinkelried 1986).

3. In 1984, a congressional amendment to the Federal Rules of Evidence was passed (704[b]) that limited the testimony of expert witnesses on the ultimate issues in insanity defense cases (Simon and Aaronson 1988).

4. The Court's opinion quotes Behringer, "Introduction, Proposals for a Model Rule on the Admissibility of Scientific Evidence," *Jurimetrics Journal* 26 (1986): 239, quoting Lacey, "Scientific Evidence," *Jurimetrics Journal* 24 (1984): 254, 264, on this.

5. The quotation from Popper is from his *Conjectures and Refutations: The Growth of Scientific Knowledge,* 5th ed. (New York: Harper and Row, 1989), 37. Blackmun also cites Green, "Expert Witnesses and Sufficiency of Evidence in Toxic Substances Litigation: The Legacy of Agent Orange and Bendectin Litigation," *Northwestern University Law Review* 86 (1992): 645: "Scientific methodology today is based on generating hypotheses and testing them to see if they can be falsified; indeed, this methodology is what distinguishes science from other fields of human inquiry" (Blackmun 483).

6. See S. Jasanoff, *The Fifth Branch: Science Advisers as Policymakers* (Cambridge, Mass.: Harvard University Press, 1990), 61–76.

7. On the topic of peer review and publication, Blackmun also references Horrobin, "The Philosophical Basis of Peer Review and the Suppression of Innovation," *Journal of the American Medical Association* 263 (1990): 1438; J. Ziman, *Reliable Knowledge: An Exploration of the Grounds for Belief in Science* (New York: Cambridge University Press, 1978), 130–33; and Relman and Angell, "How Good Is Peer Review?" *New England Journal of Medicine* 321 (1989): 827.

8. The form and content of the appellant's brief are as follows (Rehnquist 1987; Wagman 1993): Briefs may not be longer than fifty typeset pages in length (110 typewritten pages), with typefaces, type size, and margins the same as those in writ petitions. Each brief must contain a statement of the questions presented for review; a list of all

parties to the proceeding; a table of contents; a listing of authorities (precedents being relied upon); a table of citations of all opinions delivered in the lower courts; a concise statement of the facts of the case; a summary of the argument; the argument set forth to establish clearly the points of fact and law; and a conclusion, setting out the relief to which the party thinks he or she is entitled. "Briefs must be compact, logically arranged with proper headings, concise and free from burdensome, irrelevant, immaterial and scandalous matter. Briefs not complying with the paragraph may be disregarded and stricken by the Court" (Wagman 1993:12). The "joint appendix" is a compilation of documents from the lower courts, including docket sheets, rulings, and part of transcripts of previous Court proceedings that might be of interest or use to the justices in their review (Wagman 1993). The brief of the petitioner has a blue cover; the respondent's, a red cover; and the *amici curiae* briefs, a green cover. Friends of the Court briefs cannot exceed thirty pages (Rehnquist 1987).

9. Davis (1986) says that the only thing that has changed since the eighteenth century in the way the Supreme Court reviews the record is the use of law clerks.

10. T. Marvell, *Appellate Courts and Lawyers* (Westport, Conn.: Greenwood, 1978).

3

Abortion

Within the last twenty-five years there have been greater changes in the legal status of women in the United States than in the previous two centuries. These changes have been propelled by executive orders and congressional legislation, as well as by sweeping Supreme Court decisions, as discussed by Joan Hoff-Wilson in her book *Law, Gender, and Injustice: A Legal History of U.S. Women.*[1] Of the high-profile cases related to women's rights reviewed by the Court from 1972 to 1992, those having to do with abortion have figured among the most prominent. In order to investigate properly the Court's consideration and treatment of social science data in these cases, we should first briefly examine the legal history of abortion in the United States.

The history of abortion is the history of family planning, contraception, a woman's right to control her own body, and population control as it was originally introduced by the economist and sociologist Thomas Robert Malthus in late nineteenth century in England. This is discussed by William Davis in his 1991 article "Family Planning Services: A History of U.S. Federal Legislation," by Hoff-Wilson (1991), and by Terry Kandal in *The Woman Question in Classical Sociological Theory.* Malthus wrote extensively about the effects of overpopulation on the world, arguing that an individual's sexual urges cannot be completely suppressed and therefore unrestrained sexual intercourse would eventually lead to overpopulation of the earth and the demise of the human race (Davis 1991). To remedy the situation, Malthus argued for moral restraint, especially postponing marriage until a couple could support their offspring (Davis 1991). Radical Malthusians regarded contraception as a strategy for maintaining population within the limits of the world's capacity to produce and distribute the means of subsistence. Their opponents held that contraception was a tool that the upper classes used to interfere in the lives of the poor, to limit their numbers, and to put off needed reforms, as Kandal chronicles. As an alternative to the plea of Malthus for abstention, Francis Place, in England, offered information about contraception techniques, and Robert Dale Owen and Dr. Charles Knowlton initiated the birth control movement in the United States in 1828. Owen and Knowlton wrote about effective birth control methods and family planning techniques, and although they were broadly criticized, their book sold briskly, going through nine editions (Davis 1991).

Until 1825, abortion prior to "quickening" (feel of fetal movement) was left to the discretion of women, and termination prior to that was neither a moral nor a civil issue, as Sharon Marmon and Howard Palley discuss in their 1986 article "The Decade after Roe versus Wade: Ideology, Political Cleavage, and the Policy Process." By the mid-1830s, however, under pressure from doctors and the clergy, states began to pass laws governing abortion. In 1873, the Comstock Law was passed prohibiting the distribution of contraceptive information through the mails on the grounds that it was obscene. That law was used to prosecute Margaret Sanger at the turn of this century as she began her crusade for women's right to use contraceptive devices (Davis 1991).

Intricately related to the dissemination of information about birth control was the issue of public funding. Sanger advocated family planning and birth control so that women could free themselves from what she termed "biological slavery" (Kandal 1988:221). With relentless effort, Sanger carried on her crusade. Her endeavors resulted in the formation in 1937 of the Birth Control Council of America, which later became the Planned Parenthood Federation of America and enlisted such high-profile supporters as Eleanor Roosevelt into the battle for publicly provided birth control. That battle included efforts to allow grants to the states to be used for birth control (Davis 1991).

During the 1940s, the federal government and the general public were generally accepting of programs for birth control, while state legislatures were less supportive of such public measures. In the late 1950s, Eisenhower declared that the provision of birth control was not a "proper function of government" (Davis 1991:185). Later, however, he reversed his position, and along with Harry Truman, cochaired Planned Parenthood (Davis 1991; Halberstam 1993). Nearly fifty years later, the issue of government funding remains at the forefront of the public battle over family planning, birth control, and abortion.

In 1954, Planned Parenthood and the New York Academy of Medicine held an important conference, including participants from a variety of professions and covering many issues, as Lee Epstein and Joseph Kobylka discuss in their book *The Supreme Court and Legal Change: Abortion and the Death Penalty*. At the end of the 1950s, segments of the legal and medical communities began to explore abortion privately. Then, in 1963 Betty Friedan came out with her book *The Feminine Mystique*, which brought to the public eye the issue of women's status, including what Friedan identified as a woman's need to control her own reproductive system (Epstein and Kobylka 1992; Halberstam 1993).

In the 1960s, in addition to the events and organizations that contributed to the growth of the women's movement, many groups formed to advocate zero or even negative population growth. Members of these groups argued that large families were the primary cause of poverty and crime (Davis 1991).[2] Weighing in on the other side of the argument was the Catholic Church, which maintained that economic development and social justice, along with natural forms of contraception, would remedy the problem of overpopulation. Nevertheless, in 1964, the Johnson administration and Congress addressed family planning services in several different legislative acts. The administration used the Office of Economic Opportunity (OEO), which was part of the war on poverty, to administer the first family-planning grant at the local level. In 1965 the Supreme Court decided *Griswold v. Connecticut,* which held that it was unconstitutional to prohibit the selling of contraceptive devices to married persons, based on the right to privacy in marital relationships. In 1968, the Center for Population Research was established and began research on contraceptive development. As a result, family planning was tied to poverty, economic development, health and social concerns, and overpopulation. But the bigger decision was made in the courts, when the Supreme Court affirmed the right of women to have abortions, in *Roe v. Wade* (1973).

Specific measures were taken to provide American women access to family planning assistance. Title X, enacted in 1970, added to the Public Health Service Act categorical funding to states. In order to achieve a uniform policy for distributing information on family planning, Congress added additional specific legislation through several legislative acts—Title IV-A, Title XIX, and Title XX of the Social Security Act—passed in the early 1970s. But, teenagers' access to government-funded family planning services was, and still is, extremely limited. Many states passed legislation in the 1960s that permitted teenagers access to medical treatment without parental consent only if they were married or emancipated, in the military, or by judicial declaration. But, with the enactment of Title X, the federal government began passing policies that allowed teenage access to family planning services, and most states followed suit (Davis 1991).

In 1972, the enactment of the Twenty-sixth Amendment to the Constitution guaranteed eighteen-year-olds the right to vote, which also enlarged the legal rights of teenagers in most states. This was followed in 1974 by the Mature Minor Doctrine endorsement in many states, which stated that "a minor who is sufficiently mature to understand the nature and consequences of a medical treatment may effectively consent to it" (Davis 1991:389). By 1976, courts invalidated laws requiring parental consent for abortion for unmarried minors (though subsequent actions were to change that) and even at that time, many states continued to require parental consent. Two cases before the Supreme Court—*Planned Parenthood of Central Missouri v. Danforth* (1976) and *Bellotti v. Baird* (1979)—established that minors have rights to access sex-related health care.

Prior to 1976, federal funding for abortion was allowed under Medicaid, but in 1976, Congress passed the Hyde Amendment, which prohibited expenditure of federal funds for abortion services unless the mother's life was threatened. The number of federally funded abortions in 1979 fell nearly 100 percent, and the number of state-funded abortions similarly dropped. During the seventies, Senator Jesse Helms opposed Title X on the grounds that it was "inefficient, inappropriate, and immoral," and along with others he claimed that Title X was responsible for increased sexual activity, pregnancy, and abortions among teenagers. Efforts began in earnest to separate abortion from family planning services and to restrict teenagers' access to government-sponsored family planning.

Under the Carter administration, teenage pregnancy was directly addressed by the passage of the Adolescent Health Services and Pregnancy Prevention Act of 1978, but Carter was generally conservative on the issue of abortion, stressing instead adoption. Rosalynn Carter (1984) later said she was opposed to abortion for herself, but would have a hard time deciding for other women what is right or wrong or best for them. The Supreme Court entered the funding fray in three 1977 cases—*Poelker v. Doe, Beal v. Doe, and Maher v. Roe*—to decide in general how far states and cities could go in limiting access to abortion services. The majority opinions indicated that the justices were more than willing to defer to the states, while insisting that they were not retreating from *Roe* (Epstein and Kobylka 1992). The dissenting opinions, however, saw it differently, with Justice Marshall stating, "The effect will be to relegate millions of people to lives of poverty and despair" (*Beal*, 1977, 461–62). In 1979, in *Colautti v. Franklin*, a statute requiring a physician to preserve the life of a viable fetus was struck down as "void for vagueness" (Rosenberg 1991). These cases communicated a series of mixed messages from the Courts on abortion and related issues.

The Reagan administration attempted to change the focus of federal government policies on family planning. New policies established the importance of the family. The administration argued that previous policies had contributed to the deterioration of the family. Reagan said, "Make no mistake, abortion-on-demand is not a right granted by the Constitution. No scholar . . . has argued that the framers of the Constitution intended to create such a right" (Epstein and Kobylka 1992:138). The Reagan administration's approach was to reduce accessibility to federally sponsored family planning services, especially for teenagers, and to allow states more latitude in eligibility requirements. The administration emphasized adoption over abortion, and Title X was a focus of reform efforts.

Prior to 1981, abortion counseling was permissible. The new guidelines, however, required Title X projects to engage in "abortion-options" counseling.

In addition to the efforts to reform Title X, a new rule required providers of family planning services to notify the parents of teenage clients. Even though the Supreme Court deemed parental consent and notification laws to be unconstitutional, many states continued to enforce their own consent laws, especially those related to abortions performed on minors. The Adolescent Family Life Act (AFLA), which Congress passed in 1981, was designed to provide special services to pregnant teenagers, and grantees could not make abortion referrals. In a federal district court, in *McRae v. Harris*, the Hyde Amendment was found to be unconstitutional, but the Supreme Court, in *Harris v. McRae* (1980), ruled that the Constitution does not require Medicaid to pay for abortions. In a companion case, *Williams v. Zbaraz* (1980), the Court upheld an Illinois law prohibiting public funding for abortions except where "necessary for the preservation of the life of the woman" (Rosenberg 1991). In *H.L. v. Matheson* (1981), the Court upheld a Utah parental consent law providing that, if possible, physicians notify parents of a minor before performing an abortion.

In 1983, the Supreme Court struck the Akron ordinance ("Regulation of Abortions" Ordinance No. 160-1978, City Council of Akron), which would have required all abortions in the second or third trimester to be performed in hospitals. Justice Powell wrote that in so doing the Court reaffirmed *Roe v. Wade* (Rosenberg 1991). But then, in the cases of *Planned Parenthood of Kansas City, Missouri, v. Ashcroft* (1983), *Hodgson v. Minnesota* (1990), and *State of Ohio v. Akron Center for Reproductive Health* (1990), the Court upheld laws in three separate states that required minors to secure parental or judicial consent before obtaining an abortion. In *Webster v. Reproductive Health Services* (1989) the Court upheld a ban on the use of public employees and facilities for nontherapeutic abortions.

In 1986, in *Thornburgh v. American College of Obstetricians and Gynecologists,* the Court narrowly struck down a Pennsylvania law on the grounds that some of its provisions were designed to deter women from having abortions and that others would require doctors to risk the health of pregnant women to save late-term fetuses (Hoff-Wilson 1991). In *Planned Parenthood of Southeastern Pennsylvania v. Robert P. Casey,* in 1992, the Court altered the standards of *Roe* and permitted abortion restrictions, allowing to stand Pennsylvania's requirement that women be counseled on fetal development and alternatives to abortion and that they wait twenty-four hours before undergoing the procedure (Biskupic 1993).

On the legislative side, little has been done to amplify federal financial support for abortion. In 1989, Congress approved liberalized abortion funding in the District of Columbia's 1990 fiscal appropriations bill, which President Bush then vetoed. Congress also passed legislation modifying the Hyde Amendment by making federal funds available for poor women in cases of incest and rape, but President Bush vetoed it as well. In the fall of 1993, the Senate upheld a congressional bill to limit once again federal funding for abortions for women on Medicaid.

Findings: Social Science in Abortion Cases

Now that we have laid out the historical context leading up to and including the time period in question, we will present each of the twenty-two cases on abortion decided by the U.S. Supreme Court between 1972 and 1992. Those cases are: *Roe v. Wade, Doe v. Bolton, Bigelow v. Virginia, Planned Parenthood v. Danforth, Singleton v. Wulff, Beal v. Doe, Maher v. Roe, Poelker v. Dow, Colautti v. Franklin, Bellotti v. Baird, Harris v. McRae, Williams v. Zbaraz, H.L. v. Matheson, City of Akron v. Akron Center for Reproductive Health, Planned Parenthood Association of Kansas City, Missouri, v. Ashcroft, Simopoulos v. Virginia, Thornburgh v. American College of Obstetricians and Gynecologists, Webster v. Reproductive Health Services, Hodgson v. Minnesota, Ohio v. Akron Center for Reproductive Health, Rust v. Sullivan,* and *Planned Parenthood of Southeastern Pennsylvania v. Casey.* We will describe each case and then analyze each one for the Court's use of social science data in the opinions written. We examine opinions from the lower courts for references to social science literature and expert witnesses. For each Supreme Court case, the description of the case and the decision are taken from the syllabus.[3] The description includes the nature of the case, the lower courts' and Supreme Court's decision, the name of the justice who wrote the majority opinion as well as the names of those who wrote the concurring and dissenting opinions, and the vote. Following the summaries, we give the number of citations to social science expert witnesses and social science literature.[4]

Roe v. Wade 410 U.S. 113 (1973)

The case: A pregnant single woman (Roe) brought a class action suit challenging the constitutionality of Texas criminal abortion laws, which proscribe procuring or attempting an abortion, except on medical advice for the purpose of saving the mother's life. On appeal from the U.S. District Court for the Northern District of Texas. The Supreme Court held that the State criminal abortion laws violate the Due Process Clause of the Fourteenth Amendment, which protects against state action the right to privacy, including a woman's qualified right to terminate her pregnancy. Though the State cannot override that right, it has legitimate interests in protecting both the pregnant woman's health and the potentiality of human life, each of which interests grows and reaches a "compelling" point at various stages of the woman's approach to term:

a) For the stage prior to approximately the end of the first trimester, the abortion decision and its effectuation must be left to the medical judgment of the pregnant woman's attending physician. b) For the stage subsequent to approximately the end of the first trimester, the State, in promoting its interest in the health of the mother, may, if it chooses, regulate the abortion procedure in ways that are reasonably related to maternal health. c) For the stage subsequent to viability[,] the State, in promoting its interest in the potentiality of human life, may, if it chooses, regulate, and even proscribe abortion except where necessary in appropriate medical judgment for the preservation of the life or health of the mother. Justice Blackmun delivered the opinion of the Court, in which Chief Justice Burger and Justices Douglas, Brennan, Stewart, Marshall, and Powell joined. Chief Justice Burger, and Justices Douglas and Stewart, filed concurring opinions. Justice White filed a dissenting opinion, in which Justice Rehnquist joined. Justice Rehnquist filed a dissenting opinion. (7-2)

Roe was a logical outgrowth of the Court's 1965 decision regarding the right to privacy, in *Griswold v. Connecticut,* which struck down a state law forbidding the use of contraceptives. In 1972, *Eisenstadt v. Baird* extended the same rights to single people to use contraceptives under the Fourteenth Amendment (Epstein and Kobylka 1992; Hoff-Wilson 1991). The link from *Eisenstadt* to *Roe* was probably established when Justice Brennan wrote: "if the right of privacy means anything, it is the right of the individual . . . to be free from unwarranted governmental intrusion into matters so fundamentally affecting a person as the decision whether to bear or beget a child" (Goldstein 1988). In his concurring opinion in *Roe,* Douglas (213) says further that the right of privacy was characterized by Justice Brandeis as the right "to be let alone." That right includes the privilege of an individual to plan his own affairs, for, outside of areas that are "plainly harmful conduct, every American is left to shape his own life as he thinks best, do what he pleases, go where he pleases." Douglas (213) says: "Third is the freedom to care for one's health and person, freedom from bodily restraint or compulsion, freedom to walk, stroll, or loaf."

Justice Blackmun, in preparing to write *Roe,* did his own research on the subject by going to the Mayo Clinic in Rochester, Minnesota, to search for scientific and medical data upon which to base the opinion. During the summer before the Court considered *Roe,* he spent two weeks at the clinic virtually closeted and speaking to no one about what he was doing (Woodward and Armstrong 1981). Two things are unusual about Blackmun's initiative: first, Justice Blackmun used extralegal data, and second, he did much of the research himself. The trimester system on which Blackmun based his opinion is unique to his reasoning.

Blackmun's opinion relied on citations to medical history, including ancient attitudes, the Hippocratic Oath, and the positions of both the American Medical Association and the American Public Health Association. His opinion relied also on the tenets of Christianity and religious writings, the common law and American law, as well as the American Bar Association's position. In short, the majority opinion relied on medical, legal, philosophical, and religious literature, yet it makes no citations to the social science literature. Blackmun addresses social science issues (153), when he says that maternity may force a distressful life or future; psychological harm may be imminent; mental health may be taxed by child care; there can be the distress of an "unwanted child"; a woman may be psychologically and otherwise unable to handle pregnancy or motherhood; and there is the stigma of unwed motherhood. But Blackmun does not make any reference to the social science literature on any of those subjects.

Blackmun refers (165) to the "profound problems of the present day," making no explicit citations to evidence of those problems but apparently taking them into consideration. He also acknowledges (116) social issues of population growth, pollution, poverty, and race, which tend to complicate and not to simplify the problem, but again he makes no reference to social science. He continues by saying (116), "Our task, of course, is to resolve the issue by constitutional measurement free of emotion and of predilection . . . and in this opinion place some emphasis upon, medical and medical-legal history and what this history reveals about man's attitudes toward the abortion procedure over the centuries." The latter part of the passage is something of an apologia, or at the very least a defense of drawing upon extralegal evidence in the decision. The most interesting aspect of Blackmun's opinion is that while he cites ancient literature, he does not refer to any of the readily available current literature on abortion attitudes.

The majority opinion relies on medical literature to argue that the advances of modern medicine have made abortion relatively safe—mortality rates in the first trimester being no higher than the rates for normal childbirth. The justices conclude, in the opinion, "that the right of personal privacy includes the abortion decision, but that this right is not unqualified and must be considered against important state interest in regulation" (154). Blackmun (159) also notes that the Court need not resolve the difficult question of when life begins— "When those trained in the respective disciplines of medicine, philosophy, and theology are unable to arrive at any consensus, the judiciary, at this point in the development of man's knowledge, is not in a position to speculate as to the answer." Another issue not addressed, and which the Court said it would not judge in this decision, is the constitutionality of (1) father's rights, (2) father's permission, (3) unmarried minors, and (4) parental permission—all of which would become the basis of later suits brought before the Court on abortion.

On the Court's reliance on extralegal medical data, Burger, in his concurrence with Blackmun, said: "I am somewhat troubled that the Court has taken notice of various scientific and medical data in reaching its conclusion; however, I do not believe that the Court has exceeded the scope of judicial notice accepted in other contexts" (208). This statement seems to characterize the position of the Court, in 1973, as to its reliance on precedent and on the Constitution, and its reluctance to draw on extralegal evidence. Less troubled by the Court's incorporation of scientific data, Stewart in his concurring statement says (169) that liberty is a rational continuum. Quoting Justice Frankfurter, he writes, "Great concepts like . . . 'liberty' . . . were purposely left to gather meaning from experience. For they relate to the whole domain of social and economic fact, and the statesmen who founded this Nation knew too well that only a stagnant society remains unchanged." Stewart's reference to Frankfurter provides insight into the Court's awareness of the dynamic nature of society and the Court's acknowledgment of its own role in that dynamic nature.

In his dissent, Rehnquist notes (174) that "society's views are changing," although he does not refer to any public opinion polls or any literature on the subject, even though the findings of such polls were available. There were two particularly important points in his dissent. First, in 1868, when the Fourteenth Amendment was passed, thirty-six states or territories already had passed laws limiting abortion, and Rehnquist noted, "The only conclusion possible from this history is that the drafters did not intend to have the Fourteenth Amendment withdraw from the States the power to legislate with respect to this matter" (177). Second, past practice on statutes has been to declare them unconstitutional as applied to the fact and not simply "struck down" in their entirety, as was the case with *Roe*. In White and Rehnquist's dissent (221), they address the reasons women seek abortion, all of which are clearly social in nature, including inconvenience, family planning, economics, dislike of children, and the embarrassment of illegitimacy. In sum, neither the Supreme Court nor the district court made any references to social science literature in any of the opinions written for *Roe v. Wade.*

The *Roe* decision brought about wide-ranging changes in society, in politics, government, and medicine, and in social, religious, moral, and organizational activities (Rubin 1987). The case has been cited at least 3,700 times by other courts involved in social issues, including the right-to-die, the rights of the mentally ill, the regulation of genetic research, and a state's power to regulate social conduct (Wagman 1993). As Lieberman (1992) says: "*Roe* inflamed public opinion as few modern issues have, and the contentious and anguished debate continues unabated." Speaking to law students in September 1988 at the University of Arkansas in Little Rock, Justice Blackmun acknowledged he had been widely criticized for his majority opinion in *Roe v. Wade,* but that he would probably not alter his ideas on the issue (Drucker 1990). Blackmun claimed that his decision was based on his interpretation of the Constitution concerning a woman's right to do with her body whatever she wishes (Drucker 1990).

Briefs for *Roe v. Wade*

An analysis of the briefs indicates that considerable social science material was brought before the Court in the combined cases of *Roe* and *Doe*, even though no reference was made to social science in the opinion. At the beginning of each brief submitted to the Supreme Court, a table of contents lists the cases that were referenced and the articles, if any, that were cited, such as works from the medical, legal, or social science literature. In *Roe*, a table of contents for the appendix to the brief for the appellants lists medical and social science studies. The full text of each article was included in the appendix. Selected studies are listed below, along with the annotations as they appeared in the briefs. Although the list is not inclusive, it provides examples that illustrate the depth and breadth of the material in the briefs and the range of social science findings brought before the Court in the first of the abortion cases in 1973.

1. Bumpass, L., and C. Westoff, "The Perfect Contraceptive Population," *Science* 169 (Sept. 1970): 1177. (Demographic analysis finding high degree of unwanted fertility in the U.S. and measuring the effects of unwanted births on population trends.)

2. Forssman, H., and I. Thuwe, "One Hundred and Twenty Children Born After the Application for Therapeutic Abortion Refused," in *Abortion and the Unwanted Child*, ed. Carl Reiterman (1970). (Long-term study of the psychological development of unwanted children born after an application for abortion was denied.)

3. Lerner, R., "Geographic Distribution of Need for Family Planning and Subsidized Services in the United States," *American Journal of Public Health* 60 (Oct. 1970): 1945. (Review of a massive government survey of the availability of family planning services to low-income women which found that 85% of such women had no access to family planning programs.)

4. Margolis, A., et al., "Therapeutic Abortion Follow-Up Study," *American Journal of Obstetrics and Gynecology* 110 (May 1970): 243. (Results of a study of women who had undergone an abortion, finding no evidence of psychological damage.)

5. Muller, C., "Socioeconomic Outcomes of Restricted Access to Abortion," *American Journal of Public Health* 61 (June 1971): 1110. (Review of the impact of restricted abortion and the resultant unwanted births on a broad range of social problems.)

6. Tietze, C., "Abortion Laws and Abortion Practices in Europe," *Advances in Planned Parenthood*, 194 (Excerpta Medica International Congress Series No. 207, 1969). (Detailed analysis of abortion practices in Europe, as to safety, incidence, and patient characteristics.)

7. Walter, G., "Psychological and Emotional Consequences of Elective Abortion," *Journal of Obstetrics and Gynecology* 36 (Sept. 1970): 4832. (Review of studies of psychological reaction to abortion, finding no evidence of significant abortion-related distress.)

These studies address the important issues of (1) the low medical risk of abortion; (2) the negative consequences of and for unwanted children; (3) the inaccessibility of poor women to family planning services; (4) the effect of abortion on population trends; and (5) the low psychological risk of abortion. In another brief, a study by Gil reports that the victims of abuse are often unwanted children who live primarily in households headed by unmarried women. He found that there were deviations in social interaction and general functioning among 29 percent of abused children.

In the brief prepared on behalf of New Women Lawyer's, the Women's Health and Abortion Project, Inc., and the National Abortion Action Coalition, a number of social science authorities were also cited and relied upon, including the following:

1. *American Women: Report of the President's Commission on the Status of Women* (1963).

2. Cisler, L., "Unfinished Business: Birth Control and Women's Liberation," in *Sisterhood Is Powerful*, ed. Robin Morgan (New York: Random House, 1970).

3. Helfer, Ray E., *The Battered Child* (Chicago: University of Chicago Press, 1968).

4. Rosen, Harold, M.D., "Psychiatric Implications of Abortion: A Case Study of Social Hypocrisy," *Western Reserve Law Review* 17, 454.

5. Schulder, Diana, and Florynce Kennedy, *Abortion Rap* (McGraw-Hill, 1971).

6. Sinclair, Andrew, *The Emancipation of the American Woman* (New York: Harper Colophon Books, 1966).

7. Tietze, Dr. Christopher, "Legal Abortion in Eastern Europe," *JAMA* 175 (Apr. 1961): 1149.

The brief argues, based on the above references, that carrying, giving birth to, and raising an unwanted child can be one of the most painful and long-lasting punishments that a person can endure and that any statute that denies a woman the right to determine whether she will bear those burdens denies her the equal protection of the laws (6–7). It states further that in the United States, giving birth is seven times more dangerous than a therapeutic abortion (10). The brief notes also (17) that pregnancy limits a woman's liberty in the cases of employment and education (21). It quotes a psychiatrist (Dr. Shainess) who says that a woman who does not want to be pregnant suffers depression through the pregnancy and often afterward (38). Dr. Helfer, author of *The Battered Child*, describes unwanted pregnancies as leading to physical abuse of children (39). In the brief, the greater dangers of illegal abortion are presented (40). The brief ends (43) with this assertion: "Men (of whom the legislatures and courts are almost exclusively composed) must now learn that they may not constitutionally impose the cruel penalties of unwanted pregnancy and motherhood on women, where the penalties fall solely on them."

The briefs for *Roe* and *Doe* outline and document the effects of unwanted children on the children themselves and the effect on the mother of bearing a child she cannot afford or of giving it up for adoption. The same studies cited were available for the subsequent abortion cases, as were new studies that addressed the subject. The Court was willing to use extralegal data in the form of medical and other literature but reluctant, or unwilling, to use social science evidence.

Doe v. Bolton 410 U.S. 179 (1973)

Mary Doe was a 22-year-old Georgia citizen, married, and nine weeks pregnant. She had three living children. The two older ones had been placed in a foster home because of Doe's poverty and inability to care for them. The youngest had been put up for adoption. Her husband had recently abandoned her and she was forced to live with her indigent parents and their eight children. She and her husband had become reconciled. He was a construction worker, employed only sporadically. She had been a mental patient at the State Hospital. She had been advised that an abortion could be performed on her with less danger to her health than if she gave birth to the child she was carrying. She would be unable to care for or support the new child. Her application for abortion was denied, based on Georgia law. The Supreme Court held that those portions of the statute requiring that abortions be conducted in hospitals, or accredited hospitals, requiring the interposition of a hospital abortion committee, requiring confirmation by other physicians, and limiting abortion to Georgia residents, are unconstitutional, while the provision requiring that a physician's decision rest upon his best clinical judgment of necessity is not unconstitutionally vague. Justice Blackmun wrote the opinion for the majority. Chief Justice Burger, Justice Douglas and Justice Stewart filed concurring opinions; Justice White dissented and filed an opinion in which Justice Rehnquist joined, and Rehnquist dissented and filed an opinion. (7-2)

Doe v. Bolton is a companion case of *Roe*, decided on the same day, with the opinions essentially the same as those filed in *Roe*. The majority opinion relied heavily on *Roe*. The difference in the two cases was that Georgia had passed "new" abortion laws in 1968, and this decision by the Court invalidated additional statutes that the lower court did not act upon (Drucker 1990). The "new" Georgia abortion laws were amendments to those originally enacted in 1876. The 1968 laws banned abortion unless it was performed by a physician licensed in the state of Georgia and in his "best clinical judgment" the life of the mother was in jeopardy or the fetus would be born with a serious defect, or the pregnancy was a result of rape or incest (Drucker 1990).

The Court ruled that some provisions still in effect in Georgia violated the Fourteenth Amendment's Due Process Clause, reversing part of the lower court ruling and invalidating a number of abortion statutes left standing by the lower court (Drucker 1990). The Court struck down Georgia requirements that abortions be performed in hospitals accredited by special committees; that two other physicians and a hospital staff committee approve the decision; and that the abortion be "necessary" (Lieberman 1992). Horan, Grant, and Cunningham (1987) claim that *Doe* is frequently cited for its definition of "maternal health," which covers a broad range of factors including "general well being," as a justification for legalized abortion during the last trimester of pregnancy.

The majority opinion, as with *Roe,* was written by Blackmun, with Burger, Douglas, Brennan, Stewart, Marshall, and Powell joining. Douglas, Burger, and White (the latter on behalf of Rehnquist and himself) wrote additional opinions that applied to the combination of the two cases (Goldstein 1988). In White's dissent, joined by Rehnquist, there was one citation to previous cases and none to social science. As with *Roe,* there were no citations to social science literature in the Supreme Court or district court opinions.

Bigelow v. Virginia 421 U.S. 809 (1975)

The managing editor of a weekly newspaper published in Virginia, published a New York City organization's advertisement announcing that it would arrange low-cost placements for women with unwanted pregnancies in accredited hospitals and clinics in New York (where abortions were legal and there were no residency requirements). He was convicted of violating a Virginia statute making it a misdemeanor, by the sale or circulation of any publication, to encourage or prompt the processing of an abortion. The Supreme Court of Virginia affirmed the conviction. The Court invalidated the state ban on advertising for abortion. Justice Blackmun delivered the opinion of the Court, in which Chief Justice Burger and Justices Douglas, Brennan, Stewart, Marshall, and Powell joined. Justice Rehnquist filed a dissenting opinion, in which Justice White joined. (7-2)

Virginia v. Bigelow is often not included in discussion of abortion cases because it is considered, as the Virginia Supreme Court claimed, a "First Amendment case—not an abortion case." It is included here, however, because it is about abortion. The Supreme Court of Virginia said the statute's goal was "to ensure that pregnant women in Virginia who decided to have abortions come to their decisions without the commercial advertising pressure usually incidental to the sale of a box of soap powder," and it further claimed that nothing in *Roe* or *Doe* mentioned "abortion advertising." The Court argued that the activity advertised pertained to "constitutional interests" (822). In addition the Court said that the advertisement conveyed information of potential interest and value to any readers possibly in need of the services, those concerned with the laws of another state, and readers seeking reform in Virginia. The Court refers to a 1947 article stating that "liberty of the press is in peril as soon as the government tries to compel what is to go into a newspaper" (829).

Rehnquist's dissent, with White (831), argues that the newspaper announcement was advertising, and that the abortion service was charging women a fee for a procedure that is done free by Women's Liberation, Planned Parenthood, and others, and that the Virginia Supreme Court's position was to prevent commercial exploitation of those women who elect to have an abortion. He quoted legislation that said that "at the expense of desperate, frightened women these agencies are making a huge profit—some, such a huge profit that our Committee members were actually shocked." He concluded (836) that the statute in question is a "reasonable regulation that serves a legitimate public interest." The rest of the Court differed, suggesting that the statute was a thinly veiled attempt to prevent women from obtaining information on getting an abortion. The same seven justices joined in the majority opinion on this as on *Roe*, with Rehnquist and White dissenting, as with *Roe*. No references were made to social science literature or expert witnesses in the Supreme Court or in the state supreme court opinions.

Planned Parenthood of Central Missouri v. Danforth 428 U.S. 52 (1976)

Two Missouri-licensed physicians brought suit, along with Planned Parenthood, challenging the constitutionality of the Missouri abortion statute. The provisions under attack are 1) defining viability as being able to sustain life outside of the womb by natural or artificial means; 2) requiring informed consent; 3) requiring written spousal consent, unless the abortion is necessary to preserve the mother's life; 4) requiring parental consent to the abortion of an unmarried woman under age 18; 5) requiring the physician to exercise professional care to preserve the fetus' life and health, and if failing[,] to be guilty of manslaughter; 6) declaring an infant who survives an attempted abortion not performed to save the mother's life or health an abandoned ward of the State, depriving the mother and a consenting father of parental rights; 7) prohibiting after the first 12 weeks of pregnancy the abortion procedure of saline amniocentesis as deleterious to maternal health; and 8) prescribing reporting and recordkeeping. The District Court upheld the foregoing provisions with the exception of the professional skill requirement, which was held to be unconstitutionally overbroad because it failed to exclude the pregnancy stage prior to viability. The Supreme Court upheld the definition of viability and requirement of signing a consent form, but all others were invalidated—spousal consent, parental consent, prohibiting use of saline amniocentesis abortion procedure and requiring doctor to preserve the life of the fetus. Justice Blackmun delivered the opinion in which Justices Brennan, Stewart, Marshall, and Powell joined, with some exceptions, and Justices White, Burger, and Stevens and Rehnquist dissented in part and joined in part. (5-4)

In the majority opinion, Blackmun acknowledges (69), that when *Roe* and *Doe* were decided, the Court specifically reserved decision on the question of whether a requirement for spousal or parental consent may be constitutionally imposed, thereby anticipating such cases. He notes that the Court is aware of "the deep and proper concern and interest that a devoted and protective husband has in his wife's pregnancy and in the growth and development of the fetus she is carrying. . . . Neither has this Court failed to appreciate the importance of the marital relationship in our society" (69). Moreover, the decision of aborting may have profound effects, both physical and mental, on the future of any marriage (70). Blackmun's statement regarding spousal consent (71) is often quoted:

> No marriage may be viewed as harmonious or successful if the marriage partners are fundamentally divided on so important and vital an issue. But it is difficult to believe that the goal of fostering mutuality and trust in a marriage, and of strengthening the marital relationship and the marriage institution, will be achieved by giving the husband a veto power exercisable for any reason whatsoever or for no reason at all. . . . The obvious fact is that when the wife and the husband disagree on this decision, the view of only one of the two marriage partners can prevail. Inasmuch as it is the woman who physically bears the child and who is the more directly and immediately affected by the pregnancy, as between the two the balance weighs in her favor.

While these are common subjects for a scholar of marriage and the family, no citations were made to the literature on the subject. Similarly with the issue of parental consent, Blackmun (75) takes up safeguarding the family unit and parental authority but makes no citation to social science literature. The statute regarding the woman's written consent could also be viewed as a social/psychological issue regarding stress. The other issues in the statutes were related to medical decisions, such as viability and danger to maternal health, or to administrative matters, such as recordkeeping.

Regarding parental notification, Stewart argues (91) for parental notification on the basis that abortion is a grave decision and a girl of tender years, under emotional stress, may be ill-equipped to make it without mature advice and emotional support. Judging by reports on how such abortion clinics operate, he thinks she is unlikely to get that from an attending physician. White, Rehnquist, and Burger state (93), "A father's interest in having a child—perhaps his only child—may be unmatched by any other interest in his life." Similarly, they argue (95) that parental consent is not unreasonable (or unconstitutional), and the State has a right to protect children "from their own immature and improvident decisions." They noted that in a previous opinion of Justice Stevens, he states that a minor may not "lawfully work or travel where he pleases, or even attend exhibitions of constitutionally protected adult motion pictures," or marry without parental consent, even when the young woman is pregnant (95). No social science literature is cited to support these social assertions. But, a number of references are made to medical expert witnesses regarding the use of saline amniocentesis.

White asserts (98), "I am not yet prepared to accept the notion that normal rules of law, procedure, and constitutional adjudication suddenly become irrelevant solely because a case touches on the subject of abortion." He suggests that the Court is trying to be an ex-officio medical board with powers to approve or disapprove medical and operative practices and standards throughout the United States (99). Stevens claims (103) that the parental-consent requirement is consistent with the holding in *Roe,* and the state's interest in the welfare of its young citizens. He acknowledges the importance of medical advice and then counters that the most significant consequences of the decision are not medical in nature. But Stevens uses no supporting evidence on the subject of parent-child relationships to bolster his claim, even though the district court referenced literature, as part of expert testimony, on the subject of the stressful decision of having an abortion. The district court also reported on trial testimony regarding children as young as ten years old who had sought abortions and addressing whether young people are capable of making such decisions without parental involvement. Testimony, according to the district court record, was also provided on spousal consent. The district court makes three references to social science testimony; the Supreme Court does not refer to those works or experts or to any other social science research, although a number of references are made to medical witnesses in both the district court opinion and the Supreme Court opinion.

Singleton v. Wulff 428 U.S. 106 (1976)

Two Missouri-based physicians brought action declaring the unconstitutionality of a Missouri statute that excludes abortions that are not medically indicated, involving a claim of the State's unconstitutional interference with the decision to terminate pregnancy. Held that physicians may challenge abortion funding restrictions on behalf of their female clients. Justice Blackmun delivered the opinion for a majority. Justice Stevens filed an opinion concurring in part. Justice Powell filed an opinion concurring in part and dissenting in part, in which Chief Justice Burger and Justices Stewart and Rehnquist joined. (5-4)

The opinion stated that a woman cannot safely secure an abortion without a physician, and a poor woman cannot do so without the physician's being paid by the State. Therefore, a woman's exercising of her right to an abortion is at stake in this case (117). This case did not delve into the merits of the dispute, but rather dealt with technical issues. The Court did not in this case address the issue of state funding for Medicaid patients seeking an abortion. The issue of state funding was to come later. *Danforth* also came from Missouri, where popular antagonism toward *Roe* was intense (Goldstein 1988). This case dealt with technical issues, and there was only one reference to social science, and that was in the district court.

Beal v. Doe 432 U.S. 438 (1977)

Women who were eligible for medical assistance under the Pennsylvania Medicaid plan and who were denied financial assistance for nontherapeutic abortions because state regulations limited such assistance to abortions certified by physicians as medically necessary brought action. A three-judge District Court held that the requirement did not contravene the Social Security Act, but that it did deny equal protection. The United States Court of Appeals held that the regulations were inconsistent with the Social Security Act. The Supreme Court ruled that the Social Security Act did not require the funding of nontherapeutic abortions as a condition of participation in the Medicaid program. Justice Powell wrote the opinion for the majority. Justice Brennan filed a dissent, in which Justices Marshall and Blackmun joined. Justice Marshall filed a dissenting opinion. Justice Blackmun filed a separate dissenting opinion, in which Justices Brennan and Marshall joined. (6-3)

The year after *Singleton v. Wulff*, in which the Court did not address directly the issue of funding for abortions, the Court decided three funding cases—*Beal v. Doe, Maher v. Roe*, and *Poelker v. Doe*. Both *Beal v. Doe* and *Maher v. Roe* addressed the use of state Medicaid funds—*Beal* in Pennsylvania and *Maher* in Connecticut. *Poelker* was concerned with performing abortions in St. Louis public hospitals. All three Court decisions upheld the restrictions on funding to poor women.

An issue in *Beal* was the state's willingness to fund childbirth under Medicaid for indigent women, but not abortion. The Court dealt with *Beal* on statutory grounds only: whether Title XIX requires Pennsylvania to fund under its Medicaid program the cost of all abortions that are permissible under state law. The Court concluded that denying Medicaid benefits for unnecessary abortions was not a violation of federal law, adding that the State is free to provide such coverage if it so desires (447). According to Powell (448), this left both the states and the federal government free, through the normal processes of democracy, to provide the desired funding, which "should be resolved by the representatives of the people, not by this Court" (Powell, 447).

The dissent, written by Justice Brennan, reasoned to the contrary that elective abortions do constitute medically necessary treatment for pregnancy, and as such Title XIX requires that Pennsylvania pay the costs of elective abortions for women who are eligible in the Medicaid program (449). Citing *Roe v. Norton*, Brennan says (449), "Abortion and childbirth, when stripped of the sensitive moral arguments surrounding the abortion controversy, are simply two alternative medical methods of dealing with pregnancy." He adds that the *Roe v. Wade* decision dovetails with the congressional purpose under Medicaid to "avoid interference with the decision of the woman and her physician" and that "[t]his highlights the violence done the congressional mandate by today's decision" (452). The result will be to "force penniless pregnant women to have children" (Brennan, 454). Within the space of one year, the same Court that decided in *Singleton* that for "a doctor who cannot afford to work for nothing, and a woman who cannot afford to pay him, the State's refusal to fund an abortion is as effective an 'interdiction' of it as would ever be necessary" (454), ruled in *Beal* that Medicaid funding could be withheld and be considered in the same light.

Marshall's dissent was the same for *Beal, Maher,* and *Poelker.* He asserts (455) that it is all too obvious that the governmental actions ostensibly taken to "encourage" women to carry pregnancies to term are in reality intended to impose a moral viewpoint that no state may constitutionally enforce. "Since efforts to overturn these decisions have been unsuccessful, the opponents of abortion have attempted every imaginable means to circumvent the commands of the Constitution and impose their moral choices upon the rest of society" (455). He adds (455), "The present cases involve the most vicious attacks yet devised." The impact of this attack falls tragically, Marshall says, upon those least able to help or defend themselves, and it will prevent nearly all poor women from obtaining a safe and legal abortion. Marshall quotes Tietze on abortions, an authority frequently cited in the opinions of the lower courts. Marshall also cites abortion surveillance data from the U.S. Department of Health, Education, and Welfare and from the Centers for Disease Control regarding cases of women forced into illegal, often deadly, abortions. Marshall says that such enactments will produce thousands of unwanted minority children, who will spend blighted lives. Marshall remarks (457) on the Court's insensitivity to the human dimension.

In his dissent, Marshall says (459) that he realizes that poverty alone does not entitle a class to claim governmental benefits but thinks it is a relevant factor, coupled with the fact of minority status. He quotes HEW statistics and census figures on rates of abortion and how it is disproportionately minority women who are dependent upon Medicaid for their health care. Marshall notes (461) in his impassioned dissent the following: "When this Court decided *Roe v. Wade* and *Doe v. Bolton,* it properly embarked on a course of constitutional adjudication no less controversial than that begun by *Brown v. Board of Education.* . . . The effect [of today's decision] will be to relegate millions of people to lives of poverty and despair. When elected leaders cower before public pressure, this Court, more than ever, must not shirk its duty to enforce the Constitution for the benefit of the poor and powerless."

The majority opinion contained no citations to social science. The dissent, written by Brennan (with Marshall and Blackmun joining), made one reference to social science. It was to the "Special Subcommittee on Human Resources of the Senate Committee on Labor and Public Welfare Report of the Secretary of Health, Education, and Welfare Five Year Plan for Family Planning Services and Population Research Program," in which it was stated that: "Though far less than an ideal family-planning mechanism, elective abortions are one method for limiting family size and avoiding the financial and emotional problems that are the daily lot of the impoverished" (452). Marshall's dissent contained eight citations to social science. Blackmun's dissent (with Brennan and Marshall joining) made one reference to social science. In sum, the Supreme Court's dissenting opinions had nine citations to social science. The district court made one citation to social science, which was merely an acknowledgment of the concept of "worthy" poor in the late nineteenth century—those who were thought to be worthy of public assistance versus those who were not thought to be worthy. The appeals court made no reference to social science.

Maher v. Roe 432 U.S. 464 (1977)

In Connecticut, indigent women brought suit challenging a regulation prohibiting the funding of abortions that were not medically necessary. Mary Poe, a 16-year-old high school junior[,] had obtained an abortion at a Connecticut hospital. Because of her inability to obtain a certificate of medical necessity, the hospital was denied reimbursement by the Department of Social Services, thus pressing Poe to pay the hospital bill of $244. Susan Roe, an unwed mother of three children[,] was unable to obtain an abortion because of her physician's refusal to certify that the procedure was medically necessary. The Supreme Court held that the equal protection clause did not require a state participating in the Medicaid program to pay the expenses incident to nontherapeutic abortions for indigent women simply because it had made a policy choice to pay expenses incident to childbirth. Powell wrote the opinion for the majority (6-3). Chief Justice Burger filed a concurring statement. Justice Brennan filed a dissent, in which Justices Marshall and Blackmun joined. Justice Marshall wrote a separate dissent. Justice Blackmun wrote a dissenting opinion, in which Justices Brennan and Marshall joined. (6-3)

Powell wrote (469) that the Constitution imposes no obligation on the states to pay the pregnancy-related medical expenses of indigent women, or indeed to pay any of the medical expenses of indigents, and that this case involves no discrimination against a suspect class. Powell continued (471): "An indigent woman desiring an abortion does not come within the limited category of disadvantaged classes so recognized by our cases." Further this "Court has never held that financial need alone identifies a suspect class for purposes of equal protection analysis." Accordingly, as Powell states (471), the question is whether the regulation "impinges upon a fundamental right explicitly or implicitly protected by the Constitution." Powell states (472) that *Roe* afforded constitutional protection against state interference with privacy, including a woman's decision to terminate her pregnancy. He defended *Danforth* (473) by saying that spousal consent was unconstitutional because it granted the husband unilateral prevention of aborting, which was an absolute obstacle. By contrast, he argues, the Connecticut regulation placed no obstacles, absolute or otherwise, in the pregnant woman's path to an abortion. It has placed no restriction on access to abortions that was not already there. Powell continues (474): "The indigency that may make it difficult and in some cases, perhaps, impossible for some women to have abortions is neither created nor in any way affected by the Connecticut regulation. We conclude that the Connecticut regulation does not impinge upon the fundamental right recognized in *Roe.*"

In the majority opinion, Powell goes on to say that the dissenters see the decision as being inconsistent but he does not, noting that "[t]here is a basic difference between direct state interference with a protected activity and state encouragement of an alternative activity consonant with legislative policy" (476). The majority opinion actually carries the argument further regarding funding of births. It claims that a state may have legitimate demographic concerns about its rate of population growth and its future (479), quoting Justice Holmes that the "legislatures are the ultimate guardians of the liberties and welfare of the people in quite as great a degree as the courts" (480). Then, as in *Beal,* the opinion notes that the state is free through normal democratic processes to decide that such benefits should be provided. Justice Burger, concurring, says (481) that encouragement of childbirth and child care is not a novel undertaking and that various governments, in this and other countries, have made such a determination for centuries.

Brennan's dissent (with Marshall and Blackmun, 483) says that a "distressing insensitivity to the plight of impoverished pregnant women is inherent in the Court's analysis." The state operates to coerce indigent pregnant women to bear children they would not otherwise choose to have. He quotes (483) Justice Frankfurter, who, like a latter-day Anatole France, said that "[t]he law, in its majestic equality forbids the rich as well as the poor to sleep under bridges, to beg in the streets, and to steal bread." Brennan says "[n]one can take seriously the Court's assurance that its conclusion signals no retreat from *Roe v. Wade*" (483). Brennan views it instead as "an unconstitutional infringement of the fundamental right of pregnant women to be free to decide whether to have an abortion." The regulation unconstitutionally impinges upon their claim of privacy derived from the Due Process Clause (484). As with *Beal*, he sees it as an "interdiction." Thus, he sees this decision as flatly inconsistent with the Court's decision in *Roe, Doe,* and *Danforth* (487).

The district court found the state regulation unconstitutional. The appeals court reversed that finding. The district court noted that the birth of a child to a welfare mother increases the burden of the state's welfare coffers, a point that seemed to be overlooked by the other courts, referring only to covering the "cost of the birth" and not the costs of child-rearing. The cost of the birth is little compared to that of raising the child. The district court also suggested that the state was refusing to pay on the basis that it morally opposes such an expenditure.

In *Maher v. Roe,* the majority opinion made no references to social science. The Brennan dissent (with Marshall and Blackmun) made none to social science literature. Marshall's dissent (the same for the two companion cases) made eight references to social science. Blackmun's dissent (with Brennan and Marshall—the same as for the two companion cases) made none to social science, nor did the appeals courts or district courts.

Poelker v. Doe 432 U.S. 519 (1977)

Indigent pregnant woman brought class action alleging that St. Louis' refusal to provide publicly financed hospital services for nontherapeutic abortions violated equal protection, after going through several courts. The Supreme Court held that the city's refusal to provide publicly financed hospital services for nontherapeutic abortions, while providing such services for childbirth, did not deny equal protection. The majority opinion was unsigned. Justice Brennan filed a dissenting opinion, in which Justices Marshall and Blackmun joined. Justice Marshall filed a dissenting opinion, and a separate dissenting opinion of Justice Blackmun was joined by Brennan and Marshall, both of which were the same for *Beal* and *Maher*. (6-3)

The majority opinion simply says that for the reasons set forth in *Maher*, it similarly finds no constitutional violation by the city of St. Louis in electing to provide publicly financed hospital services for childbirth without providing corresponding services for nontherapeutic abortions. In his dissent, Brennan (with Marshall and Blackmun, 523) cites statistics from Sullivan, Tietze, and Dryfoos showing that only about 18 percent of public hospitals in the country provided abortion services in 1975, which reveals the difficulties faced by indigent pregnant women who desire abortions. Sullivan, Tietze, and Dryfoos note that it is poor, rural, and very young women who are most likely to be denied abortions and that the city policy constitutes "coercion of women to bear children which they do not wish to bear" (523). It is obvious from the appeals court rulings that that court thought it was carrying out the Supreme Court's position in *Singleton, Doe,* and *Roe* when upholding a woman's right to an abortion and finding the denial of payment for such services to be unconstitutional, referring to what the appeals court thought were "clear dictates of the Supreme Court." The court of appeals (548) refers to "wanton disregard for the constitutional rights of the women in St. Louis" and the fact that the city has been obdurate and obstinate in compelling these women to conform to the mayor's (Poelker) personal belief, that is, that "abortion is murder." Justice Blackmun's dissent (with Brennan and Marshall joining, 462–63) says: "The Court today, by its decisions in these cases, allows the States, and such municipalities as choose to do so, to accomplish indirectly what the Court in *Roe* and *Doe* by a substantial majority and with some emphasis, I had thought—said they could not do directly. . . . For the individual woman concerned, indigent and financially helpless[,] . . . the result is punitive and tragic." Blackmun (463) also says that the mayor is imposing his own concepts of the "socially desirable, the publicly acceptable and the morally sound," which is "not the kind of thing for which our Constitution stands." He also notes (463), as did the district court in *Maher*, that the cost of a nontherapeutic abortion is far less than the cost of maternity care and holds no comparison with the welfare costs in the long, long years ahead. In closing, Blackmun (463), who wrote the opinion for *Roe*, says: "[a]nd so the cancer of poverty will continue to grow. This is a sad day for those who regard the Constitution as a force that would serve justice to all evenhandedly and, in so doing, would better the lot of the poorest among us."

The unsigned majority opinion made no citations to social science. Marshall's opinion made nine references to social science. Blackmun and Brennan's dissents had none. The appeals court made no references to social science.

Colautti v. Franklin 439 U.S. 379 (1979)

Section 5(a) of the Pennsylvania Abortion Control Act requires every person who performs an abortion to make a determination based on his experience, judgment or professional competence that the fetus is not viable. If such person determines that the fetus is viable or if there is sufficient reason to believe that the fetus may be viable, then he must exercise the same care to preserve the fetus' life and health as would be required in the case of a fetus intended to be born alive, so long as a different technique is not necessary to preserve the mother's life or health. The District Court declared it unconstitutional. The Supreme Court held it to be vague both with respect to the viability determination requirement and the stated standard of care. Justice Blackmun wrote for the majority and Justice White, with whom Chief Justice Burger and Justice Rehnquist joined, filed a dissenting opinion. (6-3)

This case speaks to the issue of fetal viability, as did Missouri's *Danforth* case. As with *Danforth,* the Court determined that neither the legislature nor the courts may proclaim one of the elements of viability, be it weeks of gestation, fetal weight, or any other single factor (Drucker 1990). That is up to the woman's physician. Blackmun, writing as he had in *Roe,* found the "standard of care" provision to be impermissibly vague and the section on viability to be ambiguous. Blackmun reaffirmed the principles of the determination of viability, as in *Roe,* as being left with the physician. Justice White's dissent (with Rehnquist and Burger) claimed that the Court was backtracking on the permission for abortion it had granted in *Roe* and *Danforth.* While Burger had voted with the majority in *Roe,* he dissented and joined White and Rehnquist on the question of viability in *Colautti.*

Considerable medical testimony and many witnesses were quoted in the Supreme Court opinion regarding likelihood of fetus survival, and since the justices were dealing only with viability questions, it is not surprising that they made no reference to social science witnesses. There were, however, such witnesses at the district court level, testifying to other parts of the Pennsylvania Abortion Control Act. One was a sociologist, Amitai Etzioni, who testified for the state that although it is often beneficial for the marital relationship for the husband to be informed and consulted with respect to the abortion decision, the husband should not have absolute veto power (566). Other witnesses testified about parental consent, and the state's own witnesses did not support the state's view that parents must be involved.

The majority opinion made no references to social science, nor did the dissenting opinion. The district court made two references to social science expert witness testimony.

Bellotti v. Baird 443 U.S. 622 (1979)

Mary Moe (pseudonym) was pregnant, residing at home with her parents, and desirous of obtaining an abortion without informing them. She represented the "class of unmarried minors in Massachusetts who have adequate capacity to give a valid and informed consent to abortion, and who do not wish to involve their parents." The statute being challenged required parental consent prior to an abortion on an unmarried woman who is under the age of 18. If one or both of the parents refuse to grant consent, the abortion may be obtained by order of a judge of the superior court if good cause can be shown by the minor. In separate opinions, the Supreme Court held that the statute unconstitutionally burdened the right of the pregnant minor to seek an abortion. Several opinions were filed, along with one dissent by Justice White.

As with *Planned Parenthood of Central Missouri v. Danforth*, this case dealt with parental consent and again found such a requirement to be unconstitutional.[5] The concern of the Court was that the statute provided an absolute veto by the parents or a judge, even if the minor were mature. In Justice Powell's opinion (623), he says that there are three reasons that the constitutional rights of children cannot be equated with those of adults: the peculiar vulnerability of children; their inability to make critical decisions; and the importance of the guiding role of parents. Justice White, the only dissenter, expressed concern (657) with the inconsistency with which the court was handing down decisions, and Rehnquist (652) also said that "literally thousands of judges cannot be left with nothing more than the guidance offered by a truly fragmented holding of this Court." Justice Powell says (638) that there are many competing theories about the most effective way for parents to fulfill their central role in assisting their children on the way to adulthood, but he does not cite any social science data on the subject, though considerable pertinent literature exists. The Supreme Court made no references to social science in this case, but the district court did. The plaintiff's expert at trial testified that if a teenager met with parental disapproval and then went to a judge, that experience could be severely detrimental to the teenager (1001). The defendants' own expert expressed the opinion that if she did go to the court and was successful, the experience would be likely to destroy what was left of the family relationship, and the defendant would likely be in a worse position. Another expert testified that a last-minute state-compelled consultation would probably not be effective if the communication were not already there between parent and child (1003). From the plaintiff's exhibits, a considerable number of statistics were cited regarding teenage pregnancy and sexual activity among teenagers. One of the defendants' experts testified that a substantial number of minors would refuse to consult with their parents under any circumstances (1110). Another concern with the statute was that there was no allowance for children who feared going to their parents. The plaintiff's expert said the children's fears are *usually* unfounded (1012). In sum, the Supreme Court made no reference to social science, though the district court made ten references to social science expert witness testimony.

Harris v. McRae 448 U.S. 297 (1980)

In New York, an indigent pregnant women sued to challenge the Hyde Amendment which subsidized maternity costs for the poor but not their abortion costs, even if medically necessary. The Hyde Amendment was challenged as a denial of due process, equal protection, freedom of religion, and as an establishment of Roman Catholic dogma in violation of the First Amendment. The District Court invalidated the amendment on constitutional grounds, but the Supreme Court held that 1) a state is not obligated under Title XIX of the Social Security Act to fund medically necessary abortions for which federal reimbursement was unavailable under the Hyde Amendment and that 2) the funding restrictions of the Hyde Amendment did not violate either the Fifth Amendment or the establishment clause of the First Amendment. Mr. Justice Stewart wrote for the majority, with Justice White filing a concurring opinion. There were four dissents with Justice Brennan filing a dissent with Justices Marshall and Blackmun and each of the Justices—Marshall, Blackmun and Stevens—filing separate dissents. (5-4)

Harris v. McRae was another crucial funding case, as were *Beal, Maher,* and *Poelker,* which considered whether restriction of public funding blocks the constitutional right of a woman to have an abortion under *Roe. Harris* has been considered the most significant Supreme Court case on abortion outside of *Roe* (Hoff-Wilson 1991). It is particularly significant for the present study because more social science evidence was produced at the district court level than in any of the other previous abortion cases. The case is also noteworthy because of the voluminous case material (over two hundred pages) produced by the district court, including an appendix containing the debates over the Hyde Amendment. Other district court decisions in these cases typically average twenty to thirty pages in length. The case was combined and is dealt with as a companion case to *Williams v. Zbaraz,* with the dissents applicable to both cases.

Justice Stewart (for the majority, 316) concludes that the Hyde Amendment places in the path of a woman who chooses to terminate her pregnancy no governmental obstacle that would not otherwise be there, and that it does not follow that a woman's freedom of choice carries with it a constitutional entitlement to the financial resources to avail. Governments may not place obstacles in the path of a woman's exercise of her freedom of choice, but it need not remove those not of its own creation, and indigence falls within that category. Even though the ruling disproportionately affects poor people, Stewart argues (316) that poverty is not a "suspect classification." The district court also argued that teenage women were a "suspect class," but the plurality of the Supreme Court disagreed, saying (324) that the Hyde Amendment is neutral as to age, restricting funding for abortions for women of all ages. Stewart (315) agrees that the Hyde Amendment—by unequal subsidization of abortion, including withholding funds for medically necessary abortions—encourages alternative activity deemed in the public interest.

Justice Brennan (joined by Marshall and Blackmun) states emphatically (330) that "[t]he Hyde Amendment's denial of public funds for medically necessary abortions plainly intrudes upon this constitutionally protected decision, for both by design and in effect it serves to coerce indigent pregnant women to bear children that they would otherwise elect not to have." This position is diametrically opposed to that of the plurality. The two sides simply do not see, or refuse to see, the issue in the same way. Brennan stresses (330) the need to put the congressional decision in human terms (which is clearly not done in the majority opinion). He says that the Hyde Amendment is a deliberate effort to discourage the exercise of a constitutionally protected right and is an attempt to achieve indirectly what *Roe* said it could not do directly. He asserts that the amendment is a transparent attempt by the legislative branch to, as he had stated before, "impose the political majority's judgment of the morally acceptable and socially desirable preference on a sensitive and intimate decision that the Constitution entrusts to the individual" (332). In other words, the Hyde Amendment, according to Brennan (333), deprives the indigent woman of her freedom to choose abortion, thereby impinging on the due process liberty right that was recognized in *Roe v. Wade*.

Justice Marshall, in his dissent (338), says that the Hyde Amendment will result in a significant increase in the "number of poor women who will die or suffer significant health damage because of an inability to procure necessary medical services." He says plainly that the Court's decision marks a retreat from *Roe v. Wade* and "represents a cruel blow to the most powerless members of our society" (338). While Marshall refers to social issues, he never cites social science. He concludes (348) by saying that the consequence of the decision is a devastating impact on poor women; he asserts, "I do not believe that a Constitution committed to the equal protection of the laws can tolerate this result."

In dissent, Justice Blackmun (348) said that the "cancer of poverty will continue to grow, and the lot of the poorest among us, once again, and still, is not to be bettered." Justice Stevens, who had voted with the majority in restrictive Medicaid funding in *Maher*, wrote a separate dissent in *Harris*. In it, he says that the denial of benefits for medically necessary abortions will cause serious harm to excluded woman, and as such is a form of punishment (354). He refers to case examples in expert medical testimony. Concluding, he says (357) that he sees the amendment as an "unjustifiable, and indeed blatant, violation of the sovereign's duty to govern impartially."

The district court record on this case is extraordinary in its depth and references to social science evidence. The range of references covers clinical and case data, government statistics, reports of national and international surveys and studies, public opinion polls, and testimony by psychiatric, medical, and social science experts. There are 159 citations to social science and related medical data. Previous district court cases on abortion referred to social science no more than ten times. As outlined in the table of contents of the district court record, the information covers the statistical background on abortion; medical problems arising in pregnancy, related to poverty and "unwantedness," age, and delay; mental health problems related to pregnancy; poverty as an aggravating stress; familial circumstances related to unwanted pregnancy and childbirth, including fetal abnormality; age and pregnancy; and rape and incest. The citations present sound, well-documented scientific studies and reports on these topics.

The data are used to point out, among other things, the risks of teenage childbirth; the effects on children of being unwanted; the increase of suicide among teenagers who do not want to be pregnant; the failure rate of contraception devices; the rates of abortion versus live births; the increase of deaths with illegal abortions; abuse among unwanted children; the ways that having children at a young age affects the mother's education and socioeconomic status; psychological and physical ramifications of unwanted pregnancy, especially for the poor; and data on the disproportionate number of minority women among the poor. Considerable testimony was given concerning the effects of rape on victims who become pregnant and cannot get an abortion. The public opinion polls reported show repeatedly that there is support for abortion, particularly if the mother's life is in danger. The district court also covers religious, political, and legal issues. An appendix includes the debates leading to the enactment of the Hyde Amendment.

Three case examples provided in expert testimony and included in the district court decision illustrate the types of cases resulting if abortions cannot be provided for indigent women who require or desire them (674). The first example was a sixteen-year-old Hispanic welfare recipient who spoke no English; she had two children, suffered from rheumatic heart disease with a loud murmur, and became pregnant when her contraceptive foam failed. A second was a thirty-three-year-old mother of three children, furloughed from a state mental hospital after nine months of treatment for depression. Though provided with a diaphragm prior to the furlough, she became pregnant. Her husband had only intermittent employment, and the family was on public assistance. In a third case, the patient had married at sixteen and by age twenty-six already had four children. Her husband was addicted to heroin and was soon to be released from prison. She was pregnant by a married man and feared that her husband would kill her when he was released. Her two school-age children were emotionally disturbed. The patient was depressed and agitated, suffered from insomnia, had tried unsuccessfully to abort the baby herself, and spoke of killing herself if she could not obtain an abortion.

In spite of the extensive and unprecedented coverage of social science data at the district court level, where 159 citations were made, the Supreme Court opinion made no reference to social science.

Williams v. Zbaraz 448 U.S. 358 (1980)

Class action was brought challenging an Illinois statute prohibiting the use of state funds for abortion, except where necessary to preserve the life of the woman undergoing abortion. The Supreme Court ruled that a participating state was not obligated under Title XIX of the Social Security Act to pay for those medically necessary abortions for which federal reimbursement was unavailable under the Hyde Amendment, and the restrictions in the Illinois statute did not violate the equal protection clause. Justice Stewart wrote the opinion, with Justice Brennan (with Marshall and Blackmun) and Justices Marshall, Blackmun and Stevens filing separate dissents. (5-4)

The same dissenting opinion filed for *Harris* was filed for its companion case, *Williams v. Zbaraz*. But it was clear that if the Court upheld the statute allowing withholding of funding for abortions if the mother's health were at risk, as in *Harris*, the Court would uphold the statute prohibiting use of state funds except for preserving the life of the woman. A short opinion written by Stewart made no references to social science, nor did the dissents or the district court.

H.L. v. Matheson 450 U.S. 398 (1981)

An unmarried 15-year-old girl living with her parents in Utah and dependent upon them for her support discovered she was pregnant and consulted with a social worker and a physician. The physician advised her that an abortion would be in her best medical interest but refused to perform the abortion without first notifying her parents, under the Utah statute. The statute being challenged required the physician to notify, if possible, the parents of a minor seeking an abortion. The District Court and Supreme Court of Utah found the statute to be constitutional. The Supreme Court held that the statute did not violate any guarantees of the Constitution. Chief Justice Burger wrote for the majority, joined by Justices Stewart, White, Powell and Rehnquist. Justice Powell (with Justice Stewart) and Justice Stevens each wrote concurring opinions. Justice Marshall (joined by Justices Brennan and Blackmun) wrote a dissenting opinion. (6-3)

The majority argued that because the statute required parental notification and not consent, it did not permit an absolute veto over the abortion. As such, this decision was considered consistent with *Roe, Danforth,* and *Bellotti.* Further, the majority argued that the parent could provide valuable information on the child's medical condition. *H.L. v. Matheson* is the first abortion case in which the majority opinion includes citations to social science or where an opinion joined by Rehnquist, Burger, Stewart, White, or Powell refers to social science. The majority justices state (1172) that the medical, emotional, and psychological consequences of an abortion are serious and lasting, especially when the patient is immature. They cite three reports in support of that statement: Maine, "Does Abortion Affect Later Pregnancies" (*Family Planning Perspectives* [1979]: 98); Wallerstein, Kurtz, and Var-Din, "Psychosocial Sequelae of Therapeutic Abortion in Young Unmarried Women" (*Archives of General Psychiatry* 27 [1972]: 828); and Babikian and Goldman, "A Study in Teen-Age Pregnancy" (*American Journal of Psychiatry* 128 [1971]: 755).

While the majority opinion made three citations to social science, the dissenting opinion made twenty-five, the most of any opinion up to that point. The citations to bolster the dissent included Furstenberg's *Unplanned Parenthood: The Social Consequences of Teenage Childbearing* (1976) as well as a reference to that fact that when a young girl becomes pregnant, her family often refuses to allow her back into their home, a point made by Osofsky and Osofsky in "Teenage Pregnancy: Psychosocial Considerations"(*Clinical Obstetrics and Gynecology* 21 [1978]). In a study by Bedger, a large majority of pregnant minors who were sampled predicted parental opposition to their abortions. Cates was quoted in "Adolescent Abortions in the United States" (*Adolescent Health Care* [1980]:18). Bracken and Kasl's "Delay in Seeking Induced Abortion: A Review and Theoretical Analysis" (*American Journal of Obstetrics and Gynecology* [1975]) was also referenced. Teicher's "A Solution to the Chronic Problem of Living: Adolescent Attempted Suicide" (*Current Issues in Adolescent Psychiatry*) was quoted; that study showed that approximately one-fourth of female minors who attempt suicide do so because they are or believe they are pregnant.

In contrast to *McRae v. Harris,* where the district court made 159 references to social science, no references to social science were made at the lower court level (the State Supreme Court of Utah) in *H.L. v. Matheson.* But, for the first time, all of the U.S. Supreme Court justices took part in an opinion that referred to social science data. The majority opinion made 3 references to social science; the dissent, with Justices Marshall, Brennan, and Blackmun, made 25.

City of Akron v. Akron Center for Reproductive Health, Inc.
462 U.S. 416 (1983)

An Akron, Ohio, ordinance was challenged which 1) required all abortions performed after the first trimester of pregnancy be performed in a hospital, 2) prohibits
a physician from performing an abortion on an unmarried minor under 15 without
consent of one parent or court order, 3) requires that doctor say life begins at conception, details medical risks, and abortion alternatives before abortion, 4) requires a
24-hour waiting period after information and abortion, and 5) requires disposing of
the fetus in a "humane and sanitary manner." The case was brought from the District
Court and Court of Appeals. The Supreme Court held all parts of the statute to be
unconstitutional. Justice Powell delivered the opinion, in which Chief Justice Burger
and Justices Brennan, Marshall, Blackmun and Stevens joined. Justice O'Connor
filed a dissenting opinion with White and Rehnquist joining. (6-3)

This was the first abortion case in which Justice O'Connor participated, having been appointed (in 1981) to succeed Justice Stewart. In the case of *Roe*, Justices Douglas and Stewart had voted with the majority, but with both Douglas
and Stewart gone (in 1975 and 1981, respectively), and with O'Connor and
Stevens (appointed 1975) then on the bench, there was a strong possibility that
the Court would shift on abortion. Everyone was waiting to see how Justice
O'Connor would vote; the 6-3 division for striking down abortion restrictions
could become a 5-4 division against such restriction (Goldstein 1988). O'Connor
not only voted for restrictions but also wrote the dissent in *Akron*, with White
and Rehnquist joining. Justice Burger, deviating from *Danforth* and *Colautti*,
however, voted with the majority against the restriction, and Stevens also went
against the restrictions, as he had in *Harris v. McRae, Williams v. Zbaraz*, and
Colautti, even though he had reversed and supported restriction in *H.L. v.
Matheson*. Not only did O'Connor dissent, but she essentially recommended
overturning *Roe*. She also proffered that restrictions on abortion be struck down
only if they provided an "undue burden," and she found none of the restrictions sufficiently burdensome to qualify for that test and would have upheld
every one (Friedman 1993). Further, she urged the Court to hold the state interest from the time of conception.

   Powell, writing for the majority, states (420) that they "today reaffirm *Roe v.
Wade*." In footnote 1 (420) he says of O'Connor's dissent that, while she stops
short of arguing flatly that *Roe* should be overruled, her reasoning would
accomplish precisely that result. She does not, for example, see that a hospi-
talization requirement rises to the level of "official interference" with the abortion decision. Powell continues in footnote 1 (420) that "it appears that the dis-

sent would uphold virtually any abortion regulation under a rational-basis test. . . . This analysis is wholly incompatible with the existence of the fundamental right recognized in *Roe v. Wade.*" The opinion cites medical research on the problems of second-trimester abortions and the difficulty and greater cost if a woman must travel some distance to get one. They note also that the American Public Health Association no longer suggests that second-trimester abortions be performed in a hospital. Some of the medical research cited in the opinion is oriented toward social psychology, and includes consideration of depression, illegal abortions, the availability of abortions, and the dangers in waiting.

In Justice O'Connor's dissent, she bolsters her argument by quoting considerable medical research, some of which is also oriented toward social psychology. She says that the Court does not have the authority to strike down laws because they do not meet "our standards of desirable social policy, 'wisdom,' or 'common sense'" (453, quoting Burger's dissent in *Plyler v. Doe*). She does not consider the trimester approach either a legitimate or a useful framework for accommodating women's rights and the state's interest. Those demarcations, she asserts, have been blurred as technological advancement has made abortion procedures safer; thus it is no longer possible to rely on a "bright line" that separates permissible from impermissible regulation (454–55). At footnote 4 (456), O'Connor says, "Irrespective of the difficulty of the task, legislatures, with their superior factfinding capabilities, are certainly better able to make the necessary judgments than are courts." This assumption overlooks entirely the role of briefs and the lower court's cases, which provide equally comprehensive material to the justices. Relying on a prior case (*Missouri, K. & T. R. Co. v. May* in 1904), O'Connor advances this argument: "In determining whether the State imposes an undue burden, we must keep in mind that when we are concerned with extremely sensitive issues, such as the one involved here, the appropriate forum for their resolution in a democracy is the legislature. We should not forget that legislatures are ultimate guardians of the liberties and welfare of the people in quite as great a degree as the courts" (465). It is not that the Court should defer to state legislatures, she argues, but it should pay careful attention to how the other branches of government address the same problem.

The district court presents a strange and unusually convoluted case, delving into evolution, religion, Sunday closing laws, Arkansas "monkey laws," and issues regarding the sperm and the egg and when life begins. The district court found no aspect of the statute to be unconstitutional. The appeals court found some aspect to be. The Supreme Court's majority opinion makes two references to social science. The dissent makes three. The appeals court makes one and the district court none.

Planned Parenthood Association of Kansas City, Missouri, v. Ashcroft
462 U.S. 476 (1983)

Abortion clinic and others brought action challenging constitutionality of several provisions of Missouri abortion statutes. The District Court and Court of Appeals had found some portions constitutional and some unconstitutional. The Supreme Court held the 1) requirement that abortions after 12 weeks of pregnancy be performed in a hospital unconstitutional and 2) requirement of a pathology report for each abortion performed, the requirement that a second physician be present during abortions performed after viability and requirement that a minor secure parental consent or a court order were constitutional. Justice Powell wrote the opinion. Justices Blackmun, Brennan, Marshall and Stevens joined and filed opinion concurring in part and dissenting in part. Justice O'Connor (Justices White and Chief Justice Rehnquist joining) filed an opinion concurring in part and dissenting in part.

The Court was widely divided in *Ashcroft,* as it had been in *Bellotti.* In fact, three cases were decided the same day—*Akron, Ashcroft,* and *Simopoulos v. Virginia.* Powell, who generally supported the abortion right, voted to uphold the state restrictions in both *Ashcroft* and *Simopoulos. Ashcroft,* like *Danforth* before it, came out of Missouri. The Court upheld the statute for parental consent (or court ruling) because it allowed for a judgment of the minor's being "mature"; thus, it was not an absolute veto. The new conditions required a second physician after viability and a pathology report for each abortion, even in the first trimester. In footnote 9 of the opinion, a citation is made to Stroh and Hinman's "Reported Live Births Following Induced Abortion: Two and One-Half Years' Experience in Upstate New York" (*American Journal of Obstetrics and Gynecology* [1976]:126), which reported that during the period studied, there were thirty-eight live births of aborted fetuses, including one who survived.

In the dissent, Blackmun (with Brennan, Marshall, and Stevens) (495) would have all of the regulations struck as unconstitutional. O'Connor (with White and Rehnquist) on the other hand would find all of the restrictions to be constitutional, arguing that they would not impose an "undue burden"—the same arguments she advanced in *Akron.* The dissenting opinion argued that a second physician was not necessary, in that the physician performing the abortion could deal with both a viable fetus and a pathology report. Further, the need for a pathology report could price the abortion beyond reach. The district and appeals courts refer to a number of medical experts who testified and to the medical literature but not to social science experts or data. The medical testimony dealt primarily with the issue of fetal viability, abortion delay, and medical costs. There are numerous references to medical testimony and journals but none to social science in the Supreme Court opinion.

Simopoulos v. Virginia 462 U.S. 506 (1983)

In Virginia, evidence at trial had established that the physician performed a second-trimester abortion on an unmarried minor by an injection of saline solution at his unlicensed clinic, and the minor delivered the fetus alone in a motel 48 hours later. The Virginia Supreme Court affirmed the Circuit Court conviction. The Supreme Court upheld the conviction of the physician for performing a second trimester abortion in an unlicensed clinic, and found the state law requiring that all post-first-trimester abortions be either in a full-service hospital or in a licensed out-patient clinic to be constitutional. Justice Powell delivered the opinion, in which Justices Burger, Brennan, Marshall and Blackmun joined in Parts I and II of which Justices White, Rehnquist and O'Connor joined. Justice O'Connor filed an opinion concurring in part in which Justice White and Chief Justice Rehnquist joined. Justice Stevens filed a dissenting opinion. (8-1)

This case differs from prior abortion cases because it resulted from a criminal conviction. The case itself, as described by the district court (196–97), involved a seventeen-year-old woman who visited a physician and then returned to his unlicensed clinic with her boyfriend. Using her VISA card, she paid the $475 for the abortion. The physician (the defendant) administered a local anaesthetic, injected a saline solution, and gave her postinjection information and a prescription for Percodan. That afternoon, the young woman and her boyfriend filled the prescription and rented a room in a motel near the clinic. He stayed with her until 3 A.M., returned at noon, and left again at 10 P.M. Shortly after midnight, she experienced the onset of labor, and at 11 A.M. she expelled the fetus, placed it and the afterbirth in a bathroom trashcan (which the police later recovered), and went home. She later testified at trial that she had eaten "some peanut butter and jelly sandwiches" and "smoked a few cigarettes" while awaiting labor, but had not ingested any drugs or medication except the Percodan. The physician thought that she understood she should return to the hospital when she experienced labor, but she denied his telling her that, even though those instructions were on the information sheet. The conviction rested on the unlawful performing of an abortion during the second trimester and outside of a licensed hospital. This case differs from *Akron* and *Ashcroft* because Virginia defines a hospital also as an outpatient hospital; thus the Court did not see the requirement as impinging on a woman's freedom to obtain an abortion. Although Stevens was the lone dissenter, his dissent was based on a technicality, not a substantive issue. Neither the U.S. Supreme

Court nor the Supreme Court of Virginia made reference to social science literature or expert witnesses.

Thornburgh v. American College of Obstetricians and Gynecologists 476 U.S. 747 (1986)

Action was brought to challenge the Pennsylvania Abortion Control Act of 1982, which had already come before the District and Appeals Court. The Supreme Court ruled unconstitutional 1) that physician or other facility personnel recite a litany of information; 2) that public records be kept; 3) that a second physician be present to try to save the fetus with no implication of exceptions for mother's health; 4) selection of abortion techniques regarding viability; 5) informed consent. Justice Blackmun delivered the opinion of the Court, in which Justices Brennan, Marshall, Powell and Stevens joined. Stevens filed a concurring opinion. Justice White filed a dissenting opinion, which Chief Justice Rehnquist joined. Justice O'Connor filed a dissenting opinion, in which Chief Justice Rehnquist joined.

Thornburgh became a test case. By the late 1980s, the political and legal fight over abortion had become even more contentious than it had been (Friedman 1993). The close vote on the cases of *Ashcroft* and *Akron* led some states, where antiabortion sentiment was strong, to test the limits (Friedman 1993). As an indication of its interest in abortion, the Justice Department submitted a supplementary brief in *Thornburgh* arguing that *Roe* should be overruled, and it even requested an opportunity to make oral arguments, which the Court denied (Goldstein 1988).

This case drew more criticism from the justices than any other, and members of the bench who had opposed abortion expressed more disdain for the Court's previous abortion decisions (Drucker 1990). Frustration and pressures had grown to a considerable level. The case was notable for the hostility of the majority of five justices and for the strong dissents from four justices who called for reexamination or reversal of *Roe v. Wade* (Horan, Grant, and Cunningham 1987). The majority opinion voted to affirm the decision of the lower court that had invalidated many of Pennsylvania's abortion statutes. The end to this case brought an end to the Burger court, as well. In 1986, Burger stepped down after seventeen years. An ardent civil rights advocate, Burger had voted for *Roe* and in favor of abortion restrictions. Doubt about the direction of the Supreme Court after Burger's retirement was quickly put to rest by President Reagan's appointment of Justice Rehnquist to chief justice and by the subsequent appointment of Antonin Scalia to the Court.

In spite of the changes in the Court, however, in *Thornburgh*, in a 5-4 vote, the majority struck down most of the Pennsylvania state restrictions, finding them to be unconstitutional. The restrictions included (1) the litany of risks; (2) public recordkeeping; (3) attendance of a second physician to save the fetus (unlike *Ashcroft*, because it did not allow an exception for medical emergencies for the mother); and (4) requirement of doctors to risk the health of the mother to save late-term fetuses. In the majority opinion (759), Justice Blackmun said that the states are not free under the guise of protecting maternal health or potential life to intimidate women into continuing pregnancies, and that the vitality of these constitutional principles cannot be allowed to yield simply because of disagreement with them. He continued, saying that appellants claim that the statutory provisions before them further legitimate compelling interests of the state, but close analysis shows that they subordinate constitutional privacy interests in an effort to deter a woman from making a decision that, with her physician, is hers to make. The litany of information called for, Blackmun refers to as "a parade of horribles," of dubious validity, plainly designed to influence the woman's choice (760). One of the requirements was to inform the woman of the fetal characteristics at two-week intervals. This, Blackmun says (762), is plainly overinclusive, no matter how objective it may be, and such information could serve to confuse and punish her and heighten her anxiety. Under the guise of informed consent, Blackmun says (763) the Pennsylvania Abortion Control Act requires the dissemination of information that is not relevant and may be misleading, such as saying that the father is responsible for financial assistance, because theoretical financial responsibility often does not equate with the fulfillment of that responsibility. The concern about public recordkeeping is that the identity of the person would become public and that women who choose to exercise their right could be harassed (767). There are few decisions, Blackmun says (772), that are more personal, intimate, private, or basic to individual dignity and autonomy than the right to end a pregnancy. "A woman's right to make that choice freely is fundamental. Any other result, in our view, would protect inadequately a central part of the sphere of liberty that our law guarantees equally to all" (Blackmun, 772).

Stevens in his concurrence targets White's (and Rehnquist's) dissent, saying that at times White's rhetoric conflicts with his own analysis. He suggests that White's opinion may be influenced as much by his own values as his view of the allocation of decisionmaking responsibilities between the individual and the state (778). He says that while a powerful theological argument can be made for protecting fetal life, the Court's jurisdiction is limited to the evaluation of secular state interests (778). Regarding Justice White's comments on *stare decisis,* Stevens says that the Court "has not hesitated to overrule decisions, where experience, scholarship, and reflection demonstrated that their fundamental premises were not be to be found in the Constitution" (779). In the final analysis, he says it is "far better to permit some individuals to make incorrect deci-

sions than to deny all individuals the right to make decisions that have a profound effect upon their destiny" (Stevens, 781).

In Burger's dissent, he says that *Roe* should be reexamined. Justice White
(with Rehnquist) in his dissent says (785–86): "Today the Court carries forward
the difficult and continuing venture in substantive due process that began with
the decision in *Roe v. Wade* and has led the Court further and further afield in
the 13 years since that decision was handed down. I was in dissent in *Roe v.
Wade* and am in dissent today." He calls for departing from precedent and recognizing that it is time to overrule *Roe v. Wade* (788). He claims that the liberty
to choose is neither rooted in the nation's history and tradition nor implicit in
the concept of ordered liberty (793). White says (803) that there is a rationale
for state efforts to regulate the practice of professionals and not trust them to
police themselves. White (807) accuses the court of "linguistic nit-picking." He
says (813) that "the decision is symptomatic of the Court's own insecurity over
its handiwork in *Roe v. Wade* and the cases following that decision." Asserting
that the Court is creating something out of nothing, White charges there are
many who hold *Roe* to be illegitimate, which is why the Court responds defen-
sively (814); he says, "I do not share the warped point of view of the majority,
nor can I follow the tortuous path the majority treads in proceeding to strike
down the statute before us."

But there were more criticisms of the majority to come with Justice O'Connor's dissent (joined by Justice Rehnquist): "This Court's abortion decisions
have already worked a major distortion in the Court's constitutional jurisprudence. Today's decision goes further, and makes it painfully clear that no legal
rule or doctrine is safe from ad hoc nullification by this court when an occasion
for its application arises in a case involving state regulation of abortion" (814).

She alleges (814) that "the Court is not suited to the expansive role it has
claimed for itself in the series of cases that began with *Roe v. Wade.*" As with
Akron, she uses the "unduly burdensome" test and finds none of the restrictions to be unduly burdensome. In her view (833), "today's decision makes bad
constitutional law and bad procedural law."

It is remarkable that the Supreme Court introduced no extralegal data—
medical or social science—in any of the opinions or dissents in this case, even
though the issues were the same as or similar to those in other cases where
some reference had been made to social science and a great deal of reference
made to medical expert testimony and medical literature. Neither the district
court nor the appeals court referred to extralegal testimony or literature either.
Briefs were filed, however, by the American Psychological Association (APA)
and others.

Webster v. Reproductive Health Services 492 U.S. 490 (1989)

State-employed health professionals and private nonprofit corporations providing abortion services brought suit challenging the constitutionality of a Missouri statute regulating the performance of abortions: that 1) life begins at conception and confers upon the fetus the same rights as those conferred upon born children, 2) that a physician must ascertain viability if a woman is more than 20 weeks pregnant, 3) prohibits the use of public employees and facilities for abortions not necessary to save the mother's life, and 4) makes it unlawful to use public funds, employees or facilities for the purpose of encouraging or counseling a woman to have an abortion not necessary to save her life. The District Court struck down each of the provisions, and the Court of Appeals affirmed, ruling that the provisions violated *Roe* and subsequent cases. The Court delivered a split 5-4 decision, with five different opinions. The majority opinion was held by Chief Justice Rehnquist and Justices White, O'Connor, Scalia and Kennedy. The dissents were filed by Justices Blackmun, Brennan, Marshall and Stevens.

Since the 1986 *Thornburgh* decision, another change had taken place in the Court. Justice Powell had stepped down, and in 1988 Justice Kennedy, whose views on abortion were unknown, had been appointed (Goldstein 1988). Powell supported *Roe* and usually voted to strike state regulations on abortion. *Webster* was Justice Rehnquist's first opinion on abortion as chief justice. He delivered the majority opinion. Justice Kennedy voted in favor of the law, along with Rehnquist and White. Justice O'Connor also supported the law. Justice Scalia went further, explicitly voting to overrule *Roe*, insisting it was wrongly decided and the entire matter should be left to the political process to determine (Friedman 1993). Although *Webster* did not explicitly overturn *Roe*, it allowed states to place new and severe restraints. The decision was regarded as a reconsideration of *Roe* and the result viewed as encouraging states to pass restrictive legislation that would make it more difficult for poor women, rural women, and teenagers to obtain abortions (Hoff-Wilson 1991). Part of the reason for the decision was the change in the Court composition, but another may have been the increase in the activism of the prolife movement, as evidenced by the number of briefs filed. For example, in *Roe*, there were five *amicus* briefs filed by prolife positions; for *Webster* that figure rose to forty-six (Epstein and Kobylka 1992).

There were large numbers of demonstrators outside the Court on the day of oral arguments in *Webster*. Police arrested some prochoice demonstrators who would not remain behind the barricades, and the Court attracted one of the largest press contingents in its history (Epstein and Kobylka 1992). Some observers believed the decision embodied a continuum relative to *Roe*'s representing the plurality of the Court, from the position of Scalia in favor of overturning *Roe;* to O'Connor's taking the less extreme position (*Roe* need not be reevaluated); to Rehnquist's acting as a balance (*Roe* will be modified and narrowed) (Epstein and Kobylka 1992).

Rehnquist repeated, as the Court had said in *Danforth,* that the trimester framework has left the Court to serve as the country's "ex officio medical board with powers to approve or disapprove medical and operative practices and standards throughout the United States" (519). He admits that there is not doubt that its holding will allow some governmental regulation of abortion that would have been prohibited under the language of previous cases (521). Scalia (532) refers to the "Court's self-awarded sovereignty over a field where it has little proper business. . . . It thus appears that the mansion of constitutionalized abortion-law, constructed overnight in *Roe v. Wade,* must be disassembled doorjamb by doorjamb, and never entirely brought down, no matter how wrong it may be" (537). In Blackmun's dissent (with Brennan and Marshall), he asserts that the decision invites states to enact more and more restrictive legislation and that it foments disregard for the law and for the standing decisions (538). Never, he says, "in my memory has a plurality gone about its business in such a deceptive fashion" (538). He pleads his case:

> The plurality opinion is filled with winks, and nods, and knowing glances to those who would do away with Roe explicitly, but turns a stone face to anyone in search of what the plurality conceives as the scope of a woman's right under the Due Process Clause to terminate a pregnancy free from the coercive and brooding influence of the State. . . . I fear for the future. I fear for the liberty and equality of the millions of women who have lived and come of age in the 16 years since *Roe* was decided. I fear for the integrity of, and public esteem for, this Court. (Blackmun, 538)

Blackmun references Cates and Rochat's "Illegal Abortions in the United States: 1972–1974" (*Family Planning Perspectives* 8 [1976]: 86, 92), saying that every year hundreds of thousands of women, in desperation, defy the law and place their health and safety in the unclean and unsympathetic hands of back-alley abortionists or attempt the procedure themselves (558). Blackmun says that the plurality's tough approach is callous. To overturn a constitutional decision that secures a fundamental personal liberty of millions is a rare and grave undertaking. It would also be unprecedented in the two hundred years of constitutional history (558). He claims that abortion is the "most politically divisive domestic legal issue of our time" (559). In closing, Blackmun (560) says that "[f]or today, at least, the law of abortion stands undisturbed. For today, the women of this Nation still retain the liberty to control their destinies. But the signs are evident and very ominous, and a chill wind blows."

Justice Stevens takes exception to Scalia's notion that the abortion law was constructed overnight in *Roe* (565). Stevens (490) discusses abortion in light of population policy (an almost Malthusian approach), saying that there have been times in history when military and economic interests have been served by an increase in population; but no one, he claims, says that Missouri is asserting a societal interest in increasing its population with this legislation. Stevens (570) in a footnote makes the point that the most significant consequences of the abortion decision for a woman are not medical in character—a point usually ignored or overlooked by the Court. He contends that the divisiveness of the issue reflects the deeply held religious convictions of many participants, since no fewer than sixty-seven religious organizations submitted their views in briefs, on either side of the case, in *Webster* (571).

Briefs were filed by the American Psychological Association, but the Supreme Court majority opinion made no reference to social science, although the dissents of both Justices Blackmun and Stevens each made one. Justices Rehnquist and O'Connor referred to medical literature but not social science. Neither the appeals court nor the district court made any references to social science. The district court includes testimony of Dr. Robert Crist, who often testifies in abortion cases. He and other medical experts were frequently quoted in the district court opinion regarding viability, but no reference was made to social science.

Hodgson v. Minnesota 497 U.S. 417 (1990)

A Minnesota statute provides that no abortion shall be performed on a woman under 18 years of age until at least 48 hours after both of her parents have been notified, which is mandatory unless the woman declares that she is a victim of parental abuse or by court order or showing maturity. The District Court held the statute unconstitutional. The Court of Appeals reversed. The Supreme Court affirmed, ruling with five different opinions. The Supreme Court ruled that a law requiring two parent notification was constitutional as long as the state provided the option of a judicial hearing in lieu of parental consent or contacting one parent. Justice Stevens delivered the opinion of the Court but other opinions were written by Justices O'Connor, Kennedy and Marshall. (5-4)

For the first time since Justice O'Connor was appointed to the Court, she voted to strike down a state law on the grounds that it "unduly burdened" the constitutional right to an abortion, in this case by requiring that *both* parents be notified (Friedman 1993). On the other hand, Justice Kennedy voted to uphold all parts of the law and wrote the principal dissenting opinion (joined by Rehnquist, Scalia, and White). This is the first abortion case in which all of the opinions and all of the justices include references to social science. Briefs were filed by the APA and "274 organizations in Support of *Roe v. Wade,*" as well as by the Elliot Institute for Social Sciences Research. The opinion noted that the Minnesota statute is the most intrusive in the nation. The opinion, written by Stevens and joined by Brennan, Marshall, Blackmun, and O'Connor, in part refers to the APA brief, which notes that it is estimated that by age seventeen, 70 percent of white children born in 1980 will have spent at least some time with only one parent, and 94 percent of black children will have lived in one-parent homes; the brief cites Hofferth's "Updating Children's Life Course" (*Journal of Marriage and Family* 47 [1985]: 93).

The Court cited the district court's findings of studies indicating that family violence occurs in two million families; that battering of women is the most frequently committed violent crime in Minnesota, not including psychological or sexual abuse; and that many minors live in fear of violence by family members. The Court opinion included other references to expert testimony at the district court. This case differs markedly from the others because the district court testimony included fact witnesses, many of whom were judges or counselors who had been involved in the judicial aspect of parental permission. According to district court testimony, there was extreme nervousness among the children having to go before judges and reveal intimate personal details of their lives (442). Further, the case points out that the judicial bypass approves the procedure in almost every instance anyway, making the law largely irrelevant. Dr. Lenore Walker, an expert at the district court in this and other abortion cases, is quoted by the Supreme Court as testifying that the most common reason for not notifying the second parent was that the parent was a child batterer or spouse batterer and that notifying such a person would be like "showing a red cape to a bull" (451).

Justice Marshall (joined by Justices Brennan and Blackmun) relies extensively upon social science data, including the following (464–68):

1. Cartoof and Klerman, "Parental Consent for Abortion: Impact of the Massachusetts Law," *American Journal of Public Health* 76 (1986).

2. Cates, Schulz, and Grimes, "The Risks Associated with Teenage Abortion," *New England Journal of Medicine* (1983). (Finding that delays in abortions increase health risks).

3. Clary, "Minor Women Obtaining Abortions: A Study of Parental Notification in a Metropolitan Area," *American Journal of Public Health* 72 (1982). (Finding that many minors chose not to inform parents voluntarily because of fear of negative consequences, such as physical punishment or other retaliation.)

4. The Court quotes District Court trial testimony of Dr. Steven Butzer stating that involuntary disclosure is disruptive to family and has almost universally negative effects in accord with the minor's expectations.

5. The Court quotes testimony of Dr. Elissa Benedek in District Court that indicates that minors usually accurately predict parental reaction to news about their daughters' pregnancies.

6. The Court quotes testimony of Dr. Lenore Walker at District Court that forced notification in dysfunctional families is likely to sever communication patterns and increase the risk of violence.

7. Greydanus and Railsback, "Abortion in Adolescence," *Seminars in Adolescent Medicine* (1985). (One hundred times greater death rate for women who obtain illegal abortions than for those who obtain legal ones; minor's overall risk of dying from childbirth is 9 times greater than risk of dying from legal abortion.)

8. Lewis, "Minors' Competence to Consent to Abortion," *American Psychologist* 42 (1987). (Pregnancy continuation poses far greater psychological, physical, and economic risks to the adolescent than does abortion; noting absence of a judicial standard for assessing maturity.)

9. Melton, "Legal Regulation of Adolescent Abortion: Unintended Effects," *American Psychologist* 42 (1987). (Stating that in many families, compelled parental notification is unlikely to result in meaningful discussion about the daughter's predicament.)

10. National Research Council, *Risking the Future: Adolescent Sexuality, Pregnancy, and Childbearing* (ed. C. Hayes, 1987) (The risks are especially significant because adolescents already delay seeking medical care until relatively late in their pregnancies.)

11. Osofsky and Osofsky, "Teenage Pregnancy: Psychosocial Considerations," *Clinical Obstetrics and Gynecology* 21 (1978). (The disclosure of a daughter's intention to have an abortion often leads to a family crisis, characterized by severe parental anger and rejection.)

12. Torres, Forrest and Eisman, "Telling Parents: Clinic Policies and Adolescent's Use of Family Planning and Abortion Services," *Family Planning Perspectives* 12 (1980). (51 percent of minors discussed abortion with parents in the absence of a parental consent or notification requirement; 9 percent of minors attending family planning clinics would have a self-induced or illegal abortion rather than tell a parent; 9 percent of minors would carry a child to term rather than inform parents of decision to abort.)

Such lengthy development and presentation of citations to social science findings and the quoting of social science experts is unprecedented in the Supreme Court opinions. Justice Scalia, on the other hand, quotes no social science and says (480) that he continues "to dissent from this enterprise of devising an Abortion Code, and from the illusion that we have authority to do so." Justice Kennedy in his dissent, joined by White and Scalia, states that "[w]e have been over much of this ground before." Unlike the other cases, the district court makes considerable reference to expert and fact witnesses, summarizing their testimony at the end of its opinion. At least thirty-seven witnesses spoke to the issue of whether pregnant minors would notify their parents or go to court. Only two experts related facts from which a court could reasonably infer that the statute does young women more good than harm, and the justices note that neither of these witnesses has any direct contact with minors or performs abortions. Of the remaining witnesses, all but four are personally involved in Minnesota in implementing the statute, as judges, defenders, guardians, or counselors. None testified that there was a beneficial effect upon the minors, and some testified that there was a negligible effect upon intrafamily communication and on the well-being of the minors. The district court concluded that five weeks of trial produced no factual basis for the statute. In sum, the Supreme Court made ten references to social science literature and testimony in the majority opinion and twenty in the dissent. The appeals court made none, but the district court relied heavily upon social science testimony—both factual and expert—with ten cites.

Ohio v. Akron Center for Reproductive Health, Inc. 497 U.S. 502 (1990)

Challenging an Ohio statute making it a crime for a physician to perform an abortion on an unmarried, unemancipated minor woman, unless minor's parents or a juvenile court issues an order authorizing the minor to consent. Federal District Court prevented the enforcement, and the Court of Appeals affirmed, concluding that various of the statute's provisions were constitutionally defective. The Supreme Court reversed, holding that the state law requiring notification of one parent was constitutional. Justice Kennedy delivered the opinion with Chief Justice Rehnquist and Justices White, Stevens, O'Connor and Scalia joining in parts. Justices Scalia and Stevens each filed concurring opinions. Justice Blackmun filed a dissenting opinion, in which Justices Brennan and Marshall joined. (6-3)

Briefs were again filed by the APA and "274 Organizations in Support of *Roe.*" Justice O'Connor voted with Justices Kennedy, Rehnquist, White, Stevens and Scalia to uphold state restrictions, and Justices Blackmun, Brennan, and Marshall were the usual dissenters to prevent state restrictions. Kennedy notes that the justices have decided five cases addressing parental notice—*Danforth, Bellotti, H.L., Ashcroft,* and *Akron*—but that this case turns on the adequacy of the judicial bypass, rather than parental consent. In support of the state legislature's decision, Kennedy writes (520) that a free and enlightened society may decide that members should have a clear "understanding of the profound philosophic choices confronted by a woman who is considering whether to seek an abortion." He continues: "[i]t is both rational and fair for the State to conclude that, in most instances, the family will strive to give a lonely or even terrified minor advice that is both compassionate and mature" (Kennedy, 520). In a concurring statement, Justice Scalia claims that the Constitution contains no right to abortion.

Justice Blackmun, writing the dissent, with Justices Brennan and Marshall joining, asserts that the state of Ohio has acted with particular insensitivity and created a tortuous maze by placing its pattern of obstacles that are merely "poorly disguised elements of discouragement for the abortion decision" (525–26). He says that as a practical matter, a notification requirement will have the same deterrent effect as a consent statute. He would assume that the goal of the court is to assist, not entrap, the young pregnant woman, and he refers to the judicial bypass as a "ridiculous pleading scheme" (528). He cites Torres et al., who said that the majority of minors voluntarily tell their parents about their pregnancy anyway (536). He quotes the APA brief regarding the one million children suffering harm from parental abuse or neglect (537). Justice Blackmun chides the Court for referring to the "compassionate and mature" advice the minor will receive, countering with information about what happens to unwanted babies—born to youngsters who are children themselves, with little opportunity, education, or life skills—who themselves continue a cycle of poverty, despair, and violence (537). He accuses the Court of hyperbole that can have but one result: "to further incite an American press, public, and pulpit already inflamed by the pronouncement of *Webster*" (541). He notes that there is another world out there that the Court either chooses to ignore or fears to recognize, a world of unfortunate citizens who need the protection of the legislature instead of having life made difficult (541). There are few instances, Blackmun says (542), "where the injustice is so evident, and the impediments so gross as those inflicted by the Ohio Legislature on these vulnerable and powerless young women."

The majority and concurring opinions made no reference to social science, but the dissent made four citations to social science literature. Neither the district court nor the court of appeals referred to social science literature or social science expert testimony. This is surprising in light of the fact that it was a parental notification case on which the Court previously used social science evidence, particularly in *Hodgson*.

Rust v. Sullivan 11 S.Ct. 1759 (1991)

Suits challenging regulations of the Department of Health and Human Services (HHS) which prohibit Title X projects from engaging in abortion counseling, referral, and activities advocating abortion as a method of family planning. The District Court of New York upheld the regulations, and the Court of Appeals affirmed. The Supreme Court also affirmed holding that 1) regulations were permissible, 2) they do not violate First Amendment free speech rights of Title X fund recipients, and 3) do not violate a woman's Fifth Amendment right to choose whether to terminate a pregnancy or infringe on the doctor-patient relationship. Chief Justice Rehnquist wrote for the majority—Justices White, Kennedy, Scalia, and Souter. Justice Blackmun filed a dissenting opinion in which Justices Marshall, Stevens and O'Connor joined in part. Justices Stevens and O'Connor filed dissenting opinions. (5-4)

This would be Justice Marshall's last abortion case and Justice Brennan had resigned from the Court in 1990, leaving only Justice Blackmun from the original seven justices who supported *Roe*. Brennan had been replaced by Souter, whose views on abortion were not known until the *Rust* decision. Based on Souter's vote, he is not expected to be prochoice in the future. In *Rust*, his was the swing vote that provided Rehnquist with the majority, which they would not have had otherwise with Brennan gone (Epstein and Kobylka 1992).

Social science was not referred to at any court level in this case—Supreme Court, district court, or court of appeals. One set of statistics, cited at the district court, however, revealed that Title X is the single largest federally funded family-planning program, serving 4.3 million people and targeting 14.5 million women at risk of unintended pregnancy, including 5 million adolescents, all of whom have an income below the poverty level (415—data from "The Title X Family Planning Gag Rule: Can the Government Buy Up Constitutional Rights?" *Stanford Law Review*, 1989).

Planned Parenthood of Southeastern Pennsylvania v. Robert P. Casey
112 S. Ct. 2791 (1992)

Abortion clinics and physician challenged on due process ground the constitutionality of Pennsylvania abortion statute. The District Court held that several sections of the statute were unconstitutional. The Court of Appeals affirmed in part and reversed in part. The Supreme Court held that 1) the doctrine of stare decisis requires reaffirmance of *Roe v. Wade's* essential holding recognizing a woman's right to choose an abortion before fetal viability; 2) the undue burden test, rather than the trimester framework, should be used in evaluating viability; 3) the medical emergency definition was sufficiently broad that it did not impose an undue burden; 4) the informed consent requirements, the 24-hour waiting period, parental consent provision, and the reporting and recordkeeping requirements of the Pennsylvania statute did not impose an undue burden; and 5) the spousal notification provision imposed an undue burden and was invalid. Justices O'Connor, Kennedy and Souter wrote the opinion and other concurring and dissenting opinions were entered.

Planned Parenthood is the last of the abortion cases to be taken up in the twenty years under examination here. The *Planned Parenthood* decision is remarkable for a number of reasons, including the decision itself, the votes of the new members of the Court, the curious alliances among justices, the highly charged emotionalism of the opinions, and the use of social science in support of the judgment. First, neither Souter nor Thomas (the latter appointed to the court in 1991) had voted before, so while they were expected to be prolife, no one knew for sure. Second, the joint opinion of Justices O'Connor, Kennedy, and Souter, which decided the case outcome, was the big surprise, since O'Connor and Kennedy had previously voted to uphold restrictions, and Souter was an unknown (Friedman 1993). Also, these justices made it clear that the opinion was delivered by each of them—not by one writing for the other two. In it, they struck down the trimester system. Four justices—Rehnquist, White, Scalia, and Thomas—announced they would overrule *Roe v. Wade* altogether. Justice Blackmun, the author of *Roe,* and the strongest defender of the right to abortion, issued a personal statement of concern over the opinion. Also, this was the first abortion decision since *Roe* in which Justice Marshall did not participate.

Justices O'Connor, Kennedy, and Souter concluded that the essential holding of *Roe v. Wade* should be retained and reaffirmed (2804). Arguing (2807) that the ability of women to participate equally in the economic and social life of the nation has been facilitated by their ability to control their reproductive lives, they cite R. Petchesky's *Abortion and Woman's Choice* (1990). It is in the area of spousal consent that they used social science findings. In an unprecedented approach, they cite one reference after another to social science literature. The first citations are directly from the district court's opinion, which utilized expert witness testimony. The justices cite eighteen of the district court's references to social science expert witness testimony on battered women and say that these findings are supported by studies of domestic violence, published by the American Medical Association Council on Scientific Affairs ("Violence against Women" [1991]). That article indicates that approximately two million women are the victims of severe assaults by their male partners, according to a 1985 survey. The same study finds that in families where wife beating takes place, child abuse is often present as well (though the justices do not refer to that finding when they take up parental consent issues later). Another reference is to N. Shields and C. Hanneke's "Battered Wives' Reactions to Marital Rape, in the Dark Side of Families" (*Current Family Violence Research,* D. Finkelhor, R. Gelles, G. Hataling, and M. Straus, eds., 1983).

Considerable evidence had been provided in the district court trial by Dr. Lenore Walker, whose work was cited in this opinion. Walker's book *The Battered Woman Syndrome* (1984) was also cited regarding the psychological abuse of forced social and economic isolation, in addition to physical abuse. "Staying with an Abusive Relationship: I. How and Why Do Women Stay?," an article by Herbert, Silver, and Ellard (*Journal of Marriage and the Family* 53 [1991]), was included to show that women stay in abusive relationships. The women may return to their partners because of economic reasons, as Aguirre reveals in "Why Do They Return? Abused Wives in Shelters" (*Journal of the National Association of Social Work* 30). The statistic that 8.8 percent of all homicide victims are killed by their spouses was quoted from Mercy and Saltzman's "Fatal Violence among Spouses in the United States 1976–85" (*American Journal of Public Health* 79 [1989]). The opinion notes further that 30 percent of females murdered are at the hands of their male partners, as revealed in a Senate hearing. The opinion also cites information from Ryan and Plutzer's "When Married Women Have Abortions: Spousal Notification and Marital Interaction" (*Journal of Marriage and the Family* 51 [1989]: 41, 44), which indicates that the vast majority of women notify their husbands about their abortions, and that if they do not, it is because they fear violence (2830). The opinion summarizes some thirty social science citations by saying that this information in the district court's findings reinforces what common sense would suggest—that in well-functioning marriages, spouses discuss decisions, but there are millions of women who have good reasons for not informing their husbands and for whom notification would impose a substantial obstacle (2830–31). Ironically, when the Court turns to the decision of parental notification, it cites no social science data, even though there was considerable social science to quote from the district court findings and from previous cases and briefs.

Justice Blackmun laments the fact that four members of the Court appeared poised to cast into darkness the hopes and visions of every woman in this country who had come to believe that the Constitution guaranteed her the right to reproductive choice. He believes that all that remained between the promise of *Roe* and the darkness of the plurality was a single, flickering flame, and that the decisions since *Webster* gave little reason to "hope that this flame would cast much light. . . . But now, just when so many expected the darkness to fall, the flame has grown bright" (2844). While he says he does not underestimate the significance of the joint opinion, he fears "for the darkness as four Justices anxiously await the single vote necessary to extinguish the light" (2844). He says that at long last the chief justice and those who have joined him admit that they believe "that *Roe* was wrongly decided, and that it can and should be overruled consistently with our traditional approach to *stare decisis* in constitutional cases." Blackmun (2853) says, "If there is much reason to applaud the advances made by the joint opinion today, there is far more to fear from the Chief Justice's opinion," an opinion that he says follows from Rehnquist's "stunted conception of individual liberty." In short, Blackmun asserts, "The Chief Justice's view of the State's compelling interest in maternal health has less to do with health than it does with compelling women to be maternal" (2853).

For all the passion expressed in his opinion, Justice Blackmun makes no citations to social science in his opinion. But he refers (2854), to Rehnquist's assertion that the record lacks any "hard evidence" to support the joint opinion's contention that a large fraction of women who prefer not to notify their husbands are battered women and victims of unreported spousal assault. Yet, the chief justice never explains what "hard evidence" is or how large a fraction is required. Blackmun says that in one sense the Court's approach is worlds apart from that of Rehnquist and Scalia and yet in another sense the separation between them is very narrow—a single vote (2854). Blackmun (2854–55) closes by saying: "I am 83 years old. I cannot remain on this Court forever, and when I do step down, the confirmation process for my successor well may focus on the issue before us today. That, I regret[,] may be exactly where the choice between the two worlds will be made."

Chief Justice Rehnquist, joined by Justices White, Scalia, and Thomas, says that *Roe* continues to exist but "only in a way a storefront on a western movie set exists: a mere facade to give the illusion of reality" (2860). Rehnquist makes clear that the judicial branch derives its legitimacy not from public opinion but from the doctrine of *stare decisis* and it should not be subject to the vagaries of public opinion (2865). Justice Scalia (joined by Justices Rehnquist, White, and Thomas) reiterates that the Constitution does not require "abortion on demand" (2873). Scalia says the issue is whether it is a liberty protected by the Constitution, and he is sure it is not because the Constitution says absolutely nothing about it and longstanding traditions have permitted it to be legally proscribed (2874). He accuses the court of using not reasoned judgment but personal predilection (2876). Then he takes Justice O'Connor to task for the "amorphous concept of undue burden" (2876). It is here that he notes that the joint opinion's conclusion on the spousal notice requirement was based on "detailed findings of fact," which the justices set out at great length (2879–80).

Scalia makes clear that he has no objection to facts that are contained in the record or that are properly subject to judicial notice. But the justices in the joint opinion highlight only certain facts that strike them as particularly significant in establishing (or refuting) the existence of undue burden, and then, after describing the facts, they simply announce that the provision does or does not impose an undue burden (2880). In his accompanying footnote 6, Scalia says that the joint opinion is not entirely faithful to this principle either, because it relies on nonrecord materials and adds a number of factual conclusions of its own. Scalia suggests that because this additional fact finding pertains to matters that are subject to reasonable dispute according to Federal Rules of Evidence 201(b), the joint opinion must be operating on the premise that these are legislative rather than adjudicative facts—Rule 201(a). Footnote 6 concludes (2880): "But if a court can find an undue burden simply by selectively string-citing the right social science articles, I do not see the point of emphasizing or requiring 'detailed factual findings' in the District Court."

As impassioned as Blackmun is—and Marshall was—on abortion as a constitutional right, Scalia is equally impassioned in his belief that the Court should not be in the abortion business. He is particularly sensitive to threats of influence from the public, believing that *Roe* brought to life an issue that has inflamed our national politics in general (2882). Scalia (2882) is distressed at the political pressure on both sides of the issue and at the political pressure (which he expressed in *Webster*) directed to the Court: "the marches, the mail, the protests aimed at inducing us to change our opinions." He believes that people on both sides of the abortion issue think that the justices should take their views into account as though they were engaged, not in ascertaining an objective law, but in determining some kind of social consensus, as if it were based on value judgments (2884). In closing (2885), Scalia says, "We should get out of this area, where we have no right to be, and where we do neither ourselves nor the country any good by remaining."

The court of appeals made some references to the social science expert testimony offered at the district court level. But in the dissent, the justices express in a footnote their disbelief that the opinion offered by a plaintiff's expert merely describes the likely behavior of most of the women in a group of unknown size, not showing how many women would be harmed by the statute of spousal consent. How, the author of the dissent asks, could it be held facially unconstitutional simply because one expert testifies that in her opinion the provision would harm a completely unknown number of women (723)?

The district court opinion in this case is extraordinary in its comprehensive coverage of social science data, through the use of expert witnesses and the presentation of that testimony. First, the judge qualifies each of the experts, discounting some testimonies and allowing others, and entering their qualifications into the record. Dr. Lenore Walker, who has testified in several of the abortion cases, is described as an expert in the area of family violence and the effects of battering on women, children, and other members of their families (1332). She is reported to be a licensed psychologist with more than twenty years of experience; she was one of the first scientists in the country to conduct clinical research on intrafamily violence and one of the foremost experts on the psychology of battered women and families.

Dr. Rue on the other hand, who testified on postabortion syndrome, is said to lack the academic qualifications and scientific credentials possessed by the plaintiff's witnesses. His testimony, which is not credible, according to the judge, is based primarily on limited clinical experience, and his admitted personal opposition to abortion suggests a possible personal bias.

The opinion includes relevant public health statistics on abortion. Evidence is also submitted to show that an abortion is twice as safe as a tonsillectomy and one hundred times safer than an appendectomy, according to trial expert testimony. In the opinion, thirty-nine social science "facts" from publications and expert testimony are delineated and numbered. It is these numbered items that are lifted and cited by the joint opinion in reference to the spousal consent statute. In sum, the joint opinion cited some thirty references to social science; Justice Blackmun's dissent made one such reference. The court of appeals made eight references, and the district court, over thirty.

Briefs for *Planned Parenthood of Southeastern Pennsylvania v. Robert P. Casey*

For *Pennsylvania,* in 1992, 35 were filed (Friedman 1993); of those, 11 were in support of abortion rights, 23 were in support of the Pennsylvania statutes restricting abortion, and 1 was neutral. The increase in the number of briefs overall is due at least in part to the presence of more "interested parties" and to more evidence, such as social science literature. The increase in the number of prolife briefs reflects the activist movement that had developed in the twenty years since *Roe.* The more frequently referenced articles and books are listed below; some of these appeared in briefs on both sides.

Alan Guttmacher Institute, *Safe and Legal: 10 Years' Experience with Legal Abortion in New York State* (1980).

Alan Guttmacher Institute, *Teenage Pregnancy in the United States: The Scope of the Problem and State Responses* (1989).

Alan Guttmacher Institute, *Abortion and Women's Health: A Turning Point for America?* (1990).

American College of Obstetricians and Gynecologists, *The Battered Woman* (1989).

Browne, A., *When Battered Women Kill* (1987).

Cates, W., "Legal Abortion: The Public Health Record," *Science* 215 (1982).

Cates, W., and Rochat, "Illegal Abortions in the United States: 1972–74," *Family Planning Perspectives* 8 (1976): 86.

Cates, W. C. Schulz, D. Grimes, and A. Tyler, "The Effect of Delay and Method Choice on the Risk of Abortion Morbidity," *Family Planning Perspectives* 9 (Nov.–Dec. 1977): 266.

Centers for Disease Control, U.S. Department of Health, Education, and Welfare, *Abortion Surveillance, Annual Summary 1972* (April 1974).

Federal Bureau of Investigation, *Crime in the United States* (1990).

Gelles. R., "Violence and Pregnancy: Are Pregnant Women at Greater Risk of Abuse?" *Journal of Marriage and the Family* 50 (1984): 84.

Gold, R., *Abortion and Women's Health: A Turning Point for America* (1990).

Gold, R., and W. Cates, "Restriction of Federal Funds for Abortion: 18 Months Later," *American Journal of Public Health* 69 (1979).

Grimes, D., "Second Trimester Abortions in the United States," *Family Planning Perspectives* 16 (1984).

Koop, C. Everett, Letter to President Reagan, January 9, 1989, reprinted as "A Measured Response: Koop on Abortion," *Family Planning Perspectives* 21 (1989).

Luker, K., *Abortion and the Politics of Motherhood* (1984).

Mohr, J., *Abortion in America* (1978).

Osofsky, H., and J. Osofsky, "The Psychological Reaction of Patients to Legalized Abortion," *American Journal of Orthopsychology* 42 (1972): 48.

Petchesky, R., *Abortion and Woman's Choice: The State, Sexuality and Reproductive Freedom* (rev. ed., 1990).

Rosen, H., *Psychiatric Implications of Abortion: A Case Study in Social Hypocrisy in Abortion and the Law* (Smith, ed., 1967).

Ryan and Plutzer, "When Married Women Have Abortions: Spousal Notification and Marital Interaction," *Journal of Marriage and the Family* 51 (1989): 42.

Straus, M., R. Gelles, and S. Steinmetz, *Behind Closed Doors: Violence in the American Family* (1980).

Tietze, C., "The Public Health Effects of Legal Abortions in the United States," *Family Planning Perspectives* 16 (1984).

Tietze, C., and S. Henshaw, *Induced Abortion: A World Review, 1986* (6th ed., 1986).

Torres, A., and J. D. Forrest, "Why Do Women Have Abortions?" *Family Planning Perspectives* 20 (1988): 169.

Tribe, L., *American Constitutional Law* (2d ed., 1990).

Walker, L., *The Battered Woman Syndrome* (1984).

All but two of the twenty-seven articles or books listed above were published after *Roe*. Rosen was cited in *Roe*, as were earlier works of Tietze. The briefs filed in *Pennsylvania* in support of the right to an abortion included discussion of the issues of (1) spousal notification, (2) parental notification, (3) making records public, and (4) observing a waiting period. Social science issues included how the statute would (1) affect women of color disproportionately, (2) affect rural women, (3) increase the dangers of the procedures by imposing a delay, (4) lead to wife battering, and (5) lead to child abuse.[6]

The argument in the brief for petitioners in support of abortion rights pointed out that marital abuse is surprisingly common in the United States, as the district court had found, and the brief quoted Dr. Walker concerning battered women. David Grimes and others, in their article "An Epidemic of Anti-Abortion Violence in the United States" (*American Journal of Obstetrics and Gynecology* 165 [1991]:1263), point out how a clinic director's sixteen-year-old daughter was threatened with kidnapping, suggesting that public disclosure in the Pennsylvania statute could lead to harassment of women seeking abortions. Rachel Gold's *Abortion and Women's Health: A Turning Point for America?* (1990) is quoted: Gold says that by 1989, sixteen million women had obtained legal abortions, and nearly half of all women of reproductive age will have had an abortion by the time they reach forty-five. Several studies are cited to show that significantly fewer deaths result from abortion than from childbirth; a woman is twenty times more likely to die from giving birth than from having an abortion. Further, employment opportunities for women with children are severely limited because the workplace doesn't accommodate parental responsibilities, according to Reskin and Hartmann (eds., 1986) in *Women's Work, Men's Work: Sex Segregation on the Job.* Most teenagers (56 percent) who become mothers do not complete high school.

The brief filed on behalf of twenty-four organizations that represent poor women of color notes that laws restricting the provision of, and access to, abortion services for poor women will necessarily affect a high percentage of women of color. African American women are five times more likely to live in poverty and three times more likely to be unemployed than white women, according to the United States Commission on Civil Rights (*The Economic Status of Black Women* [1990]). The authors of the brief conclude that the provisions of requiring a twenty-four-hour waiting period, parental consent, and spousal notification actively interfere with a woman's decision to have an abortion and limit the ability of poor women to obtain such services. Another brief supporting abortion rights was filed by 250 American historians who are united in their conviction that the Court's decision in *Roe v. Wade* is supported by American history and the lessons that history imparts. The authors cite K. Luker's *Abortion and the Politics of Motherhood* (1984) and J. Mohr's *Abortion in America: The Origins and Evolution of National Policy* (1978), both of which have been cited in other testimony.

Briefs for the respondents in support of the Pennsylvania statute were less likely to refer to social science literature than did those opposing the statute. The brief for the United States includes quotations from works by Tribe and Mohr. The brief for the Catholic Conference et al. contains citations to some medical literature discussing negative social-psychological implications, such as Fletcher and Evans's "Sounding Boards: Maternal Bonding in Early Fetal Ultrasound Examinations" (*New England Journal of Medicine* 308 [Feb. 17, 1983]: 392). Fletcher and Evans say that once women have seen the living human being inside them, they immediately abandon thoughts of abortion. The authors of the brief cite the APA's "Adolescent Abortion: Psychological and Legal Issues" (1986), which claims that compared with adults, adolescents appear to have more negative responses, on average, following abortion. The authors plead for the Court to protect the health of its citizens and the lives of their offspring.

In the reply brief for the petitioners, the writers note that the district court found that the testimony of each of the petitioners' nine expert and fact witnesses were credible in all respects, and that the court made adverse credibility determinations against two of the three witnesses offered by Pennsylvania. They found that Dr. Rue's testimony was not credible, even though the *amici curiae* continue to rely on the discredited testimony. Further, the district court documented the record evidence supporting each of its 387 findings of fact, and the court of appeals did not reverse any of them.

Summary

The abortion cases provided information that is discussed below and summarized in table 1. In these cases, decisions and opinions from prior cases were given far greater weight than was social science data. A case may have had hundreds of citations to previous cases, with only a few or none to social science. Citations to social science literature and expert testimony have increased during the twenty years in which these abortion cases came before the United States Supreme Court. *Roe*, the original case in 1973, had no citations, and *Pennsylvania* in 1992, the most recent case in the study, had thirty-one—the most citations to date. It was not until 1977, after hearing five abortion cases, however, that the Supreme Court justices cited social science data in an opinion on abortion. That citation appeared in the dissenting opinions in three companion cases (*Maher, Beal,* and *Poelker*). Then, the Court decided four more cases in which it made no reference to social science data, before it reverted to citations of social science statistics. The return to social science data occurred in 1981, in *H.L.*, in both the majority and dissenting opinions. *H.L.* was the first case in which a majority opinion made reference to social science, a trend that continued into *Akron* in 1983, where once again both the majority and dissenting opinions held references to social science.

It was seven more years and three cases later before the Court again made reference to social science in an abortion-related case. This came in the dissenting opinion in *Webster*. That decision was followed by *Hodgson* in 1990, in which the opinion held some 30 citations, 20 in the dissent and 10 in the majority. After that, *Ohio* contained 4 social science citations in the dissent, but then *Rust* had none. Beyond the sheer number of references to social science data in *Pennsylvania* (30), it is more surprising that the citations to social science in the majority opinion far outnumbered those in the dissenting opinion (1). In sum, 4 of the 22 cases made reference to social science in the majority or concurring opinions, whereas 9 of the 22 cases had social science references in the dissenting opinions. The quantity of social science data made available to the Court increased over time, as evidenced by the number and content of the briefs submitted. In 1973, in *Roe*, fewer than 20 *amicus* briefs were filed, whereas in 1989, in *Webster*, 78 were filed, and in *Pennsylvania*, 35.

Even when social science data may support a particular position, the data may not be referenced. Supporting data may be cited in one case and not in a similar case. For example, in the funding cases of *Maher, Beal,* and *Poelker,* social science was cited, but it was not repeated in the later funding cases of *Harris* and *Williams*. Similarly, social science was cited in parental permission cases prior to *Ashcroft,* but it was not referred to in *Ashcroft*. Social science data were available and could have been used in considerations of such issues as dysfunctional families; parental authority; unwanted children; stress; privacy; impact of childbirth by race, rural area, and poverty; wife battering; spousal abuse; and child abuse.

The tendency to cite social science is dependent upon the justice. Justice Scalia has never cited social science in his 5 abortion cases, nor has Justice Thomas, though he has been on only 1 abortion case to date. The only other justice who had never cited social science was Justice Douglas, but he retired in 1975, before any justice had cited social science in an abortion opinion. Justice Stewart cited social science in 1 case, in 1981, the year he retired. Justices Powell and Burger each cited social science in 2 cases, preceding their retirements in 1987 and 1986, respectively. Justices Rehnquist and White, who have each heard 22 abortion cases, referred to social science in only 2 cases, and that was in 1981 and 1983—but not since then. Justices Blackmun, Brennan, and Marshall, on the other hand, were more likely to cite social science. Those citations were usually

Table 1. Citations to Social Science in U.S. Supreme Court Decisions, 1972–92: Abortion Cases ($N = 22$)

	Roe '73	Doe '73	Bige-low '75	Dan-forth '76	Single-ton '76	Beal '77	Maher '77	Poel-ker '77	Coa-lutti '79	Bel-lotti '79
Douglas (1939–75)	0	0								
Stewart (1958–81)	0	0	0	0	0	0	0	0	0	0
Burger (1969–86)	0	0	0	0	0	0	0	0	0	0
Powell (1972–87)	0	0	0	0	0	0	0	0	0	0
Brennan (1956–90)	0	0	0	0	0	1	1	1	0	0
Marshall (1967–91)	0	0	0	0	0	9	8	9	0	0
Blackmun (1970–91)	0	0	0	0	0	1	1	1	0	0
White (1962–93)	0	0	0	0	0	0	0	0	0	0
Rehnquist (1972–)	0	0	0	0	0	0	0	0	0	0
Stevens (1975–)				0	0	0	0	0	0	0
O'Connor (1981–)										
Scalia (1986–)										
Kennedy (1988–)										
Souter (1990–)										
Thomas (1991–)										
Majority	0	0	0	0	0	0	0	0	0	0
Dissent	0	0	0	0	0	9	8	9	0	0
Total Cites	0	0	0	0	0	9	8	9	0	0
Appeals	—	—	—	0	0	0	0	0	—	—
District	0	0	—	3	1	1	0	—	2	10
State Supreme Court	—	—	0	—	—	—	—	—	—	—

in dissenting opinions. Justices Brennan and Marshall cited social science in 7 of their cases and Blackmun in 9 of the 22 on which he sat. Justice O'Connor cited social science in 3 of her 9 cases, and in the most recent case she was one of the joint opinion writers, along with Justices Stevens, Kennedy, and Souter, who cited 30 references to social science literature or experts. Justice Kennedy heard 4 cases before he was part of an opinion that referred to social science findings, and Justice Souter had heard 1 case before the most recent case.

It is difficult to discern a trend for the use of social science data by the Court and by individual justices. In general, those who would overthrow *Roe*—the strict constitutionalists, such as Justices Rehnquist, White, Scalia, and Thomas—appear least likely to utilize social science. Those who are likely to be *Roe* supporters (such as Justice Blackmun) would probably use social sci-

Harris '80	Wil-liams '80	H.L. '81	Akron '83	Ash-croft '83	Simo-poulos '83	Thorn-burgh '86	Web-ster '89	Hodg-son '90	Ohio '90	Rust '91	Pa. '92	No. Cases Soc. Sci.	No. Cases
												0	3
0	0	3										1	13
0	0	3	2	0	0	0						2	17
0	0	3	2	0	0	0						2	17
0	0	25	2	0	0	0	1	20	0			7	20
0	0	25	2	0	0	0	1	20	0	0		7	21
0	0	25	2	0	0	0	1	20	4	0	1	9	22
0	0	3	3	0	0	0	0	0	0	0	0	2	22
0	0	3	3	0	0	0	0	0	0	0	0	2	22
0	0	3	2	0	0	0	0	10	0	0	30	4	19
0			3	0	0	0	0	10	0	0	30	3	9
0							0	0	0	0	0	0	5
0							0	0	0		30	1	5
0										0	30	1	2
0											0	0	1
0	0	3	2	0	0	0	0	10	0	0	30	4	22
0	0	25	3	0	0	0	1	20	4	0	1	9	22
0	0	28	5	0	0	0	1	30	4	0	31	9	22
—	—	—	1	0	—	0	0	0	0	0	8	2	12
159	0	—	0	0	—	0	0	10	0	0	33	8	12
—	—	0	—	—	0	—	—	—	—	—	—	0	3

ence, whereas justices who would look at restrictions as not necessarily being an undue burden—for example, Justices Stevens, O'Connor, Kennedy, and Souter—may utilize social science as necessary to bolster their argument.

Social science data in abortion cases are used more in dissenting opinions than in majority opinions (see table 1). In nine of the cases on abortion, social science was cited in the dissenting opinions; in four of the cases, social science was cited in the majority or concurring opinions. There is no apparent relationship between citations in the lower courts and citations to social science by the Supreme Court. The appeals court has virtually never cited social science, whether or not the district court has. The appeals court cited social science data in only 2 of the 12 abortion cases heard. The state supreme courts did not make reference to social science in their three cases. The district court cited social science in 8 of the 19 cases and the Supreme Court in 9 of the 22. With the district court, the highest number of citations were 159 in *Harris,* and in that case, the Supreme Court made no citations to social science in either the majority or dissenting opinions. On the other hand, in the first cases where all of the justices referred to social science (*H.L.* and *Akron*), the district court had made no references to social science. In the most recent case examined (*Pennsylvania*), however, the district court had done the most thorough job of presenting social science expert testimony and references, and this was utilized by the Supreme Court. To what extent that was merely coincidental remains to be seen in future cases. When the Court cites social science, there is a preference for referring to briefs over citing expert testimony. Reference was made by the Supreme Court to studies in the briefs and to studies cited by the district court more often than to the expert testimony. Experts did not testify before the Supreme Court, but they usually participated in the preparation of the briefs.

Abortion cases dealing with parental or spousal consent were more likely to utilize social science than were the cases that concerned funding. The parental consent cases in which the Supreme Court used social science were *H.L., Akron, Hodgson,* and *Ohio.* In other words, 4 of the 7 parental notification cases used social science. Of the 2 spousal notification cases, *Pennsylvania* cited social science. More social science data are presented to the Court on these issues than on medical issues. On the other hand, there are data on the risks of waiting too long to have an abortion and the way those risks are created by certain obstacles to abortion, and this material is presented to the court. But it appears that the Court was more willing to use data on studies dealing with battered women and children and the risks such women incur in seeking parental or spousal notification or consent.

Clinical data were used more at the district court level and less at the Supreme Court level. Statistical data were used at both levels. The emotional aspects of abortion seemed to lend themselves to anecdotal data and case histories. The justices do not hesitate to cite medical literature, but they are reluctant to cite social science literature. There were no citations to public opinion polls or public attitude surveys, even though these have been available since *Roe.* Statistics in general, such as those generated by public health organizations, the census, or the FBI, are not always cited, even when they would support the argument and had been presented in the district court or in the briefs.

Social science experts and briefs were not analyzed in the Supreme Court opinions, but they were analyzed at the district court level. At that level, there was a tendency to use the standard of refereed journals but also to question bias and conflict of interest on the part of experts. Some studies were analyzed and criticized, mostly by opposing experts. In that sense, briefs did not lend themselves to evaluation as easily. Any evaluation was essentially done by opposing sides, who entered different studies into evidence. This method follows legal standards more than social science standards; in the latter, a scientist would provide both sides of the argument and the limitations of the data.

In the next chapter we will turn our attention to the history of sex discrimination. This will provide a context for our subsequent discussion of the Court's treatment of social science data in cases of sex discrimination in the workplace.

Notes

1. This "Second Woman's Movement," according to Hoff-Wilson (1991), began in the late 1960s, after the Equal Pay Act of 1963.

2. Unless otherwise noted, this section on family planning is drawn from Davis 1991.

3. The syllabus and case descriptions are taken directly from *The Supreme Court Reporter, U.S. Reports,* or *West Publishing Citation Index.* The syllabus is prepared by the Reporter of Decisions and constitutes no part of the opinion.

4. As stated earlier in this book, citations were considered to refer to social science only if they had to do with social, social-psychological, or psychological issues—not if they referred strictly to medical, religious, philosophical, ethical, and/or historical works. Much, but not all, statistical materials were considered to be social science if they were interpreted beyond the presentation of raw numbers. Public opinion polls were classified as social science.

5. Sometimes called *Bellotti II* because it first came before the Court in 1976, *Bellotti v. Baird* (1979) was remanded and went through several appeals over the three intervening years.

6. Friedman (1993) selects three briefs for each side to present in his book. He includes, for the petitioner: Brief of the American College of Obstetricians and Gynecologists; Brief of the NAACP Legal Defense and Education Fund; and Brief of 250 American Historians; for the respondents: Brief for the United States; Brief of the United States Catholic Conference; and Brief of National Right to Life. These have been relied upon, in part, in the preparation of this section on briefs for *Pennsylvania,* along with other briefs, such as that of the American Psychological Association.

4

Sex Discrimination

Extraordinary changes in gender patterns and definitions emerged in America in the late eighteenth century, following the birth of the Republic. Fueled by religious evangelicalism that gathered momentum between the 1790s and the 1830s,[1] a number of interrelated movements gradually promulgated organized reforms of established religions, the institution of slavery, the legal status of alcohol, and women's rights, all of which came before the public eye from the 1820s to the 1850s (Kandal 1988). The battle for women's rights in particular was closely allied with the antislavery movement. While interrelated, these various groups and nascent women's movements were hardly monolithic or homogeneous in their thinking and objectives: where one group of women's rights proponents would have stopped with the achievement of the vote, another group pressed forward for changes in marriage, morals, the organization of labor, and standards of dress (Kandal 1988).

At the dawn of the nineteenth century, women's position in America was weaker than it had been in colonial times. As the primary locus of economic production shifted away from the household, women were cut off from participation. Work done at home came to be valued less. Observing America in 1835, Tocqueville wrote in *Democracy in America* that democracy raised the status of women and brought them closer to equality with men; at the same time, he argued, there should be a division of labor between men and women. The Industrial Revolution widened the division of labor between men and women, yet it was the very phenomenon that provided the means for women to work toward equality of opportunity. The 1920s was a decade that, at its beginning, ushered in a new era in America with the achievement of the vote for women; by decade's end, women enjoyed more freedom than they had at any time in history (Kandal 1988), and they began to move into white-collar occupations.

During the 1930s, 20 percent of women worked outside the home (Kandal

1988). By contrast, in the early 1990s, the percentage of women working outside the home had risen to nearly 60 percent. From 1940 to 1945, women became involved in war efforts as they worked in factories. After the war, men leaving military service returned to their jobs and women were encouraged to return to their homes. The 1950s marked a retrenchment of women at home. The government as well as women's magazines pressured women to stay at home and take care of the family. Not until the 1960s did a new women's movement emerge with a renewed fight for women's rights and equality.

The 1960s bore witness to a large increase in government interest in women's rights, in both the executive and legislative branches. Congress outpaced the Supreme Court on the question of women's individual rights (Hoff-Wilson 1991). As Gerald Rosenberg points out in his book *The Hollow Hope* (1991), the courts had been criticized as being hostile to women's rights until the 1970s. But then in the 1970s, the Court began to make gender-based case-law history (Hoff-Wilson 1991). Rosenberg outlines the trajectory of legislation, beginning in 1963 when Congress passed the Equal Pay Act, which applies to all employees covered by the minimum-wage provisions of the Fair Labor Standards Act. The Equal Pay Act prohibits employers from paying different wages to men and women for equal work on jobs requiring equal skill, effort, and responsibility and performed under similar working conditions. The next year saw the passage of the 1964 Civil Rights Act, the most sweeping civil rights bill in American history. Title VII, the job discrimination section of the act, prohibited employment discrimination on the basis of race, color, religion, or national origin, with the basis of sex added to the act by amendment (Rosenberg 1991). Congress passed more women's rights legislation in the 1970s than had been passed in the history of the country (Rosenberg 1991). The Equal Employment Opportunity Commission (EEOC), created by the 1964 Civil Rights Act to administer Title VII, issued guidelines in 1968 banning sex-segregated job advertisements.

In the 1970s, the executive branch banned sex discrimination in employment and by lending institutions. The Equal Rights Amendment (ERA) was passed at the federal level on March 22, 1972 (but it was not ratified by the necessary number of states over the next ten years in order to become law). Presidents Johnson and Nixon both supported the ERA. In 1976–77, legislation was enacted banning sex discrimination in federally funded vocational programs and in credit transactions (Rosenberg 1991).

As to the success of these legislative reforms, Paul Burstein, in his 1989 article "Attacking Sex Discrimination in the Labor Market: A Study in Law and Politics," concluded that twenty years' experience of Equal Employment Opportunity (EEO) cases shows that these measures can improve conditions for women in the labor force, reducing both occupational segregation and income differences between men and women. His analysis of EEOC cases based on sex discrimination in employment between 1963 and 1985 addresses those changes.

In considering the history of judicial involvement and Court action regarding women's rights, we can go back to 1868 and the passage of the Fourteenth Amendment, which reads: "No state shall make or enforce any law which shall abridge the privileges or immunities of citizens of the United States; nor shall any State deprive any person of life, liberty, or property, without due process of law, nor deny to any person within its jurisdiction the equal protection of the laws." The first case challenging sex discrimination as a violation of the Fourteenth Amendment was *Bradwell v. Illinois* (1873). Bradwell was a married woman who wanted to join the bar in Illinois. The Court ruled that equal protection had to do with race, not sex, and that the right to practice law was not a privilege and immunity of citizenship (Hoff-Wilson 1991; Goldstein 1988; Rosenberg 1991). The opinion went on to state that women had no legal existence separate from their husbands (Hoff-Wilson 1991).

It was not until one hundred years later, in 1971, that the Supreme Court held a state statute based on gender to be unconstitutional. According to Rosenberg (1991), other cases followed for women's rights. In 1971, in *Reed v. Reed,* the Court found unconstitutional an Idaho law that established an automatic preference for males as executors of wills. A 1974 case—*Kahn v. Shevin*—upheld a Florida statute that appeared to favor women by granting a property-tax exemption to widows but not widowers. In 1976, in *Craig v. Boren,* the Court threw out an Oklahoma law that allowed eighteen-year-old females to drink beer but required that males be twenty-one to do so. In several jury-duty cases, exemptions precluding women from serving on juries were invalidated, as in *Taylor v. Louisiana* (1975) and *Duren v. Missouri* (1979). All of these cases had to do with sex discrimination, and *Reed* is the frequently cited case that started the court fight for sex-based equality.

In 1971, in *Phillips v. Martin Marietta Corporation,* the Supreme Court tentatively struck down the exclusion of women with preschool children from holding certain jobs. Briefly, the sex discrimination cases were as follows.[2] In *Frontiero v. Richardson* (1973), considered the most important, the Court held unconstitutional a federal statute that granted dependency benefits to wives of servicemen without showing dependency but required husbands to show dependency. Then in 1974, in *Cleveland Board of Education v. LaFleur,* a state requirement that teachers leave their positions when five months pregnant was held to be unconstitutional. That same year, in *Geduldig v. Aiello,* the Court upheld California's refusal to grant pregnancy disability benefits to female workers against an equal protection challenge; and again, in *General Electric v. Gilbert* (1976), the Court held that an employer's disability plan that excluded pregnancy from its coverage did not violate Title VII of the 1964 Civil Rights Act. Yet, in *Nashville Gas Co. v. Satty,* the Court found a Title VII violation in a company policy requiring pregnant employees to take pregnancy leaves, denying sick pay, and depriving them of seniority when they returned.

Califano v. Webster (1977) upheld a provision of the Social Security Act giving a higher level of monthly benefits to retired female workers than to retired male workers. In *Dothard v. Rawlinson* (1977), the Court found minimum weight and height requirements for the job of prison guard to be in violation of Title VII of the 1964 Civil Rights Act. In 1978, in *City of Los Angeles Department of Water and Power v. Manhart,* the Court found a violation of Title VII in a pension plan that required larger premiums from women than from men. In 1981, the Supreme Court *allowed* sex-based wage discrimination claims to proceed under Title VII without being limited by the equal-work standard of the Equal Pay Act in *County of Washington, Oregon, v. Gunther.* In 1986, the Court upheld EEOC regulations that interpreted Title VII as prohibiting sexual harassment as a form of sex discrimination, in *Meritor Savings Bank v. Vinson,* and in 1987, the Court upheld an affirmative action plan that took account of gender in promotions, in *Johnson v. Transportation Agency, Santa Clara County.* In 1991, the Court heard *International Union v. Johnson Controls, Inc.,* concerning an employer's gender-based fetal-protection policy with regard to possible lead poisoning in fetuses of pregnant women. The Court held that the employer's policy was facially discriminatory and did not establish that sex was a bona fide occupational qualification (BFOQ).

The net result of these cases was that the Court struck down many gender-based distinctions in the 1970s and 1980s and in so doing lowered barriers to equal opportunity for women. But in spite of the apparent progress of both Congress and the Court in prohibiting sex discrimination, women's position in the labor market remained relatively unchanged (Rosenberg 1991). One of the recurring themes in the sex-discrimination cases has been that of sameness versus difference. Should women be treated the same as men or different from men? Ironically, the first case that brought this issue before the Court—*Muller v. Oregon* (1908)—was the same case that introduced social science into the Court in the form of the "Brandeis brief." As discussed above, Louis Brandeis represented the state of Oregon and argued that women needed to be protected under the law from working more than ten hours a day in factories because it would affect their health, safety, and welfare. Muller's attorney, William D. Fenton, arguing on behalf of the employer, aptly foresaw that protecting women by limiting their working hours might turn into a general restriction of women in the workplace (Hoff-Wilson 1991). Protective legislation also reinforced the stereotype of women as the weaker sex, frail, passive, and dependent. *Muller* opened the door to future gender bias in protective legislation (Hoff-Wilson 1991; Goldstein 1988).

By 1925, all but four states had limited working women's hours: eighteen states prescribed rest periods and meal hours; sixteen states prohibited night work in certain occupations; and thirteen had minimum wage regulations, as Nancy Cott reported in her 1990 article "Historical Perspectives." In the short term, women were protected and their conditions made better, but in the long run, such limitations had a negative impact on women's overall economic opportunities. This argument was made by supporters of the Equal Rights Amendment when it was first introduced in the 1920s. The anti-ERA group argued that the laws meant the greatest good to the greatest number of women workers, whereas the pro-ERA side argued that such laws hampered women's scope in the labor market (Cott 1990). That same dichotomy continued into the campaign for the ERA in the 1970s.

The sameness-versus-difference split recurs in cases regarding maternity leave (Cott 1990; Hoff-Wilson 1991; Minow 1990; Rhode 1989; Vogel 1992). The faction that ostensibly favors and defends pregnancy and maternity leave as a recognition of women's special needs supports difference. Weighing in in favor of sameness, the opposing faction opposes sex-specific leaves because they recreate stereotypes (Minow 1990). In the mid-1970s, the Court considered whether a constitutional or statutory problem arose when employers excluded pregnancy benefits from the health care insurance granted other employees. The Court reasoned that neither the guarantee of equal protection or the ban against sex discrimination forbade this exclusion. Minow (1990) comments that only a Court with no women on it could view pregnancy as unrelated to sex. In response to the Court's statutory ruling, Congress adopted the Pregnancy Discrimination Act, which forbids discrimination on the basis of pregnancy. The choice between women's rights based on their sameness to men versus rights based on their difference is a problem in at least two ways. If women claim they are the same as men, any signs of difference can be used against them; if they claim they are different, those differences can be used to exclude them. The Family and Medical Leave Act, passed in 1993, grew out of change in traditional roles and expectations regarding pregnancy and child care; it covers fathers and mothers alike. The Family Medical and Leave Act expanded the concept of pregnancy leave by breaking down the traditional expectation that the mother is the primary or exclusive caretaker of the children.

The classic issue of sameness/difference or of equality versus difference was argued in the *Sears* case (1986), which was not a case heard by the Supreme Court. A district court held that Sears Roebuck and Company had not demonstrated a pattern or practice of discrimination against women in hiring, promotion, or pay and that alleged statistical disparities between rank or salary of women and that of men were the result of "legitimate non-discriminatory reasons" (Hoff-Wilson 1991). Two historians—experts on either side—had to answer the question, "Are women like men?" when they testified in the suit filed against Sears. Sears maintained that women did not want "male" jobs. This case is particularly interesting because (1) female experts were used on both sides and pitted against each other; (2) statistics were used in the argument and the result; and (3) the legal issue was one of sameness versus difference. Scott (1990) says that when equality and difference are paired dichotomously, they structure an impossible choice. If one opts for equality, one accepts the notion that difference is antithetical to it. If one opts for difference, one admits that equality is unattainable. Feminists cannot give up difference, because it has been their most creative analytic tool; nor can they give up equality, because it refutes the principles and values of the very political system in which they need to operate (Scott 1990).

Tocqueville's analysis of women in America in 1835 essentially outlines the sameness-versus-difference argument of today. He espoused equality of the sexes, but by adhering strongly to the differences between them, he reinforced the differences and thereby perpetuated the inequality. He saw sexual equality as a positive phenomenon—resulting in the expanded role of women in this new America—but he was comparing it to the more rigid class structure of France and looking only at white middle-class women. He believed in a division of labor based on sex, in the difference between the sexes, and in the virtue of such a difference. In Chafetz's (1990) framework of gender inequality, such thinking is what prevents change in the gender-division of labor, continuing a resource base of superior male power.

Also at issue in the fight for equal rights in the workplace is "comparable worth"—receiving the same pay for doing comparable work. Justice Oliver Wendell Holmes said in 1925, in his dissent in *Adkins et al., v. Children's Hospital of the District of Columbia:* "I confess that I do not understand the principle on which the power to fix a minimum for the wages of women can be denied by those who admit the power to fix a maximum for their hours of work. . . . It will need more than the Nineteenth Amendment to convince me that there are no differences between men and women, or that legislation cannot take those differences into account." The problem is less one of equal pay for equal work than it is one of women's holding jobs that are female-dominated and therefore underpaid industry-wide. Historically, women have prepared and trained for jobs within industries that pay poorly, with education and health care as primary examples (Ries 1992). A further problem arises with the increase in the number of women taking on roles in the public sphere, which is not automatically accompanied by an opportunity to discharge themselves of domestic responsibilities, including child care. Tong argues that because of this doubling up of responsibility, women are still not liberated because they are not free to pursue the same economic and professional goals as men (Tong 1989). Patricia Collins, in her 1990 book *Black Feminist Thought,* argues that gender roles are tied to the dichotomous construction of two mutually exclusive institutions, wherein men work and women take care of families.

Despite equal pay legislation, equal employment opportunity, and affirmative action, women in the United States still earn less than men, and it is the concentration of women in the lower-paying jobs that makes it so (Freeman and Leonard 1987). Hartmann (1987) asserts that it may be *because* the jobs are performed by women that they are viewed as unskilled and lower paid, not just that low-wage, low-skill jobs are created and women are channeled into them. Such jobs are often called "pink-collar" jobs. For example, women make up 95 percent of registered nurses; 98 percent of kindergarten and pre-kindergarten teachers; 98 percent of secretaries, stenographers, and typists; 92 percent of telephone operators; and 96 percent of child-care workers (Stoper 1991).[3] The labor force is highly segregated by sex, with a large percentage of jobs filled to 80 percent or more by persons of the same sex (Stoper 1991).

Rosenberg argues that by 1987, after two decades of Supreme Court and legislative action, the relative position of men and women in terms of income was roughly the same as it had been thirty years earlier. One study concluded that in 1984, male high-school graduates had median incomes one and one-half times greater than those of women with college and graduate degrees (Rosenberg 1991). The U.S. Commission on Civil Rights reported in 1979 that there is discrimination against women everywhere in the job market. The Rand Corporation finds that if current trends continue, women will earn only 74 percent of men's income by the year 2000 (Rosenberg 1991). According to *Employment and Earnings,* a publication of the Bureau of Labor Statistics, and *Current Population Reports,* produced by the Bureau of the Census, female participation in the labor force increased to 57.5 percent from 51.7 percent between 1980 and 1990. Even though female income, as a percentage of male income, has gone up 10 percent in each of the last three decades, in 1990 it still was not yet 60 percent of what men earned. This largely has to do with the problem that a profession or occupation that is largely comprised of women pays less. In fact there is more disparity between females' and males' earnings than among the earnings of the different races. The Courts in the last twenty years did not end sex discrimination in the area of wage discrimination or comparable worth. Rosenberg concludes that what progress there has been has more to do with congressional and executive action than with the Court.

More recent studies indicate that the gender gap in wages has been narrowing significantly since the 1980s. June Ellenoff O'Neill, in her article "The Cause and Significance of the Declining Gender Gap in Pay" (1995), argues that a finding that women's wages are 72 percent those of men overstates the wage gap. She goes on to report that when the issue is analyzed on the basis of similar work experience, the gap narrows significantly: "For example, among women and men age 27–33 who have never had a child, the earnings of women in the National Longitudinal Survey of Youth are close to 98 percent of men's" (8). Likewise, Sally Pipes, in her article "Creating a Crisis in a Free Society" (1996), puts into perspective a recent study by Dun and Bradstreet: "According to Dun and Bradstreet, there are currently 7.7 million women-owned businesses in the United States generating $1.4 trillion in sales. These firms, with more than 15 million individuals on their payrolls, employ 35 percent more people than Fortune 500 companies do worldwide. Outside of the Fortune 1000, women hold 45 percent of all managerial positions" (5). This was meant to show the enormous gains women have made in the workplace during a time period that corresponds roughly to the one under examination in the present study. Pipes looks to the future by taking stock of the status of women and education. She cites the following statistics: women received over 50 percent of all bachelor's degrees conferred in the 1980s. In 1971, 4 percent of all MBAs were conferred on women. By 1991, women accounted for over 34 percent of all MBAs granted. From 1970 to 1990, the percentage of law degrees earned by women jumped from just over 5 percent to more than 42 percent. Likewise, over the same period, the percentage of medical degrees awarded to women moved from over 8 percent to over 34 percent.

O'Neill ties the narrowing but continued difference between men's and women's wages not to discrimination against women, but to choices women make about family care, and to women's domestic responsibilities. Pipes points to the firm foundation being laid today in education for women, which will prepare them to do well in the marketplace independent of, or in spite of, the government's application and enforcement of affirmative action or other regulatory employment policies.

The Cases: Sex Discrimination against Women on the Job, 1972–92

Thirteen cases involving sex discrimination against women on the job were decided by the U.S. Supreme Court between 1972 and 1992. These cases will be described and analyzed here for their use of social science data. We also will report the opinions of the lower courts and their references to social science literature and expert witnesses. As with the abortion cases, the description of each Supreme Court case and the decision are drawn from the syllabus, which tells the nature of the case, the lower courts' and Supreme Court's decisions, the names of those who wrote the majority opinion and the concurring and dissenting opinions, along with the vote. Each case discussion includes the number of citations to social science expert witnesses and social science literature.

The sample of sex-discrimination cases is limited to those in which suit was by or on behalf of women regarding sex discrimination on the job. Other important cases decided during the same time period were brought by men, especially regarding affirmative action and "reverse discrimination" claims, but these are not part of the study. *Frontiero* is usually considered the first, most important, and most frequently cited of the sex-discrimination cases.

Frontiero v. Richardson 411 U.S. 677 (1973)

> A married woman Air Force officer sought increased benefits for her husband as a "dependent." Statutes provide, solely for administrative convenience, that spouses of male members of the uniformed services are dependents for purposes of obtaining increased quarters allowances and medical and dental benefits, but spouses of female members are not dependents unless they are in fact dependent for over one-half of their support. When her application was denied for failure to satisfy the statutory dependency standard, appellant and her husband brought suit to District Court contending that the statutes deprived service women of due process. The District Court ruled adversely. The Supreme Court reversed the judgment. Justice Brennan, joined by Justices Douglas, White and Marshall[,] wrote the plurality opinion. Justice Stewart concurred, and Justices Powell, joined by Chief Justice Burger and Justice Blackmun[,] concurred but concluded that it was inappropriate to decide at this time whether sex is a suspect classification. Justice Rehnquist dissented. (8-1)

Arguing for the American Civil Liberties Union (ACLU) as *amicus curiae* for the appellants, and urging reversal, was Ruth Bader Ginsburg, now Justice Ginsburg.[4] Appellants contended that classifications based upon sex, like classifications based upon race, alienage, or national origin, are inherently suspect and subject to close judicial scrutiny. Justice Brennan in his opinion (682) says: "We agree and, indeed, find at least implicit support for such an approach in our unanimous decision only last Term in *Reed v. Reed.*" He notes (683) that the appellee in *Reed* argued that men are more conversant with business affairs than women and in general are better qualified to act as administrators of estates.

Justice Brennan writes (684) that there can be no doubt that "our Nation has had a long and unfortunate history of sex discrimination." Such discrimination was "rationalized by an attitude of 'romantic paternalism' which, in practical effect put women, not on a pedestal, but in a cage" (684). Such notions, Brennan contends, led to gross, stereotyped distinctions between the sexes, and he compares women's position to that of blacks under the pre–Civil War slave codes. He writes (685) that neither slaves nor women could hold office, serve on juries, bring suit, own property, or serve as guardians. Black men were given the right to vote in 1870, but all women were denied even that right for fifty more years. For this argument, he draws upon and refers to the following social science sources (684–87):

1. Amundsen, K., *The Silenced Majority: Women and American Democracy* (1970).
2. Kanowitz, L., *Women and the Law: The Unfinished Revolution* (1969), 5–6.
3. Montagu, A., *Man's Most Dangerous Myth* (1964).
4. Myrdal, G., *An American Dilemma* (1962), 1073.
5. *The President's Commission on the Status of Women, American Women* (1963).
6. *The President's Task Force on Women's Rights and Responsibilities, A Matter of Simple Justice* (1970).

In addition to these items, Brennan cited several law review articles dealing with sex discrimination, equal protection, and equal pay. Brennan writes (687) that Congress has manifested an increasing sensitivity to sex-based classifications, for example, in Title VII of the Civil Rights Act of 1964 and in the Equal Rights Amendment, which it passed in 1972 and submitted to the States for ratification. As a result, Brennan points out (688–90), sex, like race and alienage, is inherently suspect and subject to strict judicial scrutiny. Powell, with Burger and Blackmun, chose to wait for the passage of the ERA, recommending that there are times when the Court should restrain from making decisions and should leave it to the democratic institutions, rather than deciding "sensitive issues of broad social and political importance at the very time they are under consideration within the prescribed constitutional processes" (692). The district court and Justice Rehnquist saw the statute as a matter of administrative convenience and not as discriminatory. Five justices refused to subscribe to this suspect-classification argument against subjecting cases involving gender discrimination to strict scrutiny under the Fourteenth Amendment, meaning that there had to be a "compelling state interest" to justify such legislation (Hoff-Wilson 1991).[5]

The Supreme Court majority opinion contained twelve references to social science. This statistic is particularly interesting because in the same year, in *Roe*, the Court made no references to social science. The district court in *Frontiero* made no references to social science.

Briefs for *Frontiero v. Richardson*

The *amicus* brief submitted for the appellants by the ACLU contained a number of social science references. The historical perspective presented was much like that presented by Justice Brennan in the plurality opinion, including the reference to Tocqueville's view of women in *Democracy in America*. The brief also used (9) Ibsen's observation from *A Doll's House* (M. Meyer trans., 1965): "A Woman cannot be herself in a modern society. It is an exclusively male society with laws made by men, and with prosecutors and judges who assess female conduct from a male standpoint." The ACLU brief quotes Kanowitz and Myrdal regarding the analogy between women and slaves, which Justice Brennan utilized as well. The ACLU also used—though Brennan did not—a frequently quoted remark by the abolitionist and former slave Sojourner Truth, which she made at a women's rights convention in Akron, Ohio, in 1851. Responding to clergymen who maintained that women held a favored position and were too weak to vote, Truth said: "The man over there says women need to be helped into carriages and lifted over ditches, and to have the best place everywhere. Nobody ever helps me into carriages or over puddles, or gives me the best place—and ain't I a woman?" (16). As pointed out in the ACLU brief (17), women's legal status has improved since the nineteenth century, but even in the 1970s, woman's place was subordinate to man's, a fact still reflected in many statutes. In 1940, 28.9 percent of women were in the labor force; in 1971, 42.7 percent were employed (25). Women earned 59.5 percent of the male median income. Many observers argue that women are secondary earners, but that is not so, with 7.6 million married males unemployed or not in the labor force in 1971. The ACLU brief also confronts the problem with *Muller* and the limitation on hours to be worked by women. There was (1) recognition of the intolerable exploitation of women workers and (2) concern for the health of the sex believed to be weaker in physical structure. But in the long run, the laws "protecting" women ended up "protecting" them from better-paying jobs and opportunities for promotion (39). Kanowitz, Myrdal, Montagu, and the President's Commission on the Status of Women, all of which were cited in the plurality opinion, were first cited in the ACLU brief. Some of the other social science articles cited in the ACLU brief—in addition to historical and feminist writings, law review articles, and Department of Labor statistical reports—included:

1. Bird, C., *Born Female: The High Cost of Keeping Women Down* (1968).
2. Citizen's Advisory Council on the Status of Women, *Report of the Task Force on Family Law and Policy* (1968).

3. Dahlstrom (ed.), *The Changing Roles of Men and Women* (1971).

4. Ferris, A., *Indicators of Trends in the Status of American Women* (1971), 103.

5. Janeway, E., *Man's World Woman's Place: A Study in Social Mythology* (1971), 7.

6. Murray, "The Rights of Women," in *The Rights of Americans: What They Are—What They Should Be* (ed. N. Dorsen, 1971).

7. Watson, *Social Psychology: Issues and Insights* (1966), 435–36.

Comparable to the analysis of the briefs submitted in *Roe*, there were in *Frontiero* a substantial number of social science references presented to the Court for its consideration. But the difference in the two cases is that in *Frontiero* the majority opinion used them, while in *Roe* the majority opinion did not. As with *Roe*, the submission of these publications in 1973 meant that they were also there for use in the cases to follow, if the justices were so inclined.

Cleveland Board of Education v. LaFleur 414 U.S. 632 (1974)

Pregnant public school teachers brought actions challenging the constitutionality of mandatory maternity leave rules of the Cleveland, Ohio[,] and Chesterfield County, VA[,] School Boards. The Cleveland rule requires a pregnant school teacher to take unpaid maternity leave five months before the expected childbirth and not return until the semester after the child is three months old. Chesterfield County requires the teacher to leave work four months before the anticipated childbirth and return after reelegible. The Court of Appeals reversed lower courts. Chesterfield was found to be constitutional and Cleveland unconstitutional. The Supreme Court held that both mandatory termination provisions violate the Due Process Clause of the Fourteenth Amendment. The Cleveland three-month rule is also unconstitutional, but Chesterfield, without unnecessary presumption, comports with due process requirements. Justice Stewart delivered the opinion[,] in which Brennan, White, Marshall and Blackmun joined. Justices Douglas and Powell, separately, concurred. Justice Rehnquist filed a dissenting opinion, in which Justice Burger joined. (7-2)

The ACLU again filed a brief urging reversal, of which Ruth Bader Ginsburg was a part. In the majority opinion, Justice Stewart wrote (640) that by acting to penalize a pregnant teacher for deciding to bear a child, overly restrictive maternity leave regulations can constitute a heavy burden on the exercise of protected freedoms. He adds that the EEOC and other federal agencies have forbidden discrimination against pregnant workers. While acknowledging the importance of continuity in instruction, the regulations were inspired by less-weighty considerations when the rule was adopted in the 1950s, according to district court testimony of the former superintendent of schools in Cleveland. According to the former superintendent, the rule was to save pregnant teachers from embarrassment at the hands of giggling schoolchildren, because some of the pupils would say: "My teacher swallowed a watermelon, things like that" (641).

Justice Stewart suggests the role of outmoded taboos in the adoption of the rules and quotes a previous case: "Whatever may have been the reaction in Queen Victoria's time, pregnancy is no longer a dirty word" (641). As for the argument that pregnancy-related medical emergencies might arise, Justice Stewart suggests they can be accommodated like any other medical emergencies, through the use of substitute teachers. Medical experts on both sides at district court are quoted in the Supreme Court opinion as generally agreeing that pregnancy leave-taking is an individual matter (646). Justice Stewart went on to say that administrative convenience alone is insufficient to make valid what otherwise is a violation of due process of law, and which cannot pass muster under the Due Process Clause of the Fourteenth Amendment (647–48). Thus, the question of leave-taking is not whether the school board's goals are legitimate, but whether the particular means infringe upon the teacher's constitutional liberty, and the Court finds that it does.

Justice Rehnquist's dissent concludes: "If legislative bodies are to be permitted to draw a general line anywhere short of the delivery room, I can find no judicial standard of measurement which says the ones drawn here were invalid" (660). The dissent in the appeals court for *Cleveland* agrees with Rehnquist's point when the judge says: "We do not sit as a super Board of Education," arguing that it is not the prerogative of the court to determine what is a better regulation (1189). The same dissent says that expert testimony established that every pregnancy impairs to some degree the ability to teach and supervise children (1189).

The Cleveland district court introduced testimony on violence in schools as another justification for the restrictions. This testimony was not included by either the appeals court or the Supreme Court. A plaintiff's witness testified that the incidence of violence in the Cleveland schools had increased, with 256 assaults the previous year, and with the confiscation of guns and knives, and argued that "[i]n an environment where the possibility of violence and accidents exists, pregnancy greatly magnifies the probability of serious injury" (1213). The district court also relied upon the 1908 case of *Muller v. Oregon,* in which the work-hour limitation statute pertaining to women took into consideration the differences in the sexes.

The Supreme Court makes no reference to social science in the majority, but made one in the dissenting opinion. The appeals court makes no reference, whereas the district court cites two references to violence that were introduced by witnesses at trial.

Geduldig v. Aiello 417 U.S. 632 (1974)

California has a disability insurance system for private employees temporarily disabled from working by an injury or illness not covered by workmen's compensation. A disability resulting from an individual's court commitment, such as that imposed on a drug addict or sexual psychopath[,] is not compensable, nor are certain disabilities attributable to pregnancy. A District Court upheld four women's contentions that the exclusion violated the Equal Protection Clause. The Supreme Court, however, reversed, saying that California's decision not to insure does not constitute an invidious discrimination in violation of the Equal Protection Clause. Justice Stewart delivered the opinion of the Court, in which Justices Burger, White, Blackmun, Powell and Rehnquist joined. Justice Brennan filed a dissenting opinion, in which Douglas and Marshall joined. (6-3)

Justice Stewart wrote the opinion, as he had done in *Cleveland*, but in this case, the opinion upheld a state disability insurance program and denied benefits for pregnancy-related disabilities. Justices Brennan, Douglas, and Marshall joined together and dissented, as they had in the abortion cases where restrictions were brought to limit the right to an abortion. Ruth Bader Ginsburg again took part in the ACLU brief filed in the case. In *Geduldig,* Justice Stewart says that since only pregnant women and nonpregnant persons, including men, were involved, there was no gender discrimination and that herein lies one of the most unusual, dichotomous classifications of people. He explicates that the program divides potential recipients into two groups—"pregnant women" and "non-pregnant persons." While the first group is exclusively female, the second can include both sexes (407). Pregnancy is just another physical condition removed from compensable disabilities, and while it is true that only women can become pregnant, it does not follow that every legislative classification concerning pregnancy is a sex-based classification, such as those in *Reed* or *Frontiero* (496).

Brennan, in dissent, vehemently disagrees, insisting that the state created a double standard for disability compensation, by singling out a disability peculiar to women for less-favorable treatment (484). Men, he adds, may be covered for uniquely male treatments, such as circumcision. He relies on statistics from the Department of Labor to show that nearly two-thirds of women who work do so of necessity and that in 1972, a woman working full time had a median income only 57.9 percent that of males (502–3). Brennan says (503) that he views the Court's decision as a retreat. As with the abortion cases, the lower courts are seen to be trying to follow the Supreme Court's ruling, as exemplified by the district court's statement (801): "Having found that the exclusion of pregnancy-related disabilities is not based upon a classification having a rational and substantial relationship to a legitimate state purpose," the court must hold the provision of excluding these benefits unconstitutional. This was reversed by the Supreme Court.

The Supreme Court majority opinion made no reference to social science; the dissenting opinion had four citations to social science findings, while the district court had none.

General Electric v. Gilbert 429 U.S. 125 (1976)

This class action was brought challenging as violative of Title VII of the Civil Rights Act of 1964 the disability plan of General Electric. The District Court held that the exclusion constituted sex discrimination, and the Court of Appeals affirmed. The Supreme Court reversed[,] saying that the plan does not exclude anyone because of gender, but rather just one physical condition—pregnancy—and does not violate Title VII because of its failure to cover pregnancy-related disabilities. Gender-based discrimination does not result simply because an employer's disability benefits plan is less than all-inclusive. Justice Rehnquist delivered the opinion[,] in which Burger, Stewart, White and Powell joined, and in which Blackmun joined in part. Stewart and Blackmun filed separate statements concurring and Brennan filed a dissenting opinion, in which Marshall and Stevens joined. (6-3)

Thomas Emerson has written, "A Supreme Court which can decide that an employment disability plan covering every form of disability except pregnancy does not discriminate against women plainly has need of education on these matters."[6] Justice Rehnquist relied heavily on Justice Stewart's classification of people in *Geduldig* into two groups, pregnant women and all others, so the majority opinion in essence held that the concept of discrimination based on sex was identical under Title VII and the equal protection clause—refusing to distinguish between the two (Hoff-Wilson 1991). The decision questioned the validity of the 1972 EEOC guideline, and it meant that less weight would be given to such guidelines. *General Electric,* in other words, dismissed the great deference that lower courts had previously given EEOC guidelines (Hoff-Wilson 1991). Sports injuries, attempted suicides, venereal disease, elective cosmetic surgery, prostate disease, circumcision, hair transplants, vasectomies, and even disabilities incurred while committing a crime were all covered by the G.E. plan, but not pregnancy-related diseases (Hoff-Wilson 1991).

The EEOC and six federal courts of appeal had found the G.E. plan discriminatory, but the Supreme Court simply fell back on *Geduldig,* where Justice Stewart had said that only pregnant women and nonpregnant persons (including men) were involved. So, there was no gender discrimination. Thus, two-thirds of the justices reiterated that there was no violation of the equal protection clause of the Fourteenth Amendment because neither insurance plan excluded anyone on the basis of gender alone (Hoff-Wilson 1991). The result was that the Supreme Court held that employers need not compensate women for maternity-related disabilities under employee insurance plans. Congress overruled this decision, however, in 1977.

Ruth Bader Ginsburg filed a brief with the Women's Law Project et al. rather than with the ACLU in this case. The majority opinion refers to statistics and testimony from the district court on G.E.'s experience that the insurance plan costs 170 percent more for females than males, but the Court based no conclusions on that information. Brennan, in dissent, accuses the Court of disregarding a history of G.E.'s practices that undercut the employment opportunities of women who become pregnant while employed, practices based on an old belief that women played only a minor and temporary role in the labor force (149–50). Brennan quotes from a 1926 G.E. policy that offered no benefit plan to its female employees because "women did not recognize the responsibilities of life, for they probably were hoping to get married soon and leave the company" (150). In the 1930s and 1940s, females were eligible to join the disability program. Quoting governmental investigations, reported in studies from the Departments of Commerce and Labor, Brennan says that pregnancy exclusions built into disability programs financially burden women and break down the continuity of the employment relationship, exacerbating women's transient role in the labor force (158).

The district court addresses the issue already raised, concerning whether pregnancy is voluntary, and concludes that it may be controlled to some extent, but that even contraception has failure rates (375). In addition, pregnancy always has some medical and possibly disabling risk. The district court concludes that the "great mass of expert testimony presented here on the subject merely confirms what appears obvious to any layman; pregnancy is not a disease, as that term is commonly understood; it is, however, at times, physically disabling, and the Court so finds" (375). The district court notes that experts testified on socioeconomic concerns, including G.E.'s assertion that benefits for pregnancy will encourage births, and that encouragement is contrary to a national policy of limited population growth. The district court found such testimony to be self-serving or irrelevant and said that broad social concerns are more appropriate for legislative consideration. Such an observation pointing to the separation of powers is a consistent theme within all the courts. The courts recognize not only that they should not be influenced by public concerns, but that such concerns are the role of the legislature.

The district court found one example of G.E.'s conflicting policies both highly amusing and dated. While the company refused to compensate disability related to pregnancy, it also announced that it would give five shares of stock to any employee who had a child born on October 15, 1953, G.E.'s seventy-fifth anniversary. G.E. estimated it would give fifteen to twenty awards; it gave 180 (379). The district court says that plaintiffs have introduced much evidence to demonstrate that G.E.'s history is dominated by male chauvinism; the Supreme Court similarly deems this legally irrelevant and makes no findings with respect to that contention (380). Nevertheless, the justices rely upon certain statistics they find relevant, such as data from G.E. and government reports regarding annual births in the working population, mothers in the labor force, and G.E.'s pregnancy-related absences.

The Supreme Court's majority opinion made no reference to social science but the dissenting opinion contained three such citations. The appeals court made no reference to social science, but the district court made three citations to social science statistics.

Dothard v. Rawlinson 433 U.S. 321 (1977)

Applicant for employment as a prison guard in Alabama filed suit after being rejected because she failed to meet the minimum 120 pound weight and 5 feet two inches height requirement. The District Court decided in appellee's favor of a prima facie case of unlawful sex discrimination. The Court ruled that being male was not a BFOQ (bona-fide-occupation-qualification) in an Alabama male maximum security penitentiary. The Supreme Court held that Title VII prohibited the height and weight requirements but because of the prison conditions in Alabama, the use of women guards in contact positions in the maximum security male penitentiaries would pose a substantial security problem directly linked to the sex of the prison guard. Justice Stewart wrote the opinion of the Court, in which Justices Powell, Stevens, Brennan and Marshall joined in parts. Justice Marshall filed an opinion concurring in part and dissenting in part, in which Justice Brennan joined. Justice White filed a dissenting opinion. (6-3)

This case turned on the issue of the tendency to discriminate against one sex (or race) if the plaintiff could present general statistical evidence on the disproportionate impact that the particular requirement has on one sex (or race). For this reason, sex-discrimination cases would be expected to contain more statistical or social science data. If 98 percent of males meet a particular requirement but only 2 percent of females do, then there is disproportionate impact (Goldstein 1988). This creates a *prima facie* case of sex discrimination, which means that the job requirement in question is then presumed to be discriminatory until proven otherwise. At that point, the burden of proof shifts to the defendant employer to prove that the requirement bears a "manifest relation to the employment in question" (Goldstein 1988). Then, the plaintiff must show that other nondiscriminatory selection devices are available to achieve the same goal as the discriminatory one, and if the plaintiff can do this, the Court is supposed to strike down the discriminatory requirement (Goldstein 1988). (Ruth Bader Ginsburg was part of the *amicus curiae* brief filed by the ACLU.)

The plaintiff (Diane Rawlinson) had no difficulty demonstrating the disproportionate impact the height and weight requirements had on women, because more than 99 percent of American men are taller than 5 feet 2 inches and weigh more than 120 pounds; only 59 percent of American women meet those requirements (Goldstein 1988). The Alabama Corrections Board argued that the height and weight requirements were meant to achieve a certain level of physical strength among prison guards but it presented no evidence to support its assumption and offered no argument why a direct strength test could not be substituted for the height and weight test. Thus, the district court concluded that the height and weight requirement violated Title VII of the Civil Rights Act (Goldstein 1988). A majority of six justices agreed but held that Alabama had bona-fide job-related reasons for excluding women guards from contact jobs within male maximum-security penitentiaries. Brennan and Marshall dissented on the latter, agreeing with the district court. Justice White dissented entirely, believing that a valid statistical demonstration of *prima facie* discrimination had not been made (Goldstein 1988).

In the majority opinion, Justice Stewart wrote that women comprise 52.75 percent of the Alabama population and 36.89 percent of its total labor force but only 12.9 percent of correctional counselor positions (329). The district court had reported statistics, which Justice Stewart repeated, showing that the height requirement would exclude 33.29 percent of women in the United States and only 1.28 percent of men, and the weight restriction would exclude 22.29 percent of women and only 2.35 percent of men. Combined, 41.3 percent of the female population and less than 1 percent of the male population would be excluded (329–330). Justice Stewart notes also that the environment in Alabama's penitentiaries is a peculiarly inhospitable one for human beings of either sex and that a "jungle atmosphere" prevails, according to a federal district court. Such "rampant violence" was found to be constitutionally intolerable (334). According to expert testimony at the district court level, sex offenders make up 20 percent of prison population.

Regarding the claim that a particular job is too dangerous for women, the rejoinder of Title VII is to allow the individual woman to make that choice for herself (335). Justice Stewart argues that a woman's ability to maintain prison security, however, could be reduced by her "womanhood" because sex offenders may assault her, or inmates deprived of a normal heterosexual environment might assault a female guard because she is a woman (335). The plaintiff's own expert, it is noted, testified that dormitory housing for aggressive inmates poses a greater security problem than single-cell lockups and that it would be unwise to use women as guards in a prison where even 10 percent of the inmates had been convicted of sex crimes. Experts on both sides testified to the risk of using women as guards in contact positions; therefore, the Court holds that being male is a BFOQ.

Justice Rehnquist comments on the statistics, agreeing that the statistics relied upon in the case were sufficient, absent rebuttal, to sustain a finding of a *prima facie* violation; these statistics reveal a significant discrepancy between the numbers of men, as opposed to women, who are automatically disqualified by reason of the height and weight requirements (338). If the defendants in a Title VII suit believe there is any reason to discredit the statistics, they need to challenge or impeach their reliability, but appellants made no such effort (339).

Justice Marshall, with Justice Brennan, agrees with the Court's analysis of height and weight but disagrees that there is a BFOQ exception. The district court provided information on the successful experiences of other states, such as California and Washington, in using female prison guards. Justice Marshall disagrees with the Court's judgment that because of the bad conditions, women should be discriminated against, which he says is like saying two wrongs make a right (320). He claims there is no evidence in the record to show that women guards would create any danger to security in Alabama prisons significantly greater than that which already exists. All of the dangers, with one exception, are inherent in a prison setting whatever the gender of the guards (342). Justice Marshall says that the appellant's witnesses ignore individual differences among members of each sex when they claim that women guards are not strict disciplinarians and are physically less capable of protecting themselves, or when they assert that inmates would take advantage of women guards as they did their own mothers but that male guards are strong father figures who easily maintain discipline (344).

Justice Marshall then takes the Court to task, saying that it justifies its decision on the basis of the belief that women as guards will provoke sexual assault; he points out that one of the most insidious of the old myths about women is that, wittingly or not, they are seductive sexual objects (345). Yet the Court provides no evidence of assaults on female guards. Justice Marshall would instead have sex offenders begin the process of adaptation by learning to relate to women guards in a socially acceptable manner. "To deprive women of job opportunities because of the threatened behavior of convicted criminals is to turn our social priorities upside down" (346). It seems odd, Justice Marshall continues (346), that state officials who have been violating the principles of human decency for years in the operation of their prisons should become concerned about inmate privacy (as it relates to female guards), which he considers a feeble excuse of discrimination.

At the district court level the cases of *Mieth* and *Dothard* were combined. Ms. Mieth was denied employment as a state trooper with the Alabama Department of Public Safety. The requirements for the trooper job were a minimum height of 5′9″ and weight of 160 pounds. The argument was that taller state troopers hold an advantage over shorter ones, and that troopers spend much time alone, patrolling the rural highways of Alabama without backup. Thus the director of the department believes that physical strength is important (1173). When Mieth met with Colonel E. C. Dothard, the director of the Department of Public Safety of the State of Alabama, requesting a waiver of height and weight restrictions, Dothard said he would "never put a woman on the road because of the dangers involved," but in a courtly gesture he presented her with a certificate making her an "Honorary State Trooper" (1174). Colonel Dothard testified at trial that he feels that women should not be state troopers (1180), which left little doubt of the intention to discriminate.

Plaintiffs at the district court offered into evidence the testimony of two experts—T. W. White and Peter B. Bloch, a statistician and a research analyst—who collaborated in publishing the study *Police Officer Height and Selected Aspects of Performance* for the Police Foundation (October 1975). Based on their findings in two police departments (Nassau County, New York, and Dallas, Texas), the experts concluded that, with one exception, there were no statistically significant effects of height upon performance. In another report, "Policewomen on Patrol" (1974), also published by the Police Foundation (a nonprofit organization funded by the Ford Foundation), the authors studied the performance of women patrol officers in Washington, D.C., and found it to be appropriate to hire women on the same basis as men.

In *Dothard,* the Supreme Court majority opinion cited social science references four times, and the dissent three times. The district court had ten citations to social science experts, literature, and statistics.

Nashville Gas Company v. Satty 434 U.S. 136 (1977)

Action was brought by employee alleging sex discrimination in employment with respect to pregnancy. The District Court entered judgment for the employee, and the employer appealed. The Court of Appeals affirmed, and the Supreme Court held that 1) the employer's policy of denying accumulated seniority to female employees returning from pregnancy leave constituted an unlawful employment practice, but 2) the case would have to be remanded to determine whether this was a mere pretext designed to effect invidious discrimination against members of one sex. Justice Rehnquist wrote the opinion. Justice Powell filed an opinion concurring in part in which Justices Brennan and Marshall joined. Justice Stevens filed an opinion concurring in the judgment. (9-0)

Justice Rehnquist wrote the opinion for a unanimous court, contending that there are two policies at issue: not giving sick pay for pregnancy and denying accumulated seniority to employees returning to work following disability caused by childbirth (138). They found the policy of denying accumulated seniority to be in violation of Title VII. The District Court differentiates between the two kinds of sex discrimination: (1) one arising under the Equal Protection Clause of the Fourteenth Amendment and (2) one arising under Title VII of the Civil Rights Act of 1964 (770). The former needs to show a "reasonable basis" for the legislative determination. The latter must be an actual business necessity for employment policies that discriminate on the basis of sex (770). Thus, for example, *Geduldig,* according to the district court, was brought under the Equal Protection Clause. The standard was one of legislative reasonableness. In this case, the defendant has introduced no proof of any business necessity so it was assumed that no such justification exists. (Ruth Bader Ginsburg again filed a brief with the ACLU.)

The Supreme Court, appeal court, and district court opinions made no references to social science in the case.

City of Los Angeles Department of Water and Power v. Manhart
553 F 2d 581 (1978)

Suit was filed for present or former female employees of petitioner Los Angeles Department of Water and Power alleging that the Department's requirement that female employees make larger contributions to its pension fund than male employees violated 703 (a)(1) of Title VII of the Civil Rights Act of 1964, which make[s] it unlawful for an employer to discriminate against any individual because of sex. The District Court held that the contribution differential violated 703 (a)(1) and ordered a refund. The Court of Appeals affirmed. The Supreme Court held that deductions by employer of larger amounts from wages of female employees than from male employees for the pension fund held a violation of federal law and that men and women must be treated equally with regard to retirement benefits. They disagreed with allowing a retroactive monetary recovery because of the grave consequences that drastic changes in legal rules can have on pension funds, which must be commanded by legislative action. Justice Stevens delivered the opinion of the Court, in which all the Justices joined, concurred and dissented in various parts. Justice Marshall filed an opinion dissenting with regard to retroactive portion. Justice Brennan took no part in the case.

Up until the time of *Los Angeles v. Manhart,* the cases regarding penalties on pregnancy had been *Cleveland, Geduldig, General Electric,* and *Nashville,* while *Dothard* dealt with equal protection. *Los Angeles v. Manhart,* on the other hand, deals with pensions, as does *Washington v. Gunther.* As with the other sex-discrimination cases discussed here, Ruth Bader Ginsburg filed a brief of *amicus curiae* for the ACLU.

Justice Stevens writes (707) that there are both real and fictional differences between women and men. For example, it is true that the average man is taller than the average woman, but it is not true that the average woman driver is more accident prone than the average man. Before the Civil Rights Act of 1964 was enacted, Justice Stevens says (707), an employer could fashion his or her personnel policies on the basis of assumptions about the differences between men and women, whether the assumptions were valid or not. In this case, he says, it is true that women live longer than men, as a class, but all individuals in those classes do not share the characteristic that differentiate the average; the question is whether the individual is discriminated against. If height is a requirement for a job, a tall woman may not be refused employment simply because women are on the average too short (708). The result of the policy was that women received smaller paychecks because of their sex.

The opinion relies on actuarial studies (709) that disclose that whatever benefits men lose in primary coverage for themselves (because they die sooner) they may regain in secondary coverage for their wives (who live longer). A study by R. Retherford, *The Changing Sex Differential in Mortality* (1975:71–82), suggests that other social causes, such as drinking, eating, or even discrimination, may affect the mortality differential. When insurance risks are grouped, the better risks always subsidize the poorer risks. The result of the water and power department's policy was a 14.48 percent differential between contributions of men and those of women (712). In one example, this meant that a woman had contributed $18,000 to her pension fund, while a similarly situated male would have contributed less than $3,000 (Goldstein 1988).

The court of appeals made a particularly convincing and tightly constructed argument, though it referenced no actuarial studies. It claimed, for example, that discriminating against women in their retirement contributions in no way affects the ability of the department to provide water and power to the citizens of Los Angeles—so there is no "relevant business function" being affected (587). The court presents previous cases to show considerations that have been found illegal, such as forcing women to retire earlier because it was thought they were not capable of performance as long as men; terminating women employees who married because it was believed they could not work effectively and keep an adequate home; or, as in *Phillips v. Martin Marietta* in 1971, refusing to hire women with preschool children because of family responsibilities.

The district court judges believe that actuarial tables do not predict the length of any particular individual's life. They refer to a *Harvard Law Review* article, "Employment Discrimination and Title VII of the Civil Rights Act of 1964" (1971). In discussing discrimination based on statistical differences and the life insurance benefit program, they find that employers must provide the same life insurance benefits to males and females, even though premiums will be higher for males due to female longevity, because Title VII requires evaluation on an individual basis rather than a prediction made on the basis of a sex-defined group (983). Each of the courts was careful to point out the problem of holding stereotypes and assumptions about women as a group.

The majority opinion of the Supreme Court made nine references to social science in the form of actuarial studies and studies of sex discrimination found in law reviews. In Burger's dissent, joined by Rehnquist, he cited social science data twice. The appeals court made no direct reference to social science, but the district court made three references, which were then referenced by the Supreme Court.

County of Washington, Oregon, v. Gunther 452 U.S. 161 (1981)

Women employed as guards in the female section of petitioner county's jail until the section was closed, filed suit under Title VII for back pay alleging that they had been paid lower wages than male guards in the male section of the jail and that part of this differential was attributable to intentional sex discrimination, since it was lower than that warranted by its own survey. The District Court rejected the claim, ruling that a sex-based wage discrimination claim cannot be brought under Title VII unless it would satisfy the equal work standard of the Equal Pay Act. The Court of Appeals reversed. The Supreme Court affirmed, ruling that the practice held violation of federal law. Justice Brennan delivered the opinion of the Court which Justices White, Marshall, Blackmun and Stevens joined. Justice Rehnquist filed a dissenting opinion in which Justices Burger, Stewart and Powell joined. (5-4)

In the particular joining of the justices, this decision is much more reminiscent of the abortion decisions than of decisions in the other sex-discrimination cases. In *Gunther,* the Supreme Court for the first time acknowledged (however narrowly) that comparable worth was a valid legal theory; it found that Title VII coverage applied even to situations in which no male employees performed substantially equal work for higher wages. Specifically the Court held that the Bennett Amendment did not limit sex-based wage discrimination claims under

Title VII to equal-work claims (Hoff-Wilson 1991). The primary difference between the majority and dissenting opinions is that the majority opinion rules that the Bennett Amendment does not restrict Title VII's prohibition of sex-based wage discrimination to claims for equal pay for equal work (161). The dissenting opinion holds that one cannot ignore the issue of comparability in jobs, as the Court did. The majority decided that the equal work limitation of the Equal Pay Act had not been incorporated into Title VII.

The "comparable worth" issue is a thorny one, a subject even the Supreme Court avoids whenever possible. While the Equal Pay Act and Title VII of the Civil Rights Act of 1964 forbid sex discrimination, it is not clear whether those laws cover comparable worth, which is often called "the civil rights issue of the 1980s" (Goldstein 1988). Comparable worth is a pressing topic on the feminist agenda. Statistics are cited to support claims that female full-time workers continue to earn only 60 percent of what males earn, and to show that this gap is largely attributable to the fact that jobs held largely by women tend to have lower wages than jobs held largely by men (Goldstein 1988). However, such statistics are now coming to be disputed by people such as June Ellenoff O'Neill and Sally Pipes, as detailed in our brief history of women's status in the workplace.

Though the Supreme Court declined to address comparable worth, the issue lurked in the background of *Gunther* (Goldstein 1988). Interestingly enough, the lower court ruled that the job in question was not substantially equal to that of male jail guards because there were fewer prisoners in the female section of the county jail. The women guards did more clerical work than the men, and the men were considered more qualified since they also actively served as deputies. The women claimed, nevertheless, that the county administrators had evaluated the women's job as worth 95 percent of the men's and then proceeded to downgrade the salary to 70 percent because they knew that women would work for less than men, thus lowering it below the degree appropriate for noncomparability of the work on the basis of sheer sex discrimination. The Court agreed, and advocates of comparable worth took comfort in the decision. Proponents hope to convince courts that paying lower wages for female-dominated jobs is not simply a response to market forces and that sex discrimination pervades the market and shapes the market forces (Goldstein 1988).

Justice Brennan, in his opinion, while delineating how the claim is not based on the "controversial concept of comparable worth" (167), nonetheless cites five references on the subject, saying it has been the subject of much scholarly debate, as to both its elements and its merits as a legal or economic principle. It is here that there is overlap between legal and social science research. The references are to legal articles, which deal with sex discrimination beyond the law; in addition there is a reference to the hearings of the EEOC on the question as well as to D. Treiman's *Job Evaluation: An Analytic Review* (1979), a study of job evaluation systems. Justice Rehnquist argues that the Bennett Amendment incorporates the equal work standard of discrimination into Title VII; he says the Court blithely ignores this and chooses rather to interpret the Bennett Amendment as incorporating only the Equal Pay Act's four affirmative defenses and not the equal work requirement, an interpretation that Justice Rehnquist believes does not survive scrutiny (198). In his dissent, Justice Rehnquist says in sum that Title VII and the Equal Pay Act, taken together, provided a balanced approach to resolving sex-based wage discrimination claims, with Title VII guaranteeing that qualified female employees will have access to all jobs and the Equal Pay Act assuring that men and women performing the same work will be paid equally (201). Whatever the arguments, the result was that the justices appeared to encourage the concept of comparable worth by allowing female prison guards to claim intentional wage discrimination even though their work was different from male guards (Hoff-Wilson 1991).

It is expected that the issue of comparable worth will remain a lively topic of discussion in Congress for some time to come. Feminists are split on the issue. A younger generation of professional women claims that paying above-market wages for women's work ensures that women will stay in those fields instead of striking out into largely male fields (Hoff-Wilson 1991). In addition, even at the end of the 1980s, statements about preserving the rapidly vanishing typical American family reverberated in the Congress and the executive branch, in spite of the fact that less than a quarter of families fit the mold of husband, nonworking, full-time housewife, and children (Hoff-Wilson 1991).

The Supreme Court majority opinion in *Gunther* makes six references to social science material while the dissenting opinion makes none. The appeals court makes two references to social science.

Hishon v. King and Spalding 467 U.S. 69 (1984)

Petitioner, a woman lawyer, was employed in 1972 as an associate with respondent law firm, a general partnership, but her employment was terminated in 1979 after respondent decided not to invite her to become a partner. Petitioner claimed that respondent discriminated against her on the basis of her sex in failing to invite her to become a partner. The District Court dismissed the complaint on the ground that Title VII was inapplicable to the selection of partners by a partnership, and the Court of Appeals affirmed. The Supreme Court reversed and held that sex discrimination in promotion to partner of a law firm held violation of federal law. Justice Burger delivered the opinion for a unanimous Court, with Justice Powell filing a concurring opinion. (9-0)

The Supreme Court held, for the first time, that under Title VII, law firms may not discriminate on the basis of sex in deciding which lawyers to promote as partners (Hoff-Wilson 1991). Unlike in the abortion cases, there was a unanimous court, and as with *Nashville,* no dissents were filed. The petitioner alleged that the prospect of partnership was an important factor in her initial decision to accept employment with the respondent, and it was in fact used as a recruiting device. Advancement to partnership after five or six years was a matter of course for associates who received satisfactory evaluations (71–72). The Supreme Court opinion says (74) that "[o]nce a contractual relationship of employment is established, the provisions of Title VII attach and govern certain aspects of that relationship" (74).

Justice Powell filed a concurring opinion to make clear his understanding that the Court's opinion does not extend Title VII to the management of a law firm by its partners, though on the other hand the firm may not evade it by labeling employees as partners. Powell refers to Fallon's "To Each According to His Ability, from None According to His Race: The Concept of Merit in the Law of Antidiscrimination" (*Boston University Law Review* 60 [1980]). In closing, Justice Powell says (81) that neither race nor sex is relevant: "The qualities of mind, capacity to reason logically, ability to work under pressure, leadership, and the like are unrelated to race or sex. This is demonstrated by the success of women and minorities in law schools, in the practice of law, on the bench, and in positions of community, state and national leadership. Law firms—and, of course, society—are the better for these changes."

The appeals court, on the other hand, had judged that a partnership is a voluntary association of lawyers, and the partners own the partnership, they are not its employees under Title VII. "But you promised" is not a sufficient claim by the appellant because the court declines to extend the meaning of employment opportunities by encroaching upon an individual's decision to voluntarily associate in a business partnership (1028).

The Supreme Court majority opinion made no reference to social science, but Justice Powell's concurring statement refers to a law review article dealing with social science issues. The appeals court made no reference to social science data.

Meritor Savings Bank v. Vinson 477 U.S. 57 (1986)

The respondent, a former employee of petitioner bank, brought action against the bank and her supervisor, claiming that during her employment, she had been subjected to sexual harassment by the supervisor in violation of Title VII of the Civil Rights Act of 1964. The District Court denied relief without resolving if respondent and supervisor had a sexual relationship, if it was voluntary, and had nothing to do with her continued employment and that respondent was not the victim of sexual harassment. Because the bank was without notice, it could not be held liable for the supervisor's alleged sexual harassment. The Court of Appeals reversed and remanded, noting that a violation of Title VII may be predicated on either 1) harassment that involves the conditioning of employment benefits on sexual favors, and 2) harassment that, while not affecting economic benefits, creates a hostile or offensive working environment, and this was the latter. Further, as to the bank's liability, the Court of Appeals held that an employer is absolutely liable for sexual harassment by supervisory personnel, whether or not the employer knew or should have known about it. The Supreme Court affirmed[,] holding that a claim of hostile environment sexual harassment is a form of sex discrimination that is actionable under Title VII. The language is not limited to economic discrimination, and EEOC guidelines fully support the view that sexual harassment leading to non-economic injury can violate Title VII. The District Court erroneously focused on voluntariness of participation. The correct inquiry is whether the advances were unwelcome, not whether her participation was voluntary. While voluntariness is no defense to a sexual harassment claim, it does not follow that such evidence is irrelevant. The Court of Appeals erred in concluding that employers are always automatically liable for sexual harassment by their supervisors. In this case, however, the mere existence of a grievance procedure in the bank and the bank's policy against discrimination, coupled with failure to invoke that procedure, do not necessarily insulate the bank from liability. Justice Rehnquist delivered the opinion for a unanimous Court, in which Justices Burger, White, Powell, Stevens and O'Connor joined. Justice Stevens filed a concurring opinion. Justice Marshall filed an opinion concurring in the judgment in which Justices Brennan, Blackmun and Stevens joined. (9-0)

This case contains a number of interesting aspects, all of which will be taken up in detail. It is noteworthy that this was the first case of sexual harassment to come before the Supreme Court. Catharine MacKinnon filed on the brief for the respondent, on an issue about which she had written in 1979—the need to classify sexual harassment as a form of sex discrimination. Judges Bork and Scalia filed a dissenting opinion to the appeals court opinion. Bork would be refused nomination to the Supreme Court. Scalia would later become a justice but would just miss sitting on this case. Justice Rehnquist wrote the opinion, even though, based on his prior dissents in the other sex-discrimination cases and in abortion cases, a dissent might have been expected.

First, the details of the case, as taken from the Supreme Court opinion, are that Vinson alleged that Taylor, her supervisor, coerced her into sexual relations, which she at first refused but later agreed to out of fear of losing her job (60). Vinson testified that Taylor touched and fondled other women employees of the bank, but the District Court did not allow that testimony. Taylor denied all allegations of sexual activity, and the conflicting testimony was never resolved. As Justice Rehnquist reviewed the decision (63):

Title VII of the Civil Rights Act of 1964 makes it an unlawful employment practice for an employer . . . to discriminate against any individual with respect to his compensation, terms, conditions, or privileges of employment, because of such individual's race, color, religion, sex, or national origin. . . . The prohibition against discrimination based on sex was added to Title VII at the last minute on the floor of the House of Representatives . . . the bill was quickly passed as amended, and we are left with little legislative history to guide us in interpreting the Act's prohibition against discrimination based on sex.

In 1980, the EEOC issued guidelines specifying that sexual harassment as there defined is a form of sex discrimination prohibited by Title VII. Parenthetically, it should be noted that Justice Thomas came to the EEOC later as chairman, serving from 1982 to 1990 (Wagman 1993). The EEOC guidelines, according to Rehnquist's opinion (65), fully support the view that harassment leading to noneconomic injury can violate Title VII. The conduct includes unwelcome sexual advances, requests for sexual favors, and other verbal or physical conduct of a sexual nature. A plaintiff may establish a violation of Title VII by proving that discrimination based on sex has created a hostile or abusive work environment (66), as written in the court of appeals in another case:[7] "Surely a requirement that a man or woman run a gauntlet of sexual abuse in return for the privilege of being allowed to work and make a living can be as demeaning and disconcerting as the harshest of racial epithets" (67).

The significant part of any sexual harassment claim is that the alleged sexual advances were unwelcome. The opinion states that testimony about the respondent's dress and personal fantasies, which the district court admitted into evidence, had no place in this litigation, according to the court of appeals. But the Supreme Court claims that such evidence is relevant (69). Regarding the employer's liability, the Court claims that the supervisor is the employer and the employer is the supervisor, so that notice to the supervisor is notice to the bank (70). As to the grievance procedure, it required first telling the supervisor, so the Court said: "It is not altogether surprising that respondent failed to invoke the procedure and report her grievance to him. Petitioner's contention that respondent's failure should insulate it from liability might be substantially stronger if its procedures were better calculated to encourage victims of harassment to come forward" (73). But the Court concluded that the court of appeals was wrong to impose absolute liability on employers for the acts of their supervisors, regardless of the circumstances (73).

In his opinion, Justice Marshall says that every court of appeals that has considered the issue has held that "sexual harassment by supervisory personnel is automatically imputed to the employer when the harassment results in tangible job detriment to the subordinate employee" (76). He claims that a supervisor is charged with the day-to-day supervision of the work environment and with ensuring a safe, productive workplace. It is because the supervisor is clothed with the employer's authority that he is able to impose unwelcome sexual conduct on subordinates (77). Therefore, Justice Marshall concludes that "sexual harassment by a supervisor of an employee under his supervision, leading to a discriminatory work environment, should be imputed to the employer for Title VII purposes regardless of whether the employee gave 'notice' of the offense" (78).

The court of appeals (146) quotes MacKinnon's 1979 book *Sexual Harassment of Working Women* (46–47) concerning the futility of a resistance requirement for a sexual harassment claim. MacKinnon's point is that so long as the supervisor has the power to force sexual attention, how can a woman resist, except to leave work, which she contends is analogous to saying that a woman has not been raped if she did not resist (46). As far as voluntariness, the court of appeals said that, according to a previous case, "a woman does not waive her Title VII rights by her sartorial or whimsical proclivities."[8] The appeals court goes beyond this case (151) to implore employers to take a more active role in warranting that employees will enjoy a working environment free from illegal sex discrimination. According to the EEOC guidelines, prevention is the best tool for eliminating sexual harassment. Steps should be taken to prevent harassment, including raising the subject, expressing strong disapproval, developing sanctions, informing employees of their rights, and sensitizing all concerned.[9]

The dissent filed by Circuit Judge Bork and joined by Circuit Judges Scalia and Starr charges that the rulings are wrong with regard to defense. The rulings deprive the charged person of any defense. Sexual dalliance, however voluntarily engaged in, becomes harassment whenever an employee sees fit. Thus, the rules of evidence are rigged so that dalliance is automatically harassment because no one is allowed to deny it (1330). On the other hand, the dissent continues, a supervisor must not introduce evidence of an employee's dress or behavior. The dissent finds such inadmissibility astonishing, in the light of all the other evidence admitted in the case (1131).

The Supreme Court made no references to social science in its unanimous opinion. The appeals court made two. Both courts made note that they were not furnished with a transcript of the district court proceedings at trial (60 [Supreme Court]; 141 [Appeals]).

Wimberly v. Industrial Relations Commission of Missouri
479 U.S. 511 (1987)

> The petitioner took pregnancy leave from her employment. Pursuant to the employer's policy, she was told that she would be rehired only if a position was available when she was ready to return to work. When she notified the employer that she wanted to return to work, she was told that there were no positions open. When she filed a claim for unemployment benefits with the Missouri Division of Employment Security,

she was denied the claim, pursuant to a Missouri statute which disqualifies a claimant who has left his work voluntarily without good cause attributable to his work or to his employer. The Missouri Supreme Court agreed, and the Supreme Court affirmed holding that 1) provision of Federal Unemployment Tax Act[,] which mandates that no person shall be denied compensation under state law solely on basis of pregnancy or termination of pregnancy[,] only prohibits state from singling out pregnancy for unfavorable treatment; it does not mandate preferential treatment for women who leave work because of pregnancy, and 2) Missouri statute denying unemployment compensation to claimant who has left his work voluntarily without good cause attributable to his work or to his employer was consistent with a section of the Federal Unemployment Tax Act providing that no state participating in federal-state unemployment compensation program shall deny compensation solely on basis of pregnancy or termination of pregnancy. Justice O'Connor delivered the opinion of the Court, in which all other members joined, except Blackmun[,] who took no part in the decision of the case. (8-0)

The issue of treating women "specially" was raised in both *Wimberly* and *Guerra*. In the former, the Supreme Court refused to grant special treatment to a woman who specifically asked for it. In the latter, as will be seen, the Supreme Court upheld special treatment in the form of mandatory maternity leaves (Hoff-Wilson 1991). Favorable treatment can have unfavorable results when it is rationalized in the name of women's special procreation capacity, and if history repeats itself, pregnant workers today might find themselves right back where women were in the era of the protective legislation following *Muller v. Oregon* in 1908 (Hoff-Wilson 1991). Women are so divided on the issue of special-versus-equal rights that they have not clearly delineated the potential limitations of both or advanced a legal resolution of this theoretical dichotomy (Hoff-Wilson 1991).

In the opinion, Justice O'Connor writes that the petitioner (Wimberly) had been employed for three years by J. C. Penney and had requested a leave of absence due to pregnancy. She was told she could have a leave without guarantee of reinstatement, meaning she would be rehired only if a position was available, according to policy. Wimberly applied for rehire one month after her child was born but was told there were no positions open. She was denied unemployment benefits on the basis that Missouri statutes disqualify all claimants who leave work for reasons that, while perhaps legitimate and necessary from a personal standpoint, were not causally connected to the claimant's work or employer (823). The opinion does point out that there is considerable disparity among the states in the treatment of pregnancy-related terminations; most states regard leave for pregnancy as a voluntary termination for "good cause," but Missouri does not.

Justice O'Connor argues that contrary to the petitioner's assertion, the plain import of the language of Congress is the intention only to prohibit states from singling out pregnancy for unfavorable treatment, providing that compensation shall not be denied under state law "solely on the basis of pregnancy" (825). Further, she writes (827) that the petitioner can point to nothing in the statute's legislative history that gives evidence of preferential treatment for women on account of pregnancy. There is no hint that Congress disapproved of a neutral rule such as Missouri's. In short, there is nothing in 3304(a)(12) of the Federal Unemployment Tax Act that requires states to afford preferential treatment to women on account of pregnancy (828). The Supreme Court opinion is based purely on legal and technical grounds of statutes and includes no reference to its impact on women. In addition, there is no dissent, so those issues are never addressed.

The same is true of the opinion of the Missouri Supreme Court, except for the dissent. Therein, Judge Blackmar states (350–51) that he believes that Congress in the 1976 amendments to the Federal Unemployment Tax Act had the purpose of extending benefits to a woman who becomes pregnant, leaves work as the anticipated delivery date appears, and then offers herself for work as soon after giving birth as she is able. Otherwise, he continues, he can see no reason for Congress to have said: "No person shall be denied compensation . . . solely on the basis of pregnancy or termination of pregnancy." What meaning would it have?

The Supreme Court made no citations to social science, but the Missouri State Supreme Court made one reference.

California Federal Savings and Loan Association v. Guerra
107 S.Ct. 683 (1987)

> Pregnant worker's employer brought suit seeking declaration asking that California statute requiring employers to provide leave and reinstatement to employees disabled by pregnancy was preempted by Title VII. The District Court granted summary judgment in their favor and the Court of Appeals reversed. The Supreme Court affirmed[,] holding that 1) Pregnancy Discrimination Act does not prohibit employment practices favoring pregnant women; 2) California statute is not inconsistent with and thus is not preempted by Title VII as amended by PDA and 3) even if PDA prohibited favorable treatment of pregnant workers, California statute would not require employers to violate Title VII. (6-3)

A woman employed as a receptionist by the petitioner, California Federal Savings and Loan Association (Cal Fed), took a pregnancy disability leave, but when she notified Cal Fed that she was able to return to work she was informed that her job had been filled and there were no similar positions available. This was the first Pregnancy Disability Act (PDA) case to be decided by the Supreme Court, and the justices upheld a California law requiring employers to grant unpaid maternity leave to pregnant workers, in effect sanctioning "special treatment" of women (Hoff-Wilson 1991). It is difficult to believe that this was decided at the same time that *Wimberly* was decided, with what seems like diametrically opposed decisions. *Guerra* and *Wimberly*, in 1987, were the first sex-discrimination cases to be decided by a newly composed Court. Justice Rehnquist had replaced Burger as chief justice, and Burger was replaced on the Court by Justice Scalia, who happened to side with the majority of six here. This grouping of justices in the decision is similar to that in the abortion cases, with Justices White, Rehnquist, and Powell dissenting.

The majority opinion, written by Justice Marshall, shows that the case was judged on the technical issues. The PDA is described as a "floor beneath which pregnancy disability benefits may not drop—not a ceiling above which they may not rise" (691). The footnotes describing the congressional hearings for the PDA touch on the more human issues of pregnancy and make it abundantly clear that the PDA was intended to provide relief for working women and to end discrimination against pregnant workers (692). In the hearings, Representative Chisholm said that the bill "affords some 41% of this Nation's labor force some greater degree of protection and security without fear of reprisal due to their decision to bear children." Representative Tsongas said the bill "would put an end to an unrealistic and unfair system that forces women to choose between family and career—clearly a function of sex bias in the law" (692). Justice Marshall says (694) that unlike the protective labor legislation prevalent earlier in this century, the California statute does not reflect archaic or stereotypical notions about pregnancy and the abilities of pregnant workers, which would be inconsistent with Title VII's goal of equal employment opportunity. He refers to B. Brown, A. Freedman, H. Katz, and A. Price's *Women's Rights and the Law* (1977) regarding the prior protective legislation.

Marshall addresses the dichotomous issue before the Court (699): Those in favor of preferential treatment urged with conviction that preferential treatment merely enables women, like men, to have children without losing their jobs. Those opposed to preferential treatment urged with equal conviction that preferential treatment represents a resurgence of the nineteenth-century protective legislation that perpetuated sex-role stereotypes and impeded women in their efforts to take their rightful place in the workplace, for example, *Muller*. The issue pitted feminists against feminists, such as the National Organization for Women versus the ACLU (Goldstein 1988). In fact, in this case the ACLU filed an *amicus brief* on the side of the employer, arguing: "Protectionist laws reflect an ideology which values women most highly for their childbearing and nurturing roles. Such laws reinforce stereotypes about women's inclinations and abilities; they deter employers from hiring women of childbearing age or funnel them into less responsible positions; and they make women appear to be more expensive, less reliable employees" (Goldstein 1988:51). On the other side, Professor Finley of the Yale Law School argued that to pretend men and women are the same is not equality; that the equal treatment argument, carried to the extreme, tries to defy social reality (Goldstein 1988). It is also a fact that women are nearly half the workforce; 90 percent of them have or will have children; and more than 60 percent have no guarantees that the job they leave for childbirth will be available to them when they are ready to return to work (Goldstein 1988). Surprisingly, neither *Guerra* nor *Wimberly* made any reference to these statistics in any of the opinions. The Supreme Court majority opinion made five references to material of a social science nature, but the dissent for the Supreme Court made none, nor did the appeals court.

International Union et al. v. Johnson Controls, Inc. 111 S.Ct. 1196 (1991)

Class action was brought challenging employer's policy barring all women, except those whose infertility was medically documented, from jobs involving actual or potential lead exposure exceeding Occupational Safety and Health Administration (OSHA) standards. The District Court granted summary judgment for employer. The Court of Appeals affirmed. The Supreme Court held that 1) employer's policy was facially discriminatory, and 2) employer did not establish that sex was a BFOQ. Justice Blackmun wrote the opinion for a unanimous court. Justice White concurred in part, which Chief Justice Rehnquist and Justice Kennedy joined. Justice Scalia filed an opinion concurring in the judgment. (9-0)

Although the measures were being taken for women (and their current or future fetuses), and although the employer's goals may have been laudable in this case, they were found to be unconstitutional and discriminatory against women. This case brings together the issues of abortion and sex discrimination. Even though the court of appeals saw the issue quite differently than did the Supreme Court, the Supreme Court was unanimous in its decision—a Court that frequently had been divided in abortion and several of the sex-discrimination cases. This is another example of a decision made solely and entirely on the basis of the law, with seeming disregard for the human side of the issues involved, which differs from the situation in the abortion debates.

Justice Blackmun wrote the opinion for the Court, arguing that the policy is not neutral because it does not apply to male employees in the same way that it applies to females, even though there is some evidence that lead exposure has a debilitating effect on the male reproductive system (1198). No matter; a malevolent motive does not convert a facially discriminatory policy into a neutral policy, as determined in *Phillips v. Martin Marietta Corp* (1198). The policy could only be defended as a BFOQ, which cannot be established because fertile women can participate in the manufacture of batteries as efficiently as anyone else (1198). Title VII, as amended by the PDA, mandates that decisions about the welfare of future children be left to the parents who conceive, bear, support, and raise them rather than to the employers who hire those parents, or to the courts (1198). Further, the unconceived fetuses, Blackmun argues, are neither customers nor third parties whose safety is essential to the business of battery manufacturing (1198).

The district court had concluded that there was disagreement among scientific experts regarding the effect of lead on the fetus (1200). Blackmun writes that the appeals court assumed that because the asserted reason for the sex-based exclusion was ostensibly benign, the policy was not sex-based discrimination, but that assumption was incorrect, he says (1203). Case law makes clear that the safety exception is limited to instances in which sex or pregnancy actually interferes with the employee's ability to perform the job, such as maintaining prison security or insuring safety of airline passengers. The Court cites statistics to show that approximately 9 percent of all fertile women become pregnant each year, and the birthrate drops to 2 percent for blue collar workers over age thirty (1208), so few women are involved. These statistics are drawn from Mary E. Becker's "From Muller v. Oregon to Fetal Vulnerability Policies" (*University of Chicago Law Review* 53 [1986]: 1219, 1233). Concern for a woman's existing or potential offspring historically has been the excuse for denying women equal employment opportunities, beginning with *Muller*. The *Johnson Controls* opinion makes clear that it is not to say that the employer cannot have a conscience. But according to the opinion, in this situation, a warning is adequate. Then the decision is up to the individual. Justice Blackmun concludes (1210): "It is no more appropriate for the courts than it is for individual employees to decide whether a woman's reproductive role is more important to herself and her family than her economic role. Congress has left this choice to the woman as hers to make."

The court of appeals concluded that because scientific data reveal that the risk of transmitting harm to unborn children is confined to fertile female employees, the sex-based distinction is based upon real physical differences between men and women and is therefore consistent with Title VII (890). The effects of limiting women's employment on this basis would have great impact because it is estimated that twenty million industrial jobs could be closed to women because the work involves substances, in addition to lead, that pose fetal risks (900). A dissenter in the appeals court conjectured that an employer might have moral qualms about endangering children, which cannot be wholly dismissed, just as people have ethical convictions about a woman's proper place being in the home. As seen from the controversy over abortion, for example, many people are passionately protective of fetal welfare, and they cannot be expected to park their passions at the company gate (905). The same dissent, quoting Elisabeth M. Landes's "The Effect of State Maximum Hours Laws on the Employment of Women in 1920" (*Journal of Political Economy* 88 [1980]: 476), notes that many modern women resent the suggestion that women have a special responsibility for perpetuating the human race.

Considerable medical testimony entered through expert witnesses at the district court level and was cited there as well as by the court of appeals. The court made the point that an employer is better situated than its workers to gather and interpret scientific data. Medical studies are difficult to evaluate, and the need to earn a living may induce employees to give too little weight to the interests of their offspring (914). Though the latter point is made only once in this case, it is surprising that more attention was not given to the belief that young people in particular would not be looking ahead. The appeals court comments on evaluating expert witnesses, saying that judges cannot unravel medical mysteries by observing scientists' demeanor on the stand, for example. This is not how scientists resolve disputes among themselves, it says. Demeanor tells the judge only whether the scientist believes what he or she says.

The appeals court continues: "Scientists formulate hypotheses, collect data, and apply statistical methods to assess them; judges and jurors find this process alien. Yet so long as the substantive rule of law requires a court to resolve scientific disagreements . . . the judge must follow the rules, which means that material disputes must be resolved at trial," and the dispute in this case concerned the degree of danger posed by exposure to lead (916). The dissent to the appeals decision asserts that *Johnson Controls* might be the most important sex-discrimination case in court since Congress enacted Title VII in 1964, because twenty million industrial jobs could be closed to women on grounds of fetal risks. This ruling would allow employers to consign more women to "women's work," while reserving better-paying but more hazardous jobs for men (921). The district court notes that there is a lack of case law on this issue, but that many legal writers have addressed the issue. It cites six articles in law journals on the subject of gender-specific regulations in the workplace, one example being Williams's "Firing the Woman to Protect the Fetus" (*Georgetown Law Journal* 69 [1981]: 641). This is frequently referenced and will be discussed in the following section. In sum, the Supreme Court's majority decision had two cites. The dissent made no references to social science, but the appeals court made fourteen, and the district court made eight references to articles on the subject in scientific and law journals.

Briefs for *Johnson Controls*

Nineteen *amicus curiae* briefs were filed in the 1991 case of *International Union v. Johnson Controls*. To demonstrate the type of briefs filed, we list the nineteen briefs in the order in which they were filed, according to the Court docket:

California and California Fair Employment and Housing Commission
Bar of the City of New York et al.
Natural Resources Defense Council
NAACP
Legal Defense and Educational Fund
Trial Lawyers for Public Justice
Massachusetts et al.
United States
American Public Health Association
ACLU
Equal Rights Advocates et al.
United States Catholic Conference
Pacific Legal Foundation et al.
Equal Employment Advisory Council et al.
Concerned Women for America
Washington Legal Foundation
Chamber of Commerce
Industrial Hygiene Law Project
National Safe Workplace Institute

The Washington Legal Foundation supported the respondent (Johnson Controls) in arguing the risk of tort liability. In spite of what the Court would say about the risk's being low, the foundation's position was that Johnson would be at risk for being sued if there was damage done to a fetus. The Catholic Conference filed, in support of the respondent, for the protection of the fetus. The Industrial Hygiene Law Project also filed for the respondent. The American Public Health Association (APHA), on the other hand, filed for the petitioners, arguing for cleaning up the work environment rather than just removing some of the workers and leaving an unhealthy environment. The NAACP also filed for the petitioner, suggesting that black children suffer disproportionately, according to Rosenberg's "The Home Is the Workplace" and Mullings's "Minority Women, Work, and Health," both of which were published in *Double Exposure* (ed W. Chavkin, 1984:229 and 121, respectively). Also, the NAACP held that African Americans—women in particular—are disproportionately represented in the blue-collar labor force. A sample of eight battery plants and lead smelters found that 52 percent of all blue-collar jobs were held by nonwhites. In one particular plant, all forty-two of the workers, most of them African American, had lead poisoning.

The works most frequently cited and found in briefs on both sides, listed under "Table of Authorities," are:

1. Baer, J., *The Chains of Protection* (1973).
2. Becker, M., "From *Muller v. Oregon* to Fetal Vulnerability Policies," *University of Chicago Law Review* 53 (1986): 1219.
3. Bertin, J., "Reproductive Hazards in the Workplace," in *Reproductive Laws for the 1990s*, ed. Cohen and Taub (1989).
4. Kessler-Harris, A., *Out to Work* (1982).
5. Landes, M., "The Effect of State Maximum Hours Laws on the Employment of Women in 1920," *Journal of Political Economy* 88 (1980): 176
6. Paul, Daniels, and Rosofsky, *Corporate Response to Reproductive Hazards in the Workplace: Results of the Family, Work and Health Survey* (1989).
7. Rosenberg, "The Home Is the Workplace," in *Double Exposure* (ed. W. Chavkin, 1984:229).
8. Williams, "Firing the Woman to Protect the Fetus: The Reconciliation of Fetal Protection with Employment Opportunity Goals under Title VII," *Georgetown Law Journal* 69 (1981): 641.

All of these items were published after *Frontiero*. Articles cited in *Frontiero* were not carried over to the *Johnson Controls* case. The *amicus curiae* of the Association of the Bar of the City of New York et al. represents the Association of Black Women Attorneys, the Committee on Women's Rights of the New York County Lawyer's Association, and the New York City Commission on Human Rights. The brief uses most of the references listed above and presents a particularly cogent case for the petitioners (International Union, United Automobile, Aerospace and Agricultural Implement Workers of America et al.) discussed below.

The brief of the New York Bar was in response to the ruling by the court of appeals in favor of Johnson Controls. In spite of the conclusions of federal regulators and health officials that both men and women face hazards to their reproductive systems and other health risks from exposure to lead, the court of appeals deferred to the company's sweeping decision to exclude only women from lead-exposure positions in its battery plants (4). The breadth of this ban on women workers of childbearing capacity is striking and presumes that all women under age seventy are fertile, absent medical proof of sterility. It even extends to jobs with no risk of lead exposure but which might lead to a promotion into such a job. The bar considers the decision a contemporary version of *Muller* in its acquiescence to outmoded notions about women's reproductive and economic lives and in its selective reliance on science to perpetuate and bolster those notions. Parenthetically, the brief of the APHA also comments on the selectivity of scientific findings, claiming that the narrow litigation focus led the employer and the court to ignore federal agencies' findings, to misconstrue evidence, to cite data selectively, and to rely on testimony contradicted in the public record (38). The APHA brief continues by saying that credibility problems of the sort apparent in this case are not confined to litigation. Individuals have institutional loyalties and personal stakes that color their views as well (38).

In the New York Bar brief it is said that the Johnson Controls policy and the decision to uphold it resurrect archaic stereotypes that have long since been rejected by Congress, the Supreme Court, and the American public. Under Title VII, such sexist assumptions about women's physical structure and maternal functions, found in *Muller,* can no longer serve as justifications for gender-based discrimination (5). Such a decision reinforces the notion that women should be childbearers and homemakers, denigrates women's participation in the work force, and assumes that only women are responsible for the health and caretaking of future generations (5). Further, it reinforces the demeaning perception that women cannot make the decisions that most vitally affect their own lives and their existing or potential families (5). *Muller* was based on "scientific myth," according to the brief, which argues that the court of appeals in this case fell prey to ideas wholly at odds with scientific fact and the reality of women's lives (5). Although the prejudice is more subtle in *Johnson Controls* than in *Muller,* the court's selective use of scientific evidence to bar women's employment is in fact a distorting of science to bolster prejudices of the day (15). In a footnote to the brief it is pointed out (15) that scholars have observed that the way science is used is often suffused with value judgments and prejudice, as noted in *Men's Ideas, Women's Realities: Popular Science 1870 to 1915,* edited by L. Newman (1984), and by S. Gould in his book *The Mismeasure of Man* (1981).[10]

It is no accident, the brief continues (17), that employers' policies excluding women based on reproductive capacity are found in industries in which women's labor is perceived as expendable (according to Becker's 1986 article cited in the list above). At the close of World War II, the U.S. Department of Labor embarked on a campaign to convince women to relinquish jobs to make room for the returning veterans, according to A. Babcock et al. in *Sex Discrimination and the Law* (1973:260). Mary Becker, as cited above, wrote in 1986 (1219): "In recent years, a number of corporations have adopted policies restricting the employment of women because of fetal vulnerability to toxic chemicals or ionizing radiation. The scope of the policies is influenced by the sexual composition of the work force. When the work force is predominantly male, some employers exclude all fertile women from hazardous jobs. When the work force is predominantly female, some employers exclude only pregnant women from hazardous jobs." It is little wonder that the New York Bar brief described above, and several others, quote Becker and Williams, as they had both prepared comprehensive reviews and syntheses of the problem in law reviews. Becker draws on feminist literature, covering everything from the Hull-House experience in 1890s Chicago to Catharine MacKinnon's view of sexual harassment as sex discrimination.

Wendy Williams in the *Georgetown Law Journal* (1981) earlier concluded that neutrality in employment policies was the only solution. She provided a history of legislation regarding women at work, beginning with *Muller* and covering the medical effect on the fetus; work and occupational history of women; women's role in society as unidimensional and relegated to the domestic sphere; and the case law on sex discrimination. She and Becker both quote statistics and social science literature extensively in their law review articles. This is an alternative way for social science to get into the court record, rather than directly through social science experts or social science literature, as the law review articles are more easily and readily relied upon by courts.

Summary

The sex-discrimination cases provided the information discussed below and shown in table 2. In these cases, prior cases are given far greater weight than social science, as judged by the number of citations to each—there may be hundreds of citations to previous cases and few or none to social science. The use of social science by the Court has not increased in sex-discrimination cases. In the first case—*Frontiero* in 1973—there were 12 citations, the most there would ever be. There were only 2 social science citations by the Supreme Court in the last case, *Johnson Controls* in 1991. Of the 13 Supreme Court cases of sex discrimination on the job, only 3 did not cite references to social science literature or experts, however. The Court used social science more consistently in the discrimination cases than it did with abortion cases, but never made as many references to social science (abortion cases had up to 31 citations to social science). The quantity of social science data brought to the Court increased, as evidenced by the increase in the number of *amicus* briefs over the twenty years in question, though the increase was less dramatic than in the abortion cases, largely because *Frontiero* started out with more social science citations than did *Roe*.

Social science is used only occasionally to support a particular position. For example, in the pregnancy leave cases, social science was cited in *Geduldig* and *General Electric*, but not in *Nashville* or *Wimberly*, later. Data presented to the Court for its use in the cases included information on stereotypes of pregnancy and women's strength, power, protection, and safety; romantic paternalism; women's wages as disproportionate to men's; women's type of work being different from that of men; exploitation of workers; the changing roles of women; children as women's responsibility; longevity differences between the sexes; and other individual differences. In all of the sex-discrimination cases, the Court could have used data on such issues as the role of women in society, the percent of women in the labor force, changes over time in occupations, and the economic need to work. Yet it did not always refer to relevant social science. As with the abortion cases, the Court only sometimes used the evidence, even though it was available.

The differences among justices were not as great on sex discrimination as they had been on abortion. Of those justices who sat on all 13 sex-discrimination cases, Justice Marshall made the most citations to social science (in 8 out of 13 cases) and Justice Rehnquist made the fewest (in 2 out of the 13 cases). Justice Scalia was part of an opinion that referred to social science, whereas he was never part of an opinion with citations to social science in abortion cases. Justices Kennedy and Souter each sat on only one sex-discrimination case, and Thomas participated in none.

Social science was not used more in dissenting opinions than in majority opinions, as was the case with the abortion cases. The majority opinions in 6 of the 13 sex-discrimination cases cited social science, and 5 of the dissenting opinions cited social science. As with abortion cases, there appeared to be no apparent relationship between citations in the lower courts and references to social science by the Supreme Court. Until *Johnson Controls*, where the appeals courts had 14 citations, the appeals court had cited social science in only 2 other sex-discrimination cases. The district court cited social science in 5 of the 8 cases it heard. The Supreme Court cited it in 10 of the 13 it heard. In *Frontiero*, the district court had no social science citations, but the Supreme Court had 12. In the last case (*Johnson Controls*), the district court had 8 citations and the appeals court had 14, but the Supreme Court had only 2. The sole case where both the lower courts and the higher court had several references was *Dothard*, where the district court had 10 and the Supreme Court had 7 cites to social science. In

Table 2. Citations to Social Science in U.S. Supreme Court Decisions, 1972–92:
Sex-Discrimination Cases ($N = 13$)

	Frontiero '73	Cleveland '74	Geduldig '74	G.E. '76	Dothard '77	Nashville '77
Douglas (1939–75)	12	0	4			
Stewart (1958–81)	0	0	0	0	4	0
Burger (1969–86)	0	1	0	0	4	0
Powell (1972–87)	0	0	0	0	4	0
Brennan (1956–90)	12	0	4	3	7	0
Marshall (1967–91)	12	0	4	3	7	0
Blackmun (1970–91)	0	0	0	0	4	0
White (1962–93)	12	0	0	0	0	0
Rehnquist (1972–)	0	0	0	0	4	0
Stevens (1975–)				0	4	0
O'Connor (1981–)						
Scalia (1986–)						
Kennedy (1988–)						
Souter (1990–)						
Thomas (1991–)						
Majority	12	0	0	0	4	0
Dissent	0	1	4	3	3	—
Total Cites	12	1	4	3	7	0
Appeals	—	0	—	0	—	0
District	0	2	0	3	10	0
State Supreme Court	—	—	—	—	—	—

other cases, the district court had none and the Supreme Court had several.

The Supreme Court is more likely to obtain its social science evidence from briefs than from expert witnesses, and the citations were more likely to be to studies in the briefs than to expert testimony. More statistical data were used in the sex-discrimination cases than were anecdotal data, and no public opinion polls or surveys were cited. The Supreme Court opinions did not evaluate experts or briefs. Some evaluation was done at the district court level, where there was comment on conflict of interest and bias among experts or criticism of study methods. The studies appeared to be evaluated according to legal standards rather than social science standards.

In chapter 5 we will examine the issue of sexual harassment, which emerged from issues of sex discrimination in the workplace.

Manhart '78	Gunther '81	Hishon '84	Meritor '86	Wimberly '87	Guerra '87	Johnson Controls '91	No.Cases Soc. Sci.	No. Cases
							2	3
9	0						2	8
11	0	0	0	0	0		3	12
9	0	1	0				3	10
—	6	0	0	0	0		5	12
9	6	0	0	0	5	2	8	13
0	6	0	0	—	5	2	4	12
9	6	0	0	0	5	0	4	13
9	0	0	0	0	0	0	2	13
11	6	0	0	0	5	2	5	10
		0	0	0	5	2	2	5
				0	5	0	1	3
						0	0	1
						2	1	1
						0⁄		0
9	6	1	0	0	5	2	6	13
2	0	—	—	—	0	0	5	13
11	6	1	0	0	5	2	10	13
0	2	0	2	—	0	14	3	9
3	—	—	—	—	—	8	5	8
—	—	—	—	1	—		1	1

Notes

1. Nancy Cott, "Passionlessness: An Interpretation of Victorian Sexual Ideology, 1790–1850," *Signs: A Journal of Women in Culture and Society* 3, no. 2 (Winter 1978): 219–36, cited in Kandal 1988.

2. Unless otherwise noted in this section concerning women who have jobs outside the home and who have young children, the cases are as described by Gerald Rosenberg in *The Hollow Hope* (Chicago: University of Chicago Press, 1991). A conversation with Rosenberg on the subject in 1993 was also extremely helpful.

3. Stoper cites statistics from the U.S. Department of Commerce, Bureau of the Census, *Statistical Abstract of the United States* (1989), 388–89.

4. Because Ruth Bader Ginsburg was a strong advocate for women's rights and involved in sex-discrimination cases, and because she now sits on the Court, it will be

noted in this chapter when she was part of one of the sex-discrimination cases before the U.S. Supreme Court prior to her appointment.

5. According to *Black's Law Dictionary*, suspect classification is with regard to the test to be used in determining whether statutory classification constitutes a denial of equal protection. "Suspect classifications" are those based on race, national origin, and sex.

6. Thomas Emerson, foreword to Catharine A. MacKinnon's *Sexual Harassment of Working Women* (1979).

7. *Henson v. Dundee*, 682 F.2d 897, 902 (1982).

8. *Bundy v. Jackson*, 205 U.S. App. D.C., 454.

9. *EEOC Guidelines*, note 30, 29 C.F.R. 1604.11(f) (1983).

10. The New York Bar brief further claims that a reliance on stereotypes of women also harms men, with the result that "[m]en get less protection, and women get fewer jobs" (6). Congress recognized that women's capacity to become pregnant had unfairly served as the greatest obstacle to women's full integration into the workplace (8). It in fact intended to strike at the entire spectrum of disparate treatment of men and women that results from sex stereotypes (9). Moreover, the brief continues (10), not even real differences between men and women, such as women's greater longevity, justify gender-based policies that disregard individual variation among women, and this extends to the use of sex-based actuarial tables in setting pension and life insurance rates in *Los Angeles v. Manhart*. The brief quotes the dissenting judge's view that protective laws and the *Muller* rationale were "museum pieces" (10). Further, it argues that the decision was based on unfounded stereotypes of women's reproductive lives, and is thus overbroad. That is, few women who are at Johnson Controls will become pregnant, since 83.2 percent of sexually active women between the ages of fifteen and forty-four of childbearing capacity, who are not seeking pregnancy, use contraceptives, according to the Statistical Abstracts of the Bureau of the Census, and the birth rate is nearly zero at age forty (11). Furthermore, it argues that the view of the court of appeals focuses on women's reproductive capacity, seeing women as marginal, nonessential members of the work force who should sacrifice their economic livelihood (15).

5

Sexual Harassment

The label "sexual harassment" dates from the mid-1970s. Although the term came into common usage, it was not clear what fell under that heading (Otten 1993). The Civil Rights Act of 1964, Title VII, did not link sexual harassment to sex discrimination (Rifkind and Harper 1993). Catharine MacKinnon, in *Sexual Harassment of Working Women* (1979), suggested that sexual harassment was a form of sex discrimination. In the present chapter, our examination of the Court's use of social science data in cases of sexual harassment will deal only with harassment of women employees in the workplace.

The Historical Context of Sexual Harassment Cases

The first survey of sexual harassment did not take place until 1975 (Segrave 1994). Seventy-eight percent of women surveyed reported emotional or physical effects from sexual harassment, according to a survey by the Working Women United Institute. Other surveys suggest that between one-third and two-thirds of working women have experienced some form of harassment. The United States Merit Protection Board reported in 1988 that 42 percent of female workers in the federal government had suffered from sexual harassment in the preceding two years (Rosenberg 1991). Other studies have shown that an estimated 85 percent of working women will be subjected to sexual harassment in their working lives (Rosenberg 1991). Working-class women are subjected to sexual harassment on the job more often than are other women (Tong 1989).

In 1980, the EEOC, under the leadership of Eleanor Holmes Norton, issued guidelines that formed the basis for defining sexual harassment (Rifkind and Harper 1993). The guidelines delineated two types of sexual harassment: quid pro quo and hostile environment. In the first, the message is: "If you sleep with me, you will get a raise; if you do not, you will not get a raise." The harasser must be the immediate supervisor or in a position to influence the career of the alleged victim, and the victim must be able to show that there has been a monetary loss; it can be a single incident (Rifkind and Harper 1993). In the second type, that of hostile environment, the harasser may be anyone in the workplace, including a coworker or customer, but the harassment cannot be just one incident; it must be continuous, and part of an overall pattern, with the work performance affected by the behavior (Rifkind and Harper 1993). The EEOC definition also includes the general criteria of unwelcome conduct that is sexual in nature (Rifkind and Harper 1993).

The first test was in 1986, in *Meritor Savings Bank v. Vinson.* Seven years earlier, MacKinnon (1979) said that sexual harassment had been not only legally allowed but "legally unthinkable." The Supreme Court in 1986 unanimously acknowledged that sexual harassment is a violation of federal antidiscrimination laws and also that employers can be held legally culpable if they fail to take action to ensure that their supervisory personnel refrain from sexual harassment of other employees (Goldstein 1988). Chief Justice Rehnquist wrote (64), "Without question, when a supervisor sexually harasses a subordinate because of the subordinate's sex, that supervisor discriminates on the basis of sex." *Meritor* was seen as a bright legal light on the horizon in gender issues. Nonetheless, verbal slurs against women—including abusive language and threats of violence— are still commonplace, and discrimination is not taken completely seriously by the public or by the courts. Many men do not see such behavior as being detrimental or offensive (Hoff-Wilson 1991). Furthermore, unlike in rape cases, the Court ruled in *Meritor* that evidence showing possible seductive or provocative behavior is permissible (Hoff-Wilson 1991). In 1988, the EEOC published additional guidelines under the *EEOC Policy Guidance Memorandum to Field Personnel,* issued on October 17 that year (Barnett 1989). The points left open by *Meritor* included whether the sexual conduct at issue was welcome; whether it is the type of conduct that constitutes actionable sexual harassment under Title VII; and whether the employer can be held liable under agency principles (Barnett 1989).

The *Meritor* case helped to define sexual harassment, so that now there is greater agreement on what constitutes sexual harassment. It is any remark or overt behavior of a sexual nature in the context of a work situation that makes a woman uncomfortable on the job, impeding her ability to do her work, or interfering with her advancement and opportunities (Otten 1993). Sexual harassment can take the form of looks, touches, jokes, innuendoes, gestures, propositions, or even the posting of pictures of naked women on the workplace walls (Otten 1993).

The issue of sexual harassment can arise even in the upper levels of government, as with Clarence Thomas. As Aaron (1993) describes the events, President Bush nominated Thomas for Supreme Court Justice in July 1991. The Senate Judiciary Committee confirmation hearings concluded on September 20, 1991.[1] On September 27, 1991, the committee reached a split vote, 7-7, on whether Clarence Thomas should be appointed to the Supreme Court. The matter was then taken before the full Senate and a vote was scheduled. Only a few days before the scheduled vote, Anita Hill's accusation that Thomas had sexually harassed her while she worked for him at the Department of Education and at the Equal Employment Opportunity Commission was made public. An additional irony was that Thomas was the person in charge, first at the Office of Civil Rights and later at the EEOC, as the nation's chief law enforcement officer for discrimination and sexual harassment (Stark 1992). Days of televised hearings to investigate the allegations brought the issue into homes of millions of Americans before Thomas was finally confirmed (Aaron 1993). The ruckus and rancor have, in fact, never settled down. The drama of Anita Hill's accusations of sexual harassment against Clarence Thomas even eclipsed discussion about what his impact would be on the Court when the Supreme Court began its 1991–92 term (Lieberman 1992).

Just weeks after Clarence Thomas's confirmation hearings focused attention on sexual harassment, Congress passed the Civil Rights Act of 1991, and President Bush signed it on November 21, 1991 (Aaron 1993). The president had first vetoed it but then signed a compromise version limiting the amount of monetary damages. Pressure on President Bush to pass it came not only as a result of the Clarence Thomas hearings, but also following the events of the Tailhook Convention in Las Vegas, wherein naval aviators were accused of sexually harassing female aviators and other women at the convention (Rifkind and Harper 1993). The 1991 Civil Rights Act made emotional distress and punitive damages, expert witness fees, and jury trials available for sexual harassment cases. Prior to this, emotional-distress damages were not available in such cases, under Title VII (Aaron 1993). With the burden of proving discrimination made easier, damages increased, and the right to a jury trial established, there were predictions of a new wave of employment discrimination (Rifkind and Harper 1993). In fact, other allegations of sexual harassment quickly followed the Thomas hearings, both inside and outside of government.

The Supreme Court's first opportunity to review a case on sexual harassment since Justice Thomas's appointment arose with *Harris v. Forklift Systems, Inc.*, the first sexual harassment case in seven years and only the second in the history of the Supreme Court. The Court decision, as discussed below, proved to be a clear win for women, not only on the issue of a hostile work environment, but also on the issue of not needing to prove psychological damage, as some of the lower courts had ruled. Women will undoubtedly now look to the courts to settle issues of sexual harassment, as they did in abortion and sex-discrimination cases before that. At the same time, the suits will not be limited to women; men have also benefited from sex-discrimination suits in the past two decades.

If we look ahead regarding issues of abortion, sex discrimination, and sexual harassment, we see that the future progress of women in the United States toward equality will be threatened by at least four factors (Hoff-Wilson 1991): (1) the ambiguity of the Supreme Court decisions; (2) the heightened conservatism in the country at large; (3) the greater hostility toward civil rights that arose in the 1980s; and (4) the unresolved conflict among feminists over special-versus-equal treatment of women. Congress was active in initiating many of the changes to ensure equality for women in social and economic areas, but, according to Aliotta's analysis (1991), much of the credit for their implementation goes to the federal courts, especially the Supreme Court in the 1970s. Yet in the 1980s, the Supreme Court and federal courts became less receptive to the issues, and so women must once again appeal to Congress and state legislatures to reverse or limit the damage created by unfavorable court decisions of that decade (Aliotta 1991). In sum, despite obvious progress in the past twenty years, women still have not achieved their coveted equal rights.

Social Science in Sexual Harassment: The Cases

Harris was the case that brought the Supreme Court justices squarely to the issue of deciding how much harassment is too much harassment. Sexual harassment, as a form of sex discrimination, had come before the Supreme Court only once before, in 1986, with *Meritor*. Because of the increasing importance and relevance of sexual harassment, we will consider here a second case, *Harris v. Forklift Systems, Inc.* (1993), even though it falls just outside of the study period for the current research. In the opinion, Justice O'Connor acknowledged the difficulty in defining sexual harassment: "This is not, and by its nature cannot be, a mathematically precise test" (*Harris* 1993:371). What is apparent from the decision is that, despite the definition of sexual harassment in *Meritor,* it is no less elusive after *Harris* than it was before (Robinson, Fink, and Allen 1994). The label that had been given to the conduct in the 1970s still begs for definition and refinement in the 1990s.

The issue of sexual harassment in the workplace began with *Meritor,* in 1986, as presented and discussed in Chapter 5. In *Meritor,* the Court unanimously held that sexual harassment was sex discrimination under Title VII of the Civil

Rights Act of 1964; *Harris* would subsequently be a hostile-environment case, as was *Meritor* (Martell and Sullivan 1994). The *Meritor* opinion, twenty-one pages in length, was written by Justice Rehnquist. No citations were made to social science in its unanimous opinion, even though the appeals court had made two references, and extensive literature was brought to the Court in the *amicus* briefs, as described below.

Briefs for *Meritor Savings Bank v. Vinson*

Ten *amicus curiae* briefs were filed in the 1986 case. They are listed below as they appeared in the Court docket:

Equal Employment Advisory Council
Boston University
EEOC
Women's Bar Association et al.
New Jersey et al.
Women's Bar Association of the State of New York
Women's Legal Defense Fund et al.
Members of Congress
AFL-CIO et al.
Working Women's Institute

The social science books and articles most frequently cited in the briefs, as given in the "Table of Authorities," include:

1. Crull, "The Stress Effects of Sexual Harassment on the Job," *American Journal of Orthopsychiatry* 52 (1982): 539.
2. Farley, L., *Sexual Shakedown: The Sexual Harassment of Women on the Job* (1978).
3. Gruber and Bjorn, "Blue Collar Blues: The Sexual Harassment of Women Auto Workers," *Work and Occupations* 9 (August 1982): 271.
4. Gutek, B., *Sex and the Workplace* (1985).
5. MacKinnon, C. A., *Sexual Harassment of Working Women* (1979).
6. Renick, "Sexual Harassment at Work," *Personnel Journal* (1980).
7. Safran, "What Men Do to Women on the Job," *Redbook,* Nov. 1976, 149.

In spite of the availability of the social science sources listed above, the Court made no reference to social science in *Meritor*. Seven years later, it would address its second case of sexual harassment, in *Harris;* we describe below the use (or nonuse) of social science in the Court's decision.

Harris v. Forklift Systems, Inc. 114 S.Ct. 367 (1993)

Former employee filed Title VII action, claiming that the conduct of the employer's president amounted to "abusive work environment" harassment on the basis of gender. The United States District Court for the Middle District of Tennessee dismissed the action pursuant to a report and recommendation of a United States Magistrate Judge. Former employee appealed. The Court of Appeals for the Sixth Circuit, 976 F.2d 733, affirmed. Certiorari was granted. The Supreme Court, Justice O'Connor, held that (1) to be actionable under Title VII as "abusive work environment" harassment, the conduct need not seriously affect an employee's psychological well-being or lead the employee to suffer injury; (2) the *Meritor* standard requires an objectively hostile or abusive environment as well as the victim's objective perception that the environment is abusive; and (3) whether an environment is sufficiently hostile or abusive to be actionable requires consideration of all the circumstances, not any one factor. Judgment of Court of Appeals reversed and case remanded. O'Connor delivered the opinion for a unanimous Court. Justices Scalia and Ginsburg filed concurring opinions.

Compared to the twenty-one pages of *Meritor,* the *Harris* decision (9-0) was short—eight pages long. It took only twenty-seven days after oral arguments to deliver the decision, a period so brief as to be virtually unprecedented, and it was an opinion so concise it has been termed "a telegram" (Sachs 1993). This was the first case heard by two female justices, Sandra Day O'Connor and Ruth Bader Ginsburg. Justice Ginsburg, as noted earlier, had been a leading women's rights advocate, and she had argued before the Court in other sex-discrimination cases. She wrote a concurring opinion in *Harris,* in which she said: "The critical issue, Title VII's text indicates, is whether members of one sex are exposed to disadvantageous terms or conditions of employment to which members of the other sex are not exposed" (372). Justice Scalia did not dissent, but he did lament the lack of preciseness in the decision. Justice Thomas voted with the majority but did not say a word during oral arguments, nor did he write any portion of the decision (Sachs 1993).

According to the opinion, the magistrate found that during Harris's time at Forklift, Hardy often insulted her because of her gender and often made her the target of unwanted sexual innuendoes. Hardy would ask Harris and other female employees to get coins from his front pants pocket; he threw objects on the ground in front of Harris and other women and then asked them to pick up the objects (369). Harris had complained about the conduct in mid-August of 1987, and he promised he would stop. But in early September, he began again. While Harris was arranging a deal with one of Forklift's customers, Hardy asked her, in front of other employees, "What did you do, promise the guy . . . some [sex] Saturday night" (369). On October 1, Harris collected her paycheck and quit (369).

The respondent's brief (for Forklift) argued that Harris voluntarily placed herself in the situations that she complained of; that she waited two years to complain and then only at a time when a business relationship between her husband and Hardy was being terminated; and that during her employment her compensation increased and that she was happy with her compensation (3).

The magistrate found that Hardy's conduct did not create an abusive environment, and while Hardy's comments would offend the "reasonable woman," they were not so severe as to be expected to seriously affect an employee's psychological well-being (370). The opinion points out that in focusing on the employee's psychological well-being the district court was following circuit court precedent, in *Rabidue v. Osceola Refining Co.* (805 F.2d 611). The Court therefore granted certiorari, according to the opinion, to resolve a conflict among the circuits on whether conduct, to be actionable as "abusive work environment," must seriously affect an employee's psychological well-being or lead the plaintiff to suffer injury (370). They concluded that a discriminatorily abusive work environment, even one that "does not seriously affect employees' psychological well-being can and often will detract from employee's job performance, discourage employees from remaining on the job, or keep them from advancing in their careers," which offends Title VII's broad rule of workplace equality (371).

The justices said the district court erred in relying on whether the conduct "seriously affected plaintiff's psychological well-being or led her to suffer injury" (371). They also stated of the district court opinion, "We need not answer today all the potential questions it raises, nor specifically address the EEOC's new [1993] regulations on the subject" (371). Justice O'Connor wrote in her opinion that they couldn't answer all the questions, and that the circumstances of a hostile or abusive environment may include "the frequency of the discriminatory conduct; its severity; whether it is physically threatening or humiliating, or a merely offensive utterance; and whether it unreasonably interferes with an employee's work performance" (371). While psychological harm, like any other relevant factor, may be taken into account, no single factor is required (371). Justice Scalia, in his concurring opinion, asserts that "[a]s a practical matter, today's holding lets virtually unguided juries decide whether sex-related conduct engaged in (or permitted by) an employer is egregious enough to warrant an award of damages" (372).

In its unanimous opinion, the Court made no references to social science, nor were any made in either concurring opinion. There were no published opinions at the lower court level, either magistrate or appeals, so there are no references to social science in any courts for the most recent case of sexual harassment. Yet, considerable social science material was brought before the Court, as evidenced below.

Briefs for *Harris v. Forklift*

Twelve *amicus curiae* briefs were filed in the 1993 case. According to the Court docket, they were:

United States
National Conference of Women's Bar Associations
NOW legal Defense and Educational Fund et al.
NAACP Legal Defense and Educational Fund, Inc., et al.
Employment Law Center et al.
Women's Legal Defense Fund et al.
American Psychological Association
Southern States Police Association
Feminists for Free Expression
National Employment Lawyers Association
American Civil Liberties Union et al.
Equal Employment Advisory Council

The articles and books most frequently cited and found in briefs under the "Table of Authorities" were:

1. Abrams, Kathryn, "Gender Discrimination and Transformation of Workplace Norms," *Vanderbilt Law Review* (1989):1182.
2. Brenneman, "Comments: From a Woman's Point of View: The Use of the Reasonable Woman Standard in Sexual Harassment Cases," *University of Cincinnati Law Review* 60 (1981): 1281.
3. Crull, "Stress Effects of Sexual Harassment on the Job: Implications for Counseling," *American Journal of Orthopsychiatry* 52 (1982): 539.
4. Ehrenreich, Nancy, "Pluralist Myths and Powerless Men: The Ideology of Reasonableness in Sexual Harassment Law," *Yale Law Journal* 99 (1990): 1177.
5. Estrich, Susan, "Sex at Work," *Stanford Law Review* 43 (1991): 813.
6. Gruber, "How Women Handle Sexual Harassment: A Literature Review," *Journal of Sociology and Social Research* 74 (1989): 3.
7. Gutek, Barbara A., *Sex and the Workplace* (1985).
8. Koss, Mary P. "Changed Lives: The Psychological Impact of Sexual Harassment," in *Ivory Power: Sexual Harassment on Campus* (ed. M. Paludi, 1990).

9. LeBreton Laurie W., and Sara S. Loevy, *Breaking New Ground: Worksite 2000, A Report Prepared by Chicago Women In Trades* (1992).

10. Linenberger, Patricia, "What Behavior Constitutes Sexual Harassment," *Labor Law Journal* 34 (1982): 238.

11. MacKinnon, Catharine A., *Sexual Harassment of Working Women* (1979).

12. Matsuda, Mari, "Public Response to Racist Speech: Considering the Victim's Story," *Michigan Law Review* 87 (1989): 2320.

13. U.S. Equal Employment Opportunity Commission, *Policy Guidance on Current Issues of Sexual Harassment* (Mar. 19, 1990).

Three of the works cited in briefs in *Harris*—those by Crull, Gutek, and MacKinnon—had been cited in *Meritor* briefs seven years earlier. However, eight of the thirteen publications listed above were written after *Meritor*.

The American Psychological Association (APA) submitted a brief that supported neither party, but the document did include a tightly reasoned argument, with social science support, about the two primary issues of the case: psychological damage and the reasonable woman. The APA brief, in fact, cites fifty-five social science articles in the "Table of Authorities." Scientific research, according to the brief, demonstrates that workplace sexual harassment inflicts substantial nonpsychological injuries, and the cost in employment opportunities for the worker and employer is high (7). Victims of sexual harassment frequently change jobs, transfer, or abandon efforts to obtain jobs in order to avoid harassment, so they may lose income, confidence, seniority, references, and reputation (7). The brief drew upon Koss's "Changed Lives: The Psychological Impact of Sexual Harassment," as given in the list above.

The brief notes that the American Psychiatric Association has taken the official position that "sexual harassment and other forms of irrational gender-based employment discrimination are potentially severe occupational stressors" (9). Further, it argues that Title VII's protection of employees from sex discrimination comes into play before the point at which victims of sexual harassment require psychiatric assistance (9). In fact, the brief says, the presence and degree of psychological injury to the victim may be more reflective of the victim's characteristics than of the severity of the offending conduct. In other words, the very individuals who are the most likely to be harmed are precisely the ones who will not do anything about it. This situation is much like the battered woman syndrome that was raised in the abortion cases, whereby the women who are least likely to tell their husbands about an abortion are those who fear abuse. Women who are the most likely to experience psychological problems in response to sexual harassment are those with low self-esteem and are also the least likely to report the harassment (13). Social science research provides considerable support for the efficacy of imposing legal sanctions on employers for creating or tolerating an intimidating, hostile, or offensive work environment (from *Meritor*, 65). That is to say, the protection needs to be built into the system.

A reply brief by the petitioner (8) relies on the APA brief in stating that the effects reported in the research include deteriorated relationships with fellow employees, decreased feelings of competence, loss of self-esteem, loss of motivation, lack of recognition for accomplishments, and lack of respect. Further, it reports that the APA brief supports the conclusion that offensive sex-based workplace conduct will alter the conditions of employment, which Teresa Harris endured at Forklift. She testified that as a result of Charles Hardy's conduct, she cried, was emotionally upset, hated going to work and, when at work, would sit in her office and shake (8).

In the petitioner's original brief, a number of references are made to social science literature, including Gutek's *Sex and the Workplace*, in which it is reported that women commonly leave the workplace and choose another to avoid the disgust and degradation of sexual harassment (25). The petitioner relied on Abrams's article from the *Vanderbilt Law Review* and on Linenberger's essay in the *Labor Law Journal*, quoting them and the EEOC in suggesting that the following factors be considered in evaluating a hostile work environment (39):

1. Whether the conduct was physical or verbal;
2. Frequency of the conduct;
3. Whether the conduct was hostile or potentially offensive;
4. Whether the harasser was a co-worker or supervisor;
5. Whether others joined in the harassing conduct; and
6. Whether the conduct was directed at more than one individual.

The brief for the Women's Bar Associations et al. provides considerable survey data on the problems of discrimination and harassment that female attorneys face in the criminal justice system. Examples included anecdotal information, such as a judge's saying to a woman attorney who was with six male lawyers: "Oh, come on now; shut up. Let's hear what the men have to say" (16). Another male judge said to a pregnant attorney, "So I see you got knocked up" (17). The National Employment Lawyers brief says that the personal experiences of lawyers in that organization validate the observations of social scientists as to the pervasiveness of sexual harassment on the job and the inability of many victims to remedy the problem on their own (9). Further, our society has yet to regard sexism with the same degree of abhorrence with which it regards racism (9). Numerous studies have shown that sexual harassment affects virtually all women (10). One survey found that 75 percent of subjects reported that sexual harassment had adversely affected their job performance (Crull 1982, quoted in the Women's Legal Defense Fund brief (13). The National Employment Lawyers brief argues that an employer should not be allowed to engage in conduct, either verbal or physical, that perpetuates the subjugation of women workers (29).

The NAACP brief pointed out that some might claim that verbal and other abuse is widespread in the workplace, and that such behavior simply reflects societal mores or values, which Title VII was not adopted to change. But the NAACP argues that this is precisely what Congress intended when, in 1964, it addressed the fact that racial bigotry abounded in work environments (15).[2] Agreeing with this position, in *Rabidue*, the dissent maintained: "I hardly believe reasonable women condone the pervasive degradation and exploitation of female sexuality perpetuated in American culture. In fact, pervasive societal approval thereof and of other stereotypes stifles female potential and instills the debased sense of self worth which accompanies stigmatization" (Martell and Sullivan 1994:199).

Women's groups were generally jubilant about the *Harris* decision. The executive director of the NOW Legal Defense Fund, Helen Neuborne, said: "We are thrilled with the Court's strong message that when women suffer sexual harassment, they will be treated exactly the same as any other group discriminated against based on race, religion or national origin" (Sachs 1993).

The American Psychological Association, in addition to addressing the issue of psychological harm, also considered the reasonableness standard. It submitted social science data about men's and women's differing perceptions of sexual harassment, which could provide a more objective test for determining whether a work environment is actionable under Title VII (6). Survey and laboratory research has shown that women are more likely than men to label sexually aggressive behavior at work as harassment (18). Studies also show that men are more likely to be tolerant of sexual harassment than women, and this may be because women see such harassment as a possible prelude to violence (19). This research relates to the question of whether to use a reasonable-man standard or reasonable-woman standard for the court.

In 1990 the EEOC adopted a reasonable-person standard that considered the victim's perspective and not stereotyped notions of unacceptable behavior, such as a workplace displaying "girlie" pictures and other offensive conduct (39). The genderless standard of reasonableness is a fairly recent development; historically, the standard has been that of a "reasonable man" (30). These issues are not merely matters of semantics. Unless the outlook of the reasonable woman is adopted, the defendants as well as the courts are permitted to sustain ingrained notions of reasonable behavior fashioned by the offenders, in this case, men (Martell and Sullivan 1994). The reasonable-person standard tends to be male-biased and systematically ignores the experiences of women (Robinson, Fink, and Allen 1994). The Court turned its back on the reasonable-women test in *Meritor* and again in *Harris*. In *Harris*, the Court used the reasonable-person terminology and did not address the reasonable-woman test as a replacement for the reasonable-person test in sexual harassment cases.

As Martell and Sullivan have written, "The development of the law of sexual harassment has been emerging from courts and administrative agencies for a considerable time, and the lack of definitional certitude is testimony to the inherent difficulty of the subject itself" (Martell and Sullivan 1994:205). The *Harris* ruling was very narrow in scope, holding that it was not necessary for a victim to prove psychological damage, and the Court did not adopt a reasonable-woman test. In the end, the *Harris* decision gave the business and legal communities little more guidance than was provided seven years earlier in *Meritor*. The Court has said what sexual harassment is not (it is not psychological damage), but it has failed to say what it is (Robinson, Fink, and Allen 1994).

Summary

No references were made to social science in the Supreme Court opinions of either sexual harassment case discussed in this chapter, although data were available through the ten briefs filed in the first case, *Meritor,* in 1986, and the twelve briefs filed in the second, *Harris,* in 1993.[3] Data in those briefs included information on the psychological impact of sexual harassment and on the nonpsychological injuries of cost. Studies of victimization, rape, and battered women were also available for reference, and an array of surveys revealed the number of women affected by sexual harassment in all sectors of government and business. Both statistical and anecdotal data were presented to the Court, but neither were used in these two cases.

There were no dissenting opinions in either case of sexual harassment, as the decisions in both cases were unanimous. In *Meritor* the appeals court had made two references to social science, but in *Harris* there were no published opinions from the lower courts to evaluate. Even though the justices referred to social science data in both abortion and sex-discrimination cases, they did not do so in the sexual harassment cases.

Notes

1. Aaron (1993) draws on two of Joan Biskupic's articles for the chronology of the Clarence Thomas confirmation hearings: "Deflecting Tough Questions, Thomas Stumps Senators," *Congressional Quarterly* 49 no. 37 (1991): 2619–23, and "With a Split

Vote Over Thomas, Panel Sends Bush a Message," *Congressional Quarterly* 49, no. 39 (1991): 2786–87.

2. An opposing view is taken in the brief of the Feminists for Free Expression, that the paternalistic project of sanitizing workplace speech in defense of women workers enshrines archaic stereotypes of women as delicate, asexual creatures who require special protection from mere words and images, and the group argues that hostile work environment theory has gone awry in relation to the First Amendment protection of free speech (13–14).

3. We do not provide a table here because *Harris* occurred outside of the twenty-year period of study and was included here for comparison only, as the second case to be heard by the Supreme Court.

Results and Conclusions

Our study shows that the Supreme Court uses social science data in its decisions, but that the Court gives far more weight to its decisions in previous cases. In table 3 we combine our findings about the Court's use of social science data in abortion and sex-discrimination cases. We discovered that hundreds of citations may be made to previous cases in an opinion, but few are made to social science. Our study bears out the theory that a major issue surrounding the citation of social science data is not the veracity or quality of the data but the appropriateness of using social science data at all.

Our findings permit us to answer our original research questions explicitly:

1. The use of social science data by the Supreme Court is not dependent upon whether such data were introduced into and considered by the lower courts.
2. The frequency of the use of data from the social sciences in opinions of Supreme Court justices does not depend on whether the opinion expressed is a majority or dissenting opinion.
3. There is a difference in the kind or nature of the social science data depending on how the information entered the courts in the form of a preference for data submitted to the courts via *amicus* briefs.
4. It does not appear that certain kinds of social science data carry more weight than others.
5. Data are used in the courtroom in a manner consistent with the standards of the legal community, not the social sciences community.

Imwinkelried (1986) said that social science is used in one-third of cases. It was used more than that in the cases studied here; citations were made in 19 of the 35 cases in this study (54 percent) that came before the Court between 1972 and 1992. Brown (1989) found that federal courts rarely cite social science re-

Table 3. Citations to Social Science in U.S. Supreme Court Decisions, 1972–92:
Abortion and Sex-Discrimination Cases ($N = 35$)

	Number of Cases				Combined Cases: Abortion and Sex Discrimination	
	Abortion		Sex Discrimination			
	With Cites	Total	With Cites	Total	With Cites	Total
Douglas (1939–75)	0	3	2	3	2	6
Stewart (1958–81)	1	13	2	8	3	21
Burger (1969–86)	2	17	3	10	5	27
Powell (1972–87)	2	17	3	12	5	29
Brennan (1956–90)	7	20	5	12	12	32
Marshall (1967–91)	7	21	8	13	15	34
Blackmun (1970–91)	9	22	4	12	13	34
White (1962–93)	2	22	4	13	6	35
Rehnquist (1972–)	2	22	2	13	4	35
Stevens (1975–)	4	19	5	10	9	29
O'Connor (1981–)	3	9	2	5	5	14
Scalia (1986–)	0	5	1	3	1	8
Kennedy (1988–)	1	5	0	1	1	6
Souter (1990–)	1	2	1	1	2	3
Thomas (1991–)	0	1	0	0	0	1
Majority	4	22	6	13	10	35
Dissent	9	22	5	13	14	35
Total Cites	9	22	10	13	19	35
Appeals	2	12	3	9	5	21
District	8	19	5	8	13	27
State Supreme Court	0	3	1	1	1	4

search in obscenity cases, and when they did it was to support the law under
review, rather than to overturn it. Acker (1987) concluded that in criminal
cases, the Supreme Court referred to social science research more frequently
than did the district court, with the Supreme Court citing it in 20 percent of its
cases and the district courts citing it in 3.3 percent of the cases. The use of social
science by the Supreme Court has increased over time, though not greatly.
References to social science increased in abortion cases, from none in *Roe,* in
1973, to 31 citations in *Pennsylvania,* in 1992. The number of social science references did not increase in the sex-discrimination cases, but these cases started
out with more citations than did the abortion cases.

The number of studies presented to the Court for its consideration increased over time, as evidenced by the briefs. For example, fewer than twenty briefs were submitted in *Roe* but there were over seventy-five in *Webster*. The number of citations at the district court level increased as well. Since the scientific process is cumulative, obviously more studies existed twenty years later, but even in the early cases there was never a lack of scientific studies on the issues, and these studies were presented to the court through experts and briefs. What is surprising is that greater use has not been made of social science. It is likely that social science will be used more in the future than it has been in the past, particularly on women's issues, because a larger percentage of those cases have already used social science than did other types of cases. Further, issues concerning women, such as sexual harassment and the continued debates on abortion, will be brought before the Court for years to come.

The justices sometimes acted as if the social science evidence did not exist. As with policymakers, however, the justices chose the studies most appropriate to their respective arguments when they did consider such evidence. A number of issues relating to this point have been raised in the literature. Rosen (1972) said that when the Court wished to uphold social welfare measures, it accepted the validity of facts of the Brandeis brief, but when it chose to reject legislation, the Court found extralegal data spurious and unconvincing. That seemed to be less the case with abortion and sex discrimination, because the justices sometimes did not use the information even when it supported a position. Tanford (1990) and Bersoff (1987) found the courts to be reluctant to use social science. But their analyses were limited to issues relating to the judicial process, such as jury selection. Imwinkelried (1986) discussed how statistics are used regarding discrimination to determine if hiring patterns are discriminatory. The Court used such information; however, the case usually did not turn on fact, but on law. To say that the justices use scientific data when it is in their best interest, as Bersoff (1987) has suggested, is to oversimplify.

There were many instances when a majority or a dissenting opinion could have relied upon existing, even previously cited, social science data to bolster an argument, but did not. Over half of the cases (19 out of 35) referred to social science data, with almost as many majority opinions as dissenting opinions containing citations. Ten of the 35 (29 percent) cases contained references to social science in the majority opinions, and 14 of the 35 cases (40 percent) made references to social science in the dissenting opinions. The justices used social science data in both types of cases. The Supreme Court referred to social science in more of the cases on sex discrimination than in those on abortion, but with fewer total citations. The justices cited social science data in 9 of the 22 (41 percent) abortion cases and in 10 of the 13 (77 percent) sex-discrimination cases. In the 22 abortion cases there were 125 citations to social science (6 per case); in the 13 sex discrimination cases there were 52 citations (4 per case), so there were more citations per case in abortion cases. The justices were more likely to cite social science in cases having to do with parental and spousal consent than in those concerning funding issues. In sex-discrimination cases, there was not a notable difference among cases. All of the justices, particularly Scalia and Rehnquist, appear reluctant to be influenced by public opinion. Epstein and Kobylka (1992) have suggested that modern court decisions reflect public opinion. To the extent that this is true, public opinion was indirectly, and not directly, reflected in the women's issues.

Public opinion should not be confused with other types of social science research. Scientific surveys can provide true reflections of public opinion and objective views of the effects of abortion, discrimination, and harassment. Other types of research—laboratory, clinical, and field studies—can also provide evidence of the effects of unwanted pregnancy or of the psychological and non-psychological impacts of both sex discrimination in hiring and sexual harassment on the job. Such information provides a basis for monitoring changes in society over time and meets the criterion of social science expressed by Justice Frankfurter, when he said that the social sciences can provide new and important insights about society (in Rosen 1972).

Friedman (1975) suggests that judges use public opinion polls, but the justices did not cite public opinion data in these cases, even though such data were available, particularly on the issue of abortion. Public opinion may or may not influence the Court through the process of "enlightenment." Friedman (1975) asserts that social science journals and law review articles that use social science are the means by which the influence of the larger society creeps into court decisions. This seems more to the point than any direct influence of public opinion. Tanford (1990) suggests that the law resists change and tends toward the *status quo*, ignoring evidence and public opinion that is to the contrary to certain ideas. This suggestion seems on point with regard to public opinion, but less so with other evidence, which the justices did use in some cases.

When given the choice, in both abortion and sex-discrimination cases, the justices appeared to favor the use of statistical data over clinical data, although opinions in the abortion cases were slightly more likely to rely on clinical data than were those in sex-discrimination cases. This is largely because the abortion issue seemed to lend itself more readily to case histories and anecdotes, and sex discrimination more to statistics. When data were evaluated, it was at the district court level, rather than at the Supreme Court level, and usually by expert witnesses on either side who criticized studies or testimony of the opposing side. Some data were reanalyzed by the lower court, and the evaluations in the lower courts were made according to both scientific and legal standards. While expert witnesses do not usually testify before the Supreme Court, they are frequently involved in the preparation of the briefs for the Court. For that reason, their evidence is admitted indirectly rather than directly. Lower courts sometimes outline the experts' credentials and then point out if they believed there was a conflict of interest or bias. Criticisms had to do with the experts' methods and with the investigators themselves, but our study could not determine which was the greatest consideration overall—the investigators, the methods, or the findings. Statistical data were questioned and sometimes reanalyzed by the lower courts, and experts were sometimes disqualified. In district court, guidelines regarding refereed journals were sometimes used, but this will change in the future because of the *Daubert* decision, which says such criteria are not necessary.

A scientifically reliable study—one that is relevant, ethically conducted, and exhibits the authors' awareness of the values and biases, provides proper disclaimers, and does not exaggerate results—is almost assured of being entered into the court record. If it is not entered in the lower courts, then it may be entered through the *amicus curiae* briefs. The *amicus* briefs appear to provide a balance in the presentation of data to the court because both sides are represented—plaintiff and respondent. Even if a particular expert witness does not provide a balanced view, opposing studies are presented to the Court through the briefs or through opposing witnesses in the lower courts. In our research, however, we found that many more studies were presented in the briefs than were cited by the Supreme Court. Social science studies that were entered into the record appeared to be the most current on the subject, and the ones cited were up-to-date. Social scientists can provide evidence on both sides of an issue; there does not have to be only "one answer" supplied to the Court from social science because the Court will pick from among the studies and data presented. Evidentiary rules and the qualifications of experts and the science they present are handled by the courts. The democratic process can be seen at work in the process of providing *amicus* briefs, when interested parties present both sides of the argument. Lindman (1989) asserted that an attorney will bring to the Court's attention only facts he desires. This does not appear to be a problem, however, because the other side will do the same. Lawyers, interested parties, and judges will make the selection of facts necessary for the final decision.

The Supreme Court sometimes used evidence from briefs not introduced by the lower courts. It is Monahan and Walker's (1986) hope that the Court be unconstrained in its ability to reevaluate any social science upon which a lower court relied, or to use research dismissed by a lower court. The justices clearly exercised such judgment in the cases studied here. The Supreme Court referred to social science in more cases than did the district courts or courts of appeals, but the district courts' treatment of social science experts and literature was more extensive. The district courts and the Supreme Court both referred to social science about half of the time, but not necessarily on the same cases. The court of appeals cited social science less often. In other words, the use of social science by the Supreme Court was not dependent upon the lower courts. The district court's use did not dictate the Supreme Court's use. The lower courts may have cited social science and the Supreme Court would not, or the Supreme Court may cite such studies and the lower courts had not. The Supreme Court quoted studies either from the lower court or from the *amicus* briefs, but more often from the briefs.

The inability of social scientists to explain all aspects of human behavior should not undermine the contributions they can provide. There is no reason that descriptive social science cannot provide the rationale for normative judicial decisions. This study confirms that it can and does. Concern that the law may fluctuate with each new data set seems unfounded in light of this study because prior cases are by far the greater contributor to the Court's decision.

The findings imply that social scientists can anticipate the possible use of their studies by the courts, some of which may be surprising. Who would have predicted that studies of wife battering, child abuse, or suicide would contribute to later decisions on abortion? Or that a study on violence in schools would be used in deciding a case on pregnancy leave in a sex-discrimination case? These cases indicate the unlimited possibilities for the Court's use of social science data. A scientific study with clearly delineated findings will almost certainly be introduced to the Court, if it is on a topic related to a particular case before the Supreme Court.

Our research revealed no indication from the justices themselves as to when they use social science, why they use it, or, conversely, why they do not use it. A survey reported by Monahan and Walker (1986) found that 40 percent of state supreme court judges did their own independent investigations. Except for Justice Blackmun's independent medical research in *Roe*, there is no evidence that any of the justices did independent investigations on abortion or sex discrimination. We can confirm Tanford's (1990) findings, gleaned from conversations with clerks, that judges almost never do proactive research. It becomes apparent, then, that there are certain limitations on the Court's use of social science data. The clerks have a role in it, by selecting the information that the justices see. Other factors are the justices' group deliberation process and the outside influences upon them. Also, the expert witnesses can have an indirect role, as can the quality of the studies. Long-held positions of the justices may also have an impact on their decisions. For example, Justice Ginsburg promised that she and Justice O'Connor would help their male colleagues "look at life a bit differently" (Sachs 1993). The *Harris* sexual harassment case may have marked the beginning of that changed view.

In sum, the use of social science data by the Supreme Court has increased over time, although its use is neither entirely predictable nor consistent. Science seeks truth, and the law seeks truth; clearly, the law can use social science in arriving at the truth. Social facts clearly aided the justices in their decisions on abortion and sex discrimination—not consistently, but these facts were crucial to their arguments at certain times. The broader question is whether the legal culture accepts the social science culture. It does, but on its own terms. The results of our study indicate that the two can and do work together.

Appendix A: Overview of the Research Design

We considered thirty-five cases on abortion and sex discrimination that the Supreme Court decided between 1972 and 1992, along with fifty-one lower court cases, for a total of eighty-six cases. We analyzed existing data by measuring the frequency of social science citations in the Court's opinions. The use of public documents and official records for sociological research dates back to Durkheim's use of death records in 1897 (Singleton et al. 1988). In our study, we employed both qualitative and quantitative methods of analysis. Such an analysis of the Supreme Court cases can provide a comprehensive understanding of how, why, and when the justices use social science, a result not possible from a citation count alone. Our analysis was based on several thousand pages of written court records.

For purposes of the research, social science was defined as information and data dealing with social, social-psychological and psychological issues. Literature that was strictly medical, religious, philosophical, ethical, or historical in nature was not classified as social science. Statistics, such as census data, were considered to be social science if they dealt with social issues and were interpreted beyond raw numbers. Public opinion polls and surveys were classified as social science.

Areas of interest that were outside the scope of the study include: (1) the effect that the group deliberation process and the sociodemographic characteristics or attitudes of the justices had on the decision; (2) the effect the justices' overall knowledge of an issue—that is, their "enlightenment"—had on their decision, since such information, if it is documented at all, exists outside the official court records and our analysis was limited to what is stated in the court records; (3) the role of expert testimony, since not as much was included about such testimony in the court record as had been anticipated; (4) the role of briefs and whether or not their number increased over time, and whether reliance on briefs increased over time, since the study was limited to examining briefs in detail in only four cases, not in the entire sample of thirty-five Supreme Court cases; (5) whether or not the quality of the social science studies had improved over the twenty years studied; and (6) the role of the justices' clerks in determining what the justices see and do not see, since the analysis was limited to the citations and the written record.

The Sample

Instead of selecting from among them, we included in our sample all cases on abortion and sex discrimination against women in the workplace that were decided by the U.S. Supreme Court from 1972 to 1992. Thus, the sample is the universe. Cases on the subjects that were decided before or after that period are not included in the quantitative analysis presented in the tables. Sex-discrimination cases were included only if they involved discrimination against women, not against men, though there were such cases. Only cases of sexual discrimination regarding employment were included—not other sex-discrimination cases, such as those regarding credit, jury duty, and alimony. To insure that all cases meeting the research criteria were included, we consulted legal citation indexes; we reviewed the later opinions of the Court for reference to all previous cases on the subjects; and we consulted other related social science studies (e.g., Drucker 1990; Epstein and Kobylka 1992; Goldstein 1988; Hoff-Wilson 1991; Horan, Grant, and Cunningham 1987; Rosenberg 1991).

In all, there were 22 Supreme Court cases on abortion and 13 Supreme Court cases on sex discrimination that met the criteria of the study design, for a total of 35 Supreme Court cases. In addition to the Supreme Court cases, the opinions of the lower courts were included. There were 32 lower court cases on abortion and 19 on sex discrimination, bringing the total of Supreme Court and lower court cases on abortion to 54 and the total of Supreme Court and lower court cases on sex discrimination to 32, for a total of 86 court cases on the combined cases of abortion and sex discrimination, as shown in table A-1.

Table A-1. Number of Cases: U.S. Supreme Court on Abortion
and Sex Discrimination, 1972–92

	Abortion	Sex Discrimination	Total
Supreme Court	22	13	35
Lower Courts	32	19	51
	54	32	86

We selected four cases for an in-depth analysis of the briefs: the first case on abortion (*Roe v. Wade*), in 1973, and the last one on abortion (*Planned Parenthood of Southeastern Pennsylvania v. Robert P. Casey*), in 1992; the first case on sex discrimination in employment (*Frontiero v. Richardson*), in 1973, and the last one on sex discrimination in employment during the study period (*International Union v. Johnson Controls*), in 1991. From this, it was possible to determine if the use of social science increased over the twenty-year period. The briefs, as compared to the opinions, list all outside evidence presented to the Court. The cases analyzed for the study are listed chronologically by subject in Appendix B.

Sexual harassment, a form of sex discrimination, had come before the Supreme Court only once during the period of 1972 and 1992 (*Meritor* in 1986). But because of its increasing importance and relevancy, a second case, *Harris v. Forklift Systems, Inc.* (1993) was added to the research.

The Analysis

Because of the Court's need for accuracy, Court opinions are an excellent source of data, providing internal consistency, reliability, and validity. The factors below were determined from both the majority and the dissenting opinions. The dissent is sometimes even richer in detail and citations than the majority opinion.

1. Citations of social science data that were relied upon
2. How the social science evidence was introduced, that is, via expert witness, briefs
3. How the studies were evaluated by the Court
4. How the expert witnesses were evaluated by the Court
5. What previous cases were relied upon

In sum, in our study we analyzed existing and available data by (1) applying a sociological model for the content analysis of the court records; (2) measuring the frequency of the appearance of social science citations; and (3) relating the citations to one another and to the other variables of the study.

Appendix B: List of Cases

Abortion

Roe v. Wade
Supreme Court: 410 U.S. 113 (1973)
Appeals: No Appeal
District: 314 F.Supp. 1217

Doe v. Bolton
Supreme Court: 410 U.S. 179 (1973)
Appeals: No Appeal
District: 319 F.Supp. 1048

Bigelow v. Va
Supreme Court: 421 U.S. 809 (1975)
Appeals: No Appeal
State Supreme Court: 214 VA 341, 200 S.E. 2d 680

Planned Parenthood of Central Missouri v. Danforth
Supreme Court: 428 U.S. 52 (1976)
Appeals: No Appeal
District: 392 F.Supp. 1362

Singleton v. Wulff
Supreme Court: 428 U.S. 106 (1976)
Appeals: 508 F.2d 1211
District: 380 F.Supp. 1137

Beal v. Doe
Supreme Court: 432 U.S. 438 (1977)
Appeals: 523 F.2d 611
District: 376 F.Supp. 173

Maher v. Roe
Supreme Court: 432 U.S. 464 (1977)
Appeals: 522 F.2d 928
District: 380 F.Supp. 726

Poelker v. Doe
Supreme Court: 432 U.S. 519 (1977)
Appeals: 497 F.2d 1063 & 515 F.2d 541
District: Dismissed

Colautti v. Franklin
Supreme Court: 439 U.S. 379 (1979)
Appeals: No Appeal
District: 401 F.Supp. 541

Bellotti v. Baird
Supreme Court 443 U.S. 622 (1979)
Appeals: No Appeal
District: 450 F.Supp. 997

Harris v. McRae
Supreme Court: 448 U.S. 297 (1980)
Appeals: No appeal
District: 491 F.Supp. 630

Williams v. Zbaraz
Supreme Court: 448 U.S. 358 (1980)
Appeals: No appeal
District: 469 F.Supp. 1212

H.L. v. Matheson
Supreme Court: 450 U.S. 398 (1981)
State Supreme Court: Utah 604 P.2d 907
District: Dismissed

City of Akron v. Akron Center for Reproductive Health, Inc.
Supreme Court: 462 U.S. 416 (1983)
Appeals: 651 F.2d 1198
District: 479 F.Supp. 1172

Planned Parenthood Association of Kansas City, Missouri, v. Ashcroft
Supreme Court: 462 U.S. 476 (1983)
Appeals: 655 F.2d 848 & 664 F.2d 687
District: 483 F.Supp. 679

Simopoulos v. Virginia
Supreme Court: 462 U.S. 506 (1983)
Appeals: No appeal
State Supreme Court: 221 VA 1059, 277 S.E. 2d 194

Thornburgh v. American College of Obstetricians & Gynecologists
Supreme Court: 476 U.S. 747 (1986)
Appeals: 737 F.2d 283
District: 552 F.Supp. 791

Webster v. Reproductive Health Services
Supreme Court 492 U.S. 490 (1989)
Appeals: 851 F.2d 1071
District: 662 F.Supp. 407

Hodgson v. Minnesota
Supreme Court: 497 U.S. 417 (1990)
Appeals: 853 F.2d 1452
District: 648 F.Supp. 756

State of Ohio v. Akron Center for Reproductive Health, Inc.
Supreme Court 497 U.S. 502 (1990)
Appeals: 854 F.2d 852
District: 633 F.Supp. 1123

Rust v. Sullivan
Supreme Court: 11 S.Ct. 1759 (1991)
Appeals: 889 F.2d 410
District: 690 F.Supp. 1261

Robert P. Casey v. Planned Parenthood of Southeastern Pennsylvania
Supreme Court: 112 S.Ct. 2791 (1992)
Appeals: 947 F.2d 682
District: 744 F.Supp. 1323

Sex Discrimination

Frontiero v. Richardson
Supreme Court: 411 U.S. 677 (1973)
Appeals: No Appeal
District: 341 F.Supp. 201

Cleveland Board of Education v. LaFleur
Supreme Court: 414 U.S. 632 (1974)
Appeals: 465 F.2d 1184 & 474 F.2d 395
District: 326 F.Supp. 1208

Geduldig v. Aiello
Supreme Court: 417 U.S. 484 (1974)
Appeals: No Appeal
District: 359 F.Supp. 792

General Electric v. Gilbert
Supreme Court: 429 U.S. 125 (1976)
Appeals: 519 F.2d 661
District: 375 F.Supp. 367

Dothard v. Rawlinson
Supreme Court: 433 U.S. 321 (1977)
Appeals: No Appeal
District: 418 F.Supp. 1169

Nashville Gas Co. v. Satty
Supreme Court: 434 U.S. 136 (1977)
Appeals: 522 F.2d 850
District: 384 F.Supp. 765

City of Los Angeles Department of Water and Power v. Manhart
Supreme Court: 435 U.S. 702 (1978)
Appeals: 553 F.2d 581
District: 387 F.Supp. 980

County of Washington, Oregon v. Gunther
Supreme Court: 452 U.S. 161 (1981)
Appeals: 602 F.2d 882 & 623 F.2d 1303

Hishon v. King and Spalding
Supreme Court: 467 U.S. 69 (1984)
Appeals: 678 F.2d 1022 (1984)
District Court: Dismissed

Meritor Savings Bank v. Vinson
Supreme Court: 477 U.S. 57 (1986)
Appeals: 753 F.2d 141

Wimberly v. Industrial Relations Commission of Missouri
Supreme Court: 107 S.Ct. 821 (1987)
State Supreme Court: Missouri 688 S.W.2d 344

California Federal Savings and Loan v. Guerra
Supreme Court: 107 S.Ct. 683 (1987)
Appeals: 758 F.2d 390

International Union v. Johnson Controls, Inc.
Supreme Court: 111 S.Ct. 1196 (1991)
Appeals: 886 F.2d 871
District: 680 F.Supp. 309

Harris v. Forklift Systems, Inc.
Supreme Court: 114 S.Ct. 367 (1993)
Appeals: 976 F.2d 733 (unpublished)
United States Magistrate Judge: Unpublished

Bibliography

Aaron, Titus E. (with Judith A. Isaksen). 1993. *Sexual Harassment in the Workplace: A Guide to the Law and a Research Overview for Employers and Employees.* Jefferson, N.C.: McFarland.

Acker, James R. 1987. "The Supreme Court's Use of Social Science Research Evidence in Criminal Cases." Ph.D. diss., State University of New York at Albany, 1987. Microfiche, Ann Arbor, Mich.: UMI, 1988.

Adler, Nancy E., Henry P. David, Brenda N. Major, Susan H. Roth, Nancy Felipe Russo, and Gail E. Wyatt. 1992. "Psychological Factors in Abortion." *American Psychologist* 47 (10): 1194–1204.

Aliotta, Jilda M. 1991. "The Unfinished Feminist Agenda: The Shifting Forum." *Annals of the American Academy of Political and Social Sciences* 515:140–50.

Anderson, Patrick R. 1987. "Scholarship in the Courtroom: The Criminologist as Expert Witness." In *Expert Witnesses: Criminologists in the Courtroom,* ed. Patrick R. Anderson and Thomas L. Winfree, 9–19. Albany: State University of New York Press.

Anderson, Patrick R., and Thomas L. Winfree, eds. 1987. *Expert Witnesses: Criminologists in the Courtroom.* Albany: State University of New York Press.

Barnes, David W. 1983. *Statistics as Proof: Fundamentals of Quantitative Evidence.* New York: Little, Brown.

———. 1986. *Statistical Evidence in Litigation: Methodology, Procedure, and Practice.* New York: Little, Brown.

Barnett, Edith. 1989. "Sexual Harassment: A Continuing Source of Litigation in the Workplace." *Trial* 25 (June): 34–38.

Barton, Anne. 1983. "My Experience as an Expert Witness." *American Statistician* 37 (4): 374–76.

Baum, David B. 1984. "Taking on the Opposing Expert: An Approach to Cross-Examination." *Trial* 20 (April): 74–78.

Belli, Melvin M., Sr. 1982. "The Expert Witness." *Trial* 17 (July): 35–37.

Bersoff, Donald N. 1987. "Social Science Data and the Supreme Court: Lockhart as a Case in Point." *American Psychologist* 47 (1): 52–58.

Biskupic, Joan. 1992. "High Court to Review Expert-Witness Standards in Product Case." *Washington Post*, Oct. 14.

———. 1993. "Court Lets North Dakota Enforce Abortion Law." *Washington Post*, Apr. 3.

Black, Donald J. 1989. *Sociological Justice.* New York: Oxford University Press.

———. 1972. "The Boundaries of Legal Sociology." *Yale Law Journal* 81:1086–1100.

Blau, Theodore H. 1984. *The Psychologist as Expert Witness.* New York: Wiley.

Block, Alan P. 1990. "Rape Trauma Syndrome as Scientific Expert Testimony." *Archives of Sexual Behavior* 19 (4): 309–23.

Brown, Allen J. 1989. "The Utilization of Social Science Research by the Federal Judiciary: A Quantitative Analysis of Obscenity Opinions." Ph.D., diss., University of Nebraska. Microfiche, Ann Arbor, Mich.: UMI.

Burstein, Paul. 1989. "Attacking Sex Discrimination in the Labor Market: A Study in Law and Politics." *Social Forces* 67 (3): 641–65.

Carleton, Francis Joseph, III. 1992. "Sex Discrimination Law and Women in the Workplace: A Feminist Analysis of Legal Ideology." Ph.D., diss., Indiana University, 1991. *Dissertation Abstracts International* 53/01A, p. 287.

Carter, Rosalynn. 1984. *First Lady from Plains.* Boston: Houghton Mifflin.

Chafetz, Janet Saltzman. 1990. *Gender Equity: An Integrated Theory of Stability and Change.* Newbury Park, Calif.: Sage.

Chan, Steve. 1982. "Expert Judgments Under Uncertainty: Some Evidence and Suggestions." *Social Science Quarterly* 63 (3): 429–44.

Chesler, Mark A., Joseph Sanders, and Debra S. Kalmuss. 1988. *Social Science in Court: Mobilizing Experts in the School Desegregation Cases.* Madison: University of Wisconsin Press.

Ciresi, Michael V., and Martha K. Wivell. 1991. "Protecting Your Evidence Against 'Junk Science' Attacks." *Trial* 27 (Nov.): 35–40.

Colker, Ruth. 1992. *Abortion and Dialogue.* Bloomington: Indiana University Press.

Collins, Patricia Hill. 1990. *Black Feminist Thought.* New York: Routledge.

Conley, John M. 1993. Review of *Deciding to Decide: Agenda Setting in the United States Supreme Court*, by H. W. Perry Jr. *Contemporary Sociology* 22 (Mar.): 2.

Copen, George. 1990. "Controlling Contests: Interpretation and Expert Testimony." *American Speech* 65 (Winter): 323–33.

Coser, Lewis A. 1977. *Masters of Sociological Thought.* New York: Harcourt Brace Jovanovich.

Cott, Nancy. 1990. "Historical Perspectives." In *Conflicts in Feminism*, ed. Marianne Hirsch and Evelyn Fox Keller, 44–59. New York: Routledge.

Craven, J. Braxton, Jr. 1975. "The Impact of Social Science Evidence on the Judge: A Personal Comment." *Law and Contemporary Problems* 39 (1): 150–56.

Davis, Kenneth Culp. 1986. "Judicial, Legislative, and Administrative Lawmaking: A Proposed Research Service for the Supreme Court." *Minnesota Law Review* 71:1–71.

Davis, William L. 1991. "Family Planning Services: A History of U.S. Federal Legislation." *Journal of Family History* 16 (4): 381–400.

Delgado, Richard. 1984. "Moral Experts in Court? The Jury Is Still Out." *The Center Magazine* 17 (Apr.): 48–64.

Diamond, Shari Seidman. 1982. "Growth and Maturation in Psychology and Law." *Law and Society Review* 17 (1): 1982.

Di Paoloa, Marianna, and Georgia Green. 1990. "Jurors' Beliefs about the Interpretation of Speaking Style." *American Speech* 65 (Winter): 304–22.

Dorram, Peter B. 1982. *The Expert Witness.* Washington, D.C.: Planners Press.

Driessen, Patrick A. 1983. "The Wedding of Social Science and the Courts: Is the Marriage Working?" *Social Science Quarterly* 64 (Sept.): 476–93.

Drucker, Dan. 1990. *Abortion Decisions of the Supreme Court, 1973 through 1989.* Jefferson, N.C.: McFarland.

Epstein, Lee, and Joseph F. Kobylka. 1992. *The Supreme Court and Legal Change: Abortion and the Death Penalty.* Chapel Hill: University of North Carolina Press.

Faigman, David L. 1989. "To Have and Have Not: Assessing the Value of Social Science to the Law as Science and Policy." *Emory Law Journal* 38:1005–95.

Faust, David, and Jay Ziskin. 1988. "The Expert Witness in Psychology and Psychiatry." *Science* 241 (July 1): 31–35.

Feder, Harold A. 1985. "The Care and Feeding of Experts." *Trial* 21 (June): 49–52.

Federal Rules of Evidence. 1988. Westbury, N.Y.: Foundation Press.

Fennelly, Lawrence J. 1983. "The Life of an Expert Witness." *Security Management* 27 (Sept.): 92–97.

Freckelton, Ian R. 1987. *The Trial of the Expert: A Study of Expert Evidence and Forensic Experts.* New York: Oxford University Press.

Freeman, Richard B., and Jonathan S. Leonard. 1987. "Unions and the Female Work Force." In *Gender in the Workplace,* ed. Clair Brown and Joseph A. Rechman, 189–216. Washington, D.C.: Brookings Institution.

Friedman, Lawrence M. 1975. *The Legal System: A Social Science Perspective.* New York: Russell Sage Foundation.

Friedman, Lawrence M., and Stewart Macaulay. 1977. *Law and the Behavioral Sciences.* Indianapolis: Bobbs-Merrill.

Friedman, Leon. 1993. *The Supreme Court Confronts Abortion: The Briefs, Argument, and Decision in* Planned Parenthood v. Casey. New York: Farrar, Straus, and Giroux.

Friloux, C. Anthony. 1975. "Another View from the Bar." In *The Jury System in America,* ed. Rita J. Simon, 217–33. Beverly Hills: Sage.

Fyfe, James. 1987. "Police Expert Witness." In *Expert Witnessess: Criminologists in the Courtroom,* ed. Patrick R. Anderson and Thomas L. Winfree, 100–118. Albany: State University of New York Press.

Gardener, William, David Scherer, and Maya Tester. 1989. "Asserting Scientific Authority: Cognitive Development and Adolescent Legal Rights." *American Psychologist* 44 (6): 895–902.

Geis, Gilbert. 1991. "The Case Study Method in Sociological Criminology." In *A Case for the Case Study*, ed. Joe R. Feagin, Anthony M. Orum, and Gideon Sjoberg, 200–223. Chapel Hill: University of North Carolina Press.

Goldstein, Leslie Friedman. 1988. *The Constitutional Rights of Women: Cases in Law and Social Change*. Madison: University of Wisconsin Press.

Granberg, Donald. 1985. "The United States Senate Votes to Uphold *Roe v Wade*." *Population Research and Policy Review* 4:115–31.

Hafemeister, Thomas L. 1988. "The Impact of Social Science Materials on the Judiciary: A Qualitative and Quantitative Analysis." Ph.D. diss., University of Nebraska, 1989. Microfiche, Ann Arbor, Mich.: UMI, 1988.

Halberstam, David. 1993. *The Fifties*. New York: Villard.

Halva-Neubauer, Glen. 1990. "Abortion Policy in the Post-*Webster* Age." *Publius* 20 (Summer): 27–44.

———. 1993. "Legislative Agenda-Setting in the States: The Case of Abortion Policy." Ph.D. diss., University of Minnesota, 1992. *Dissertation Abstracts International* 53/09A, p. 603.

Hamel, Jacques. 1992. "The Case Method in Sociology." *Current Sociology* 40 (1): 1–48.

Hans, Valerie. P. 1989. "Expert Witnessing." Review of *Mobilizing Experts in the School Desegregation Cases*, by Mark A. Chesler, Joseph Sanders, and Debra S. Kalmuss. *Science* 245 (July 21): 312–13.

Hartmann, Heidi I. 1987. "Internal Labor Markets and Gender: A Case Study of Promotion." In *Gender in the Workplace*, ed. Clair Brown and Joseph A. Pechman. Washington, D.C.: The Brookings Institution.

Hely, James. 1985. "Opponent's Experts Can Work for You." *Trial* 21 (Sept.): 64–68.

Hoff-Wilson, Joan. 1991. *Law, Gender, and Injustice: A Legal History of U.S. Women*. New York: New York University Press.

Hopper, Kim. 1990. "Research Findings as Testimony: A Note on the Ethnographer as Expert Witness." *Human Organization* 49 (2): 110–13.

Homant, Robert J. 1989. "Assessing Psychological Damages of Crime Victims." *Trial* 25 (Jan.): 86–90.

Horan, Dennis J., Edward R. Grant, and Paige C. Cunningham. 1987. *Abortion and Constitution*. Washington, D.C.: Georgetown University Press.

Horowitz, Donald L. 1977. *The Courts and Social Policy*. Washington, D.C.: Brookings Institution.

Horsley, Jack E., with John Calova. 1988. *Testifying in Court*. Oradell, N.J.: Medical Economical Books.

Howard, Perla Buhay. 1988. "A Content Analysis of Newspaper Portrayal of Abortion Topics, January 1, 1986, to December 31, 1986." Ph.D. diss., Oklahoma State University, 1989. *Dissertation Abstracts International* 49/10A, p. 2850.

Humphreys, Hugh C. 1987. "Cross-Examining the Expert." *Trial* 23 (Oct.): 75–78.

Imwinkelried, Edward J. 1986. "Science Takes the Stand." *The Sciences* (Nov.–Dec.): 20–25.

Ingraham, Barton L. 1987. "The Ethics of Testimony: Conflicting Views on the Role of the Criminologist as Expert Witness." In *Expert Witnesses: Criminologists in the Courtroom*, ed. Patrick R. Anderson and Thomas L. Winfree, 178–99. Albany: State University of New York Press.

Jones, Russell A. 1985. *Research Methods in the Social and Behavioral Sciences.* Sunderland, Mass.: Sinauer Associations.

Kandal, Terry. 1988. *The Woman Question in Classical Sociological Theory.* Miami: Florida International University Press.

Kaye, David H. 1990. "Improving Legal Statistics" (review essay). *Law and Society Review* 24 (5): 1255–75.

Kraft, Melvin D. 1982. *Using Experts in Civil Cases.* New York: Practicing Law Institute.

Langelan, Martha J. 1993. *Back Off: How to Confront and Stop Sexual Harassment and Harassers.* New York: Simon and Schuster.

Langerman, Amy G. 1990. "Making Sure Your Experts Shine." *Trial* 28 (Jan.): 106–10.

Levine, Murray. 1974. "Scientific Method and the Adversary Model." *American Psychologist* 29 (Sept.): 661–77.

Lewis, Neil A. 1993. "Thomas Still Carries Wounds." *Seattle Post-Intelligencer,* Nov. 27.

Lieberman, Jethro K. 1992. *The Evolving Constitution: How the Supreme Court Has Ruled on Issues from Abortion to Zoning.* New York: Random House.

Lindman, Constance R. 1989. "Sources of Judicial Distrust of Social Science Evidence: A Comparison of Social Science and Jurisprudence." *Indiana Law Journal* 64:755–68.

MacHovec, Frank J. 1987. *The Expert Witness Survival Manual.* Springfield, Ill.: Thomas.

Malone, David M. 1988. "Direct Examination of Experts." *Trial* 24 (Apr.): 44–49.

Mannheim, Karl. 1936. *Ideology and Utopia.* New York: Harcourt Brace Jovanovich.

Marmon, Sharon, and Howard A. Palley. 1986. "The Decade after Roe versus Wade: Ideology, Political Cleavage, and the Policy Process." *Research in Politics and Society* 2:181–209.

Marshall, Thomas R. 1991. "Public Opinion and the Rehnquist Court." *Judicature* 74 (5): 323–29.

Martell, Kathryn, and George Sullivan. 1994. "Sexual Harassment: The Continuing Workplace Crisis." *Labor Law Journal* 45 (Apr.): 195–207.

Matson, Jack V. 1990. *Effective Expert Witnessing.* Chelsea, Mich.: Lewis.

Mayer, Jane, and Jill Abramson. 1994. *Strange Justice: The Selling of Clarence Thomas.* Boston: Houghton Mifflin.

McElhaney, James. W. 1989. "Expert Witnesses." *American Bar Association Journal* (Mar.): 98–99.

McMillan, James B. 1975. "Social Science and the District Court: The Observations of a Journeyman Trial Judge." *Law and Contemporary Problems* 39 (1): 157–63.

Mead, Margaret. 1972. *Blackberry Winter: My Earlier Years.* New York: Morrow.

Melton, Gary B. 1990. "Knowing What We Do Know: APA and Adolescent Abortion." *American Psychologist* 45 (10): 1171–74.

Michelson, Stephan, Paul L. Rosen, and Stephen L. Wasby. 1980. "History and State of the Art of Applied Social Research in the Courts." In *The Use/Nonuse/Misuse of Applied Social Research in the Courts*, ed. Michael J. Saks and Charles H. Baron, 1–27. Cambridge, Mass.: Abt Books.

Minow, Martha. 1990. "Adjudicating Differences: Conflicts among Feminist Lawyers." In *Conflicts in Feminism*, ed. Marianne Hirsch and Evelyn Fox Keller, 149–63. New York: Routledge.

Mohanty, Chandra Talpada, Ann Russo, and Lourdes Torres, eds. 1991. *Third World Women and the Politics of Feminism*. Bloomington: Indiana University Press.

Monahan, John, and Laurens Walker. 1986. "Social Authority: Obtaining, Evaluating, and Establishing Social Science in Law." *University of Pennsylvania Law Review* 134 (3): 477–517.

Montgomery, Lanelle. 1983. Review of *The Methods of Attacking Scientific Evidence*, by Edward J. Imwinkelried. *American Journal of Criminal Law* 11 (July): 219–21.

Moore, Gwen, and Glenna Spitze, eds. 1986. *Research in Politics and Society*. Greenwich, Conn.: JAI Press.

Morris, Anne E., 1991. *Working Women and the Law: Equality and Discrimination in Theory and Practice*. London: Routledge.

Nader, Laura. 1969. *Law in Culture and Society*. Berkeley: University of California Press.

Olasky, Marvin. 1988. *The Press and Abortion, 1838–1988*. Hillsdale, N.J.: Lawrence Erlbaum Associates.

Olson, Walter. 1989. "The Case against Expert Witnesses." *Fortune*, Sept. 24, 133–38.

O'Neill, June Ellenoff. 1995. "The Cause and Significance of the Declining Gender Gap in Pay." In *Neither Victim Nor Enemy*, ed. Rita J. Simon, 1–13. Lanham, Md.: University Press of America.

Orum, Anthony M., Joe R. Feagin, and Gideon Sjoberg. 1991. "The Nature of the Case Study." In *A Case for the Case Study*, ed. Joe R. Feagin, Anthony M. Orum, and Gideon Sjoberg, 1–26. Chapel Hill: University of North Carolina Press.

Otten, Laura A. 1993. *Women's Rights and the Law*. Westport, Conn.: Praeger.

Palley, Marian Lief. 1991. "Women's Rights as Human Rights: An International Perspective." *Annals of the American Academy of Political and Social Sciences* 515: 163–78.

Perry, H. W., Jr. 1991. *Deciding to Decide: Agenda Setting in the United States Supreme Court*. Cambridge, Mass.: Harvard University Press.

Pipes, Sally. 1996. "Creating a Crisis in a Free Society." In *From Data to Public Policy: Affirmative Action, Sexual Harassment, Domestic Violence, and Social Welfare*, ed. Rita J. Simon, 1–6. Lanham, Md.: University Press of America.

Pliner, Anita J., and Susan Yates. 1992. "Psychological and Legal Issues in Minor's Rights to Abortion." *Journal of Social Issues* 48 (3): 203–16.

Platt, Suzy. 1992. *Respectfully Quoted*. Washington, D.C.: Congressional Quarterly, Inc.

Poythress, Norman G., Jr. 1980. "Coping on the Witness Stand: Learned Responses to 'Learned Treatises.'" *Professional Psychology* 1 (Feb.): 139–49.

Preiser, Monty L. 1989. "Cross-Examining the Expert Witness." *Trial* 25 (Jan.): 83–85.

Rehnquist, William H. 1987. *The Supreme Court: How it Was, How It Is.* New York: Quill, William Morrow.

Retherford, Robert O. 1975. *The Changing Sex Differential in Mortality.* Westport, Conn.: Greenwood.

Rhode, Deborah L. 1989. *Justice and Gender: Sex Discrimination and the Law.* Cambridge, Mass.: Harvard University Press.

Ries, Lynn Marie. 1992. "Evaluating Work: An Examination of Wage Differentials." Ph.D. diss., University of Washington.

Rifkind, Lawrence J., and Loretta F. Harper. 1993. *Sexual Harassment in the Workplace: Women and Men in Labor.* Dubuque: Kendall/Hunt.

Ritzer, George. 1992. *Contemporary Sociological Theory.* New York: McGraw-Hill.

Robinson, Robert K., Ross L. Fink, and Billie Morgan Allen. 1994. "Unresolved Issues in Hostile Environment Claims of Sexual Harassment." *Labor Law Journal* 45 (Feb.): 110–14.

Rosen, Lawrence. 1977. "The Anthropologist as Expert Witness." *American Anthropologist* 79:555–78.

Rosen, Paul L. 1972. *The Supreme Court and Social Science.* Urbana: University of Illinois Press.

Rosenberg, Gerald N. 1991. *The Hollow Hope.* Chicago: University of Chicago Press.

Rossi, Faust E. 1991. *Expert Witness.* Chicago: American Bar Association.

Rubin, Eva R. 1987. *Abortion, Politics, and the Courts: Roe v. Wade and Its Aftermath.* New York: Greenwood.

Sachs, Andrea. 1993. "9–Zip! I Love It!: A Dramatic Decision Produces New Guidelines for Judging Sexual Harassment." *Time,* Nov. 22, 44–45.

Saks, Michael J., and Charles H. Baron, eds. 1980. *The Use/Nonuse/Misuse of Applied Social Research in the Courts.* Cambridge, Mass.: Abt Books.

Scott, Jacqueline. 1988. "Attitude Strength and Social Action in the Abortion Dispute." *American Sociological Review* 53 (Oct.): 785–93.

———. 1989. "Conflicting Beliefs about Abortion: Legal Approval and Moral Doubts." *Social Psychology Quarterly* 52 (4): 319–26.

Scott, Joan W. 1990. "Deconstructing Equality-Versus-Difference: Or, the Uses of Post-structuralist Theory for Feminism." In *Conflicts in Feminism,* ed. Marianne Hirsch and Evelyn Fox Keller, 134–48. New York: Routledge.

Segrave, Kerry. 1994. *The Sexual Harassment of Women in the Workplace, 1600 to 1993.* Jefferson, N.C.: McFarland.

Seither, Michael. 1984. "Expert Witness." *Forbes,* Aug., 202–3.

Sherman, Janette D. 1983. "Women as Expert Witnesses." *Trial* 19 (Aug.): 46–47.

Simon, Rita J., and David E. Aaronson. 1988. *The Insanity Defense: A Critical Assessment of Law and Policy in the Post-Hinckley Era.* New York: Praeger.

Simon, Rita J., and Gloria Danziger. 1991. *Women's Movements in America: Their Successes, Disappointments, and Aspirations.* New York: Praeger.

Singleton, Royce, Jr., Bruce C. Straits, Margaret M. Straits, and Ronald J. McAllister. 1988. *Approaches to Social Research.* New York: Oxford University Press.

Smith, H. W., and Cindy Kronauge. 1990. "The Politics of Abortion: Husband Notification Legislation, Self-Disclosure, and Marital Bargaining." *Sociological Quarterly* 31 (4): 585–98.

Stark, Sheldon J. 1992. "Sexual Harassment in the Workplace: Lessons from the Thomas-Hill Hearings." *Trial* 28 (May): 116–22.

Stoper, Emily. 1991. "Women's Work, Women's Movement: Taking Stock." *Annals of the American Academy of Political and Social Sciences* 515:151–62.

Strodel, Robert C. 1982. "The Expert Witness." *Trial* 18 (June): 37–39, 84.

Tamney, Joseph B., Stephen D. Johnson, and Ronald Burton. 1992. "The Abortion Controversy: Conflicting Beliefs and Values in American Society." *Journal for the Scientific Study of Religion* 31 (1): 32–46.

Tanford, J. Alexander. 1990. "The Limits of a Scientific Jurisprudence: The Supreme Court and Psychology." *Indiana Law Journal* 66:136–73.

Tocqueville, Alexis de. 1902 (originally published 1835–40). *Democracy in America.* New York: D. Appleton.

Tong, Rosemarie. 1989. *Feminist Thought.* Boulder, Colo.: Westview Press.

"Trends." 1988. "Experts Can't Give Legal Conclusions." *Trial* 24 (Sept.): 97–99.

United States Bureau of the Census. 1991. "Money Income of Households, Families, and Persons in the United States: 1990." *Current Population Reports,* P-60. Washington, D.C.: U.S. Bureau of the Census.

United States Department of Labor. 1991. *Employment and Earnings: Bureau of Labor Statistics, 1990.* Washington, D.C.: U.S. Department of Labor.

van Geel, T. R. 1991. *Understanding Supreme Court Opinions.* New York: Longmans.

Vogel, Lise. 1992. Review of *Justice and Gender,* by Deborah L. Rhode. *Contemporary Sociology* 21 (5): 584–87.

Wagman, Robert J. 1993. *The Supreme Court: A Citizen's Guide.* New York: Pharos Books.

Weiss, Carol H. 1993. "The Integration of the Sociological Agenda and Public Policy." In *Sociology and the Public Agenda,* ed. William Jules Wilson. Newbury Park, Calif.: Sage.

Wetzel, Janice Wood. 1993. *The World of Women: In Pursuit of Human Rights.* New York: Macmillan.

Wilmoth, Gregory H. 1992. "Abortion, Public Health Policy, and Informed Consent Legislation." *Journal of Social Issues* 48 (3): 1–17.

Winfree, Thomas L., Jr., and Patrick R. Anderson. 1985. "Criminal Justice Scholars as Expert Witnesses: A Descriptive Analysis." *Journal of Criminal Justice* 13:279–89.

———. 1985b. "Pragmatism and Advocacy in Criminal Justice Expert Witnessing." *Justice Quarterly* 2:213–35.

Wisdom, John Minor. 1975. "Random Remarks on the Role of Social Sciences in the Judicial Decision-Making Process in School Desegregation Cases." *Law and Contemporary Problems* 39 (1): 134–63.

Wolff, Alvin A., Jr. 1988 (March). "Cross-Examination of Experts." *Trial* 24 (Mar.): 97.

Wolfgang, Marvin E. 1987. "The Social Scientist in Court." In *Expert Witnesses: Criminologists in the Courtroom*, ed. Patrick R. Anderson and Thomas L. Winfree, 20–35. Albany: State University of New York Press.

Woodward, Bob, and Scott Armstrong. 1981. *The Brethren.* New York: Avon Books.

Worthington, Everett L., David B. Larson, Marvin W. Brubaker, Cheryl Colecchi, James T. Berry, and David Morrow. 1989. "The Benefits of Legislation Requiring Parental Involvement Prior to Adolescent Abortion." *American Psychologist* 44 (12): 1542–45.

Zeitlin, Irving M. 1990. *Ideology and the Development of Sociological Theory.* Englewood Cliffs, N.J.: Prentice Hall.

Index

Rosemary J. Erickson is president of Athena Research Corporation, a Seattle-based firm that conducts research in crime and justice. Her study of violence has resulted in the books *Paroled But Not Free* and *Armed Robbers and Their Crimes* and numerous articles. Dr. Erickson is frequently called upon to testify before state and federal legislative bodies on the subject of workplace violence. She also serves as an expert witness and provides testimony, based on her research, at trials in civil litigation on premises liability.

Rita J. Simon is University Professor in the School of Public Affairs and the Washington College of Law at American University. Her books on law and society include: *The Jury and the Defense of Insanity* (1967); *The Jury: Its Role in American Society* (1980); and *The Insanity Defense: A Critical Assessment of Law and Policy in the Post-Hinckley Era* (with David Aaronson, 1988). She has written extensively on transracial adoption. Her books on that topic include *Adoption, Race and Identity* (with Howard Altstein) (1992); and *The Case for Transracial Adoption* (with Howard Altstein and Marygold Melli, 1994). Her book *The Ambivalent Welcome: Media Coverage of American Immigration* (with Susan Alexander, 1993) is one of her many writings about immigration.